The Shape of Things Known

The Shape of Things Known

Sidney's Apology in Its Philosophical Tradition

Forrest G. Robinson

Harvard University Press
Cambridge, Massachusetts
1972

To
Herschel C. Baker
and
Walter J. Ong

To

Herschel C. Baker

and

Walter J. Ong

Preface

There are nearly as many versions of Sir Philip Sidney as there are readers of his works: courtly Sidney, maker of sonnets and lover of Lady Rich; political Sidney, protégé of Leicester and martyr to the Protestant cause in the Netherlands; learned Sidney, friend of Languet and arbiter of literary fashion; grave and serious Sidney, whose Romance became a philosophical treatise; heroic Sidney, beloved of the poets and warrior par excellence. My Sidney is related to this family of types, though he is more learned than courtly and quite possibly more grave and serious than heroic. Given this much, it will come as no surprise that my Sidney is also more poetry and prose than personality.

I take my point of departure in the *Apology,* assuming — as I think we must — that Sidney's finely wrought critical treatise is a just and genuine expression of his literary values. Submerged in the rhetoric of the *Apology* is a line of reasoning that forms the psychological substructure of Sidney's aesthetics. The theory takes root in the assumption that thought is a form of internal vision and has its most important result in the persistent description of poetry as a "speaking picture," a verbal rendering of ideas visible in the poet's mind as he composes and visible in the reader's mind as he reads. Poetry is the verbal shape of visible thoughts.

My analysis of the *Apology* appears in Chapter 3. Chapter 4 is a detailed application of the theory to Sidney's poetry and prose; and Chapter 5 is a discussion of the same critical assumptions at work in seventeenth-century Character writing and in Ben Jonson's masques.

Sidney was not the first to equate seeing and knowing; rather, his use of the formula is an important aesthetic link in a philosophical and cultural tradition that stretches from classical antiquity to the present day. Throughout this study it should be understood that most of the writers discussed, if challenged, would probably have agreed that the analogy between thought and sight has grave limitations. It remains true, however, that they were rarely challenged and that visual analogies have almost completely dominated European habits of thinking about thought. Chapter 1 traces the philosophical background from the pre-Socratic period to the Renaissance. Chapter 2 concerns itself with more broadly cultural developments in the decades that preceded the composition of the *Apology*. I have organized these preliminary materials with two objectives in mind: first, to set Sidney's critical formulations in their historical perspective, thereby offering new approaches to a correct appreciation of his art; second, to provide a more thorough understanding of the place of vision in Renaissance thought and culture. Certainly the first objective could have been achieved with less historical preparation than the second. Accordingly, those readers interested primarily in Sidney's poetry and poetic theory may be content with a survey of the introductory and concluding remarks in Chapter 1 and with a brisk reading of Chapter 2 or its summary. Intellectual historians, on the other hand, will probably want to read these pages more carefully.

Preface

My debts to historians, philosophers, and literary critics are extensive and will be found in the notes. Research could not have gone forward without the accumulated wisdom of scholars too numerous to mention here, but it would have been utterly impossible in the absence of friendly advice and assistance from sources closer to home. David Kalstone first introduced me to Sidney and helped me to penetrate the finer textures of his verse. His early encouragement was the impetus for this study. Renato Rosaldo and David Thomas, friends on the Charles and elsewhere, had to sit through endless discussions of visual epistemology. The first helped me to see the relevance of what I was doing, and the second admits that he has finally seen the light. At an intermediate stage Jeremy Adams applied his learning and tact to Chapters 1 and 2. His criticism and encouragement were invaluable. At the same time, during several lively debates in the Maine woods, Fred Schneider and Frank Birmingham offered advice that resulted in several major revisions. To my friends and colleagues at Santa Cruz, and particularly to Harry Berger, I am grateful for advice and warm enthusiasm. Nancy Sullivan has been a tireless typist, editor, and friend. From the outset I have had the cooperation and guidance of Miss Carolyn Jakeman and her staff at the Houghton Library of the Harvard College Library. Annette Gordon, my good mother-in-law, has brought her experience and skill to the index. Harvard University has provided financial assistance at crucial steps along the way. A Knox Memorial Fellowship relieved me from teaching duties for a year of research and writing in England, and Cannaday and Clark Fellowships provided additional support after the journey home. More recently, I am grateful to the University of California at Santa Cruz for timely assistance.

Walter J. Ong has been a constant source of inspiration, both by the example of his scholarship and by his warm encouragement. Throughout my work I have had the benefit of Father

Preface

Ong's learning and friendship. Herschel C. Baker has been my mentor from beginning to end. Without his enthusiasm, advice, tireless reading of drafts of the manuscript, and transatlantic good will, the work might never have been completed. Finally, closest to home, my wife, Margaret, contributed humor, patience, and much more, without which all of this would have been intolerable.

F. G. R.

June, 1971
Santa Cruz, California

Contents

The Shape of Things Known

Introduction

There will always be men of ideas, or at least men who pretend to the possession of ideas, and even some who seek new ideas; but nearly all of these men would hesitate if asked to describe what an idea is. We dwell almost exclusively on the "what" of knowledge, perhaps by choice, but possibly because the "how" of knowledge defies an easy or obvious explanation. The search might frustrate us beyond our endurance. I have no definite answers to the "how" question, but it remains a fact that others have tackled the problem and that many believed they had found the answers. In fact, thinkers for thousands of years found similar solutions and described the activity of knowing in roughly the same way. Until the seventeenth century at any rate, it was the almost undisputed view that ideas were mental objects, things somehow insubstantial but nevertheless very closely analogous to material objects seen by material vision.

Roger Bacon, for example, wrote that "the active intellect is primarily God, and secondarily the angels, who illuminate us. For God is to the soul just as the sun is to the eyes, and the angels are just as the stars." [1] The comparison of the sun with God was one of the staples of medieval Franciscan thought, a part of Christian tradition that had its most important early expression in Augustine's doctrine of illumination. The archetype for all such comparisons is, of course, Plato's alignment of the Good with the sun in Chapter XXIII of the *Republic*. Bacon's analogy rests on the assumption that the processes of seeing and thinking are similar — more specifically, that to the physical eyes (*oculi corporales*) of visual sensation there corresponds an eye of the mind (*oculus mentis*) for the purposes of thought. Bacon and many of his peers invested the comparison with far more than figurative significance. Medieval natural philosophers believed that the stars (usually meaning the planets in their spheres) were inhabited by angels, and Scripture provided ample evidence that "God is light." Just as the movements of the stars regulate the ebb and flow of nature, thus revealing God's plan to human view, so the angelic intelligences mediate between divine and human thought, thereby illuminating God's design to the eyes of the mind. The radii of divine light inform and define the worlds of nature and spirit, representing the factual basis for Bacon's equation of God and the sun, angels and stars, thinking and seeing. The third of these equations, the association of thought and vision, or what I term "visual epistemology," will be a central consideration in the pages that follow.

The metaphysical axioms that supported Bacon's analogies had lost much of their force by the time of the Renaissance, but a residuum of scientific lore and theological tradition remained, along with an increasingly common tendency to construe thought as a form of internal vision. The currency of many of these ideas

1. Cited from *Opus Tertium* by D. E. Sharp in *Franciscan Philosophy at Oxford in the Thirteenth Century* (London, Oxford University Press, 1930), p. 161. Translation mine.

is apparent in *Paradise Lost*, where Milton, fusing doctrine with myth, describes Adam's transcendent vision.

> But to nobler sights
> *Michael* from *Adams* eyes the Filme remov'd
> Which that false Fruit that promis'd clearer sight
> Had bred; then purg'd with Euphrasie and Rue
> The visual Nerve, for he had much to see;
> And from the Well of Life three drops instill'd.
> So deep the power of these Ingredients pierc'd,
> Eevn to the inmost seat of mental sight,
> That *Adam* now enforc't to close his eyes,
> Sunk down and all his Spirits became intranst.[2]

To be sure, what Adam has to see is purely spiritual, a result of divine grace, and not the ordinary thought processes. Almost invariably, however, men of the Renaissance describe ordinary cogitation as the movement of an internal eye across mental objects, ideas, conceits, very often Beauty or Truth or one of many vices and virtues. Milton urges us to "see the ingenuity of truth" and assures Charles Diodati that it is his "habit day and night" to pursue the *"idea of the beautiful,* as for a certain image of supreme beauty."[3] James I claimed that it was his earnest desire "to set *cor regis in oculis populi,"*[4] which is to say he wanted to make his ideas and feelings clear to his subjects (the heart, as the seat of all the faculties, was the receptacle for mental images). Similarly, the Muse admonishes Astrophil ("looke in thy heart and write") to turn his inward gaze on the idea of Stella as a well of invention for his "trewand pen."[5]

2. John Milton, *Paradise Lost*, XI, 411–420, in *The Student's Milton*, ed. Frank Allen Patterson (New York, Appleton-Century-Crofts, Inc., 1933), p. 341.

3. John Milton, *Areopagitica*, in *The Student's Milton*, ed. Patterson, pp. 739–740; and Letter to Diodati, p. 1080.

4. Cited by Godfrey Davies, *The Early Stuarts*, 2nd ed. (Oxford, The Clarendon Press, 1959), p. 32.

5. Sir Philip Sidney, *Astrophil and Stella*, I, 13–14. Citations of Sidney's poetry are from *The Poems of Sir Philip Sidney*, ed. William A. Ringler

Sidney's writing is a clear example of the way in which visual epistemology, freed from its moorings in traditional philosophy, drifted into the varied currents of Renaissance culture. A hymn from the *Arcadia* illustrates one direction that such variations might take.

> Apollo great, whose beames the greater world do light,
> And in our little world dost cleare our inward sight,
> Which ever shines, though hid from earth by earthly shade,
> Whose lights do ever live, but in our darknesse fade.
>
> (OA, 26, 1–4)

Although the poetry is submerged in pagan myth, Sidney's theme is clearly Christian. God is the sun of the macrocosm, and His light is partially obscured, presumably by trees, clouds, perhaps even night. But God is also the light of the microcosm, the little world of man, where He illuminates the "inward sight" of the mind. Because of the Fall, man's nobler part, his reason, is the prisoner of mortal flesh ("earthly shade") and thus realizes but a dull glimmering of God's eternal brilliance. Of course, the passage can be interpreted allegorically. "Our darkness," for example, can be understood as a metaphor for the pitfalls of carnal desire. Such transparent moralizing is one among several indications that we are reading a serious young poet of the Protestant Renaissance, and not a medieval metaphysician; but it does nothing to obscure the fact that Sidney, by aligning *Sol* with *Deus* as the luminaries of external and internal vision, has retained the substance of doctrine as Bacon understood it.

An identical division between moral and immoral vision is an important theme in *Astrophil and Stella*. Indeed, the title of the sequence (literally, "Star Lover and Star") is an obvious reminder that the sonnets have to do with the skyward gaze of an ardent

---

(Oxford, The Clarendon Press, 1962). Hereafter citations will employ the following symbols: *AS* (*Astrophil and Stella*); *OA* (poems from the *Old Arcadia*); *CS* (*Certain Sonnets*); and *OP* (*Other Poems*). On the heart in Elizabethan psychology, see Ringler's note, p. 459.

lover. The unity of the cycle arises in part from Sidney's skillful manipulation of the thematic comparison of Stella's eyes with the stars.[6] From the beginning Astrophil is aware that love is a mixed blessing; that "A strife is growne betweene *Vertue* and *Love*" (*AS*, 52, 1) because there are two important ways of looking at Stella. At times the sight of her beauty can be an incitement to moral purity; at others to agonizing lust; and at others, through a deceptive double vision, Astrophil mixes purity and lust by parading innocent motives in the name of passionate desire. But the relationship between thinking and seeing was much more for Sidney than a convenient device for delineating the conflict between virtuous and vicious love. The so-called "conventional eye conceit" of *Astrophil and Stella* is only one manifestation of the poet's convictions about the psychology of perception and communication. In fact, it is one of my most important objectives in this study to illustrate that the epistemological doctrines recurring in Sidney's verse were more than casual allusions to tested philosophical conventions. From one point of view, the sonnets can be read as a dramatization of some of the main arguments set forth in the *Apology*. For example, in one of the most familiar passages in the *Apology*, poetry is defined as "an art of imitation, for so Aristotle termeth it in this word *mimesis*, that is to say, a representing, counterfeiting, or figuring forth — to speak metaphorically, a speaking picture — with this end, to teach and delight." [7] Sidney's conception of "delight" is not to be understood as merely "pleasing" or "appealing." Rather, it is intimately bound up with his notion that poetry is "a speaking

---

6. Lisle C. John, *The Elizabethan Sonnet Sequences* (New York, Columbia University Press, 1938), p. 152. Cf. also p. 154: "Although the sonneteers who follow Sidney often compare the eyes of the lady to stars or show the influence of the stars upon the mortal, none executes them with the skill or motivation of Sidney."

7. Sir Philip Sidney, *An Apology for Poetry*, ed. Forrest G. Robinson (Indianapolis, The Bobbs-Merrill Company, Inc., 1970), p. 18. Hereafter page numbers from this edition will be given in the text.

picture." The poet delights his reader when he is able to evoke vivid images, when he "figures forth" the precepts of moral philosophy in such a way that his audience can see them. The psychology of the reader's response is described in the Seventh Song of *Astrophil and Stella*, where, except for those who have "leaden eyes," "wooden wits," "muddy minds," and "frothy thoughts," sight produces knowledge, knowledge produces love, and love results in movement. Just as Stella stimulates a chain reaction in Astrophil, so a good poem will be designed to set off a similar pattern of responses in the reader. Of course, the poet deals with subjects other than virtue and love, but Sidney is confident that in any delightful description, regardless of its content, sight will be followed by knowledge, and knowledge will result in an appropriate emotion and an appropriate action. In short, the persistent assertion that poetry is a "speaking picture" proceeds from the assurance that art has ethical activity as its end and from a well-integrated theory of perception that guarantees the achievement of that end. We are constantly reminded that the poet presents a picture of "all virtues, vices, and passions so in their own natural seats laid to the view that we seem not to hear of them, but clearly to see through them" (p. 29), or that poetry is a "feigning notable images of virtues, vices, or what else" (p. 21), simply because it was such a crucial consideration in Sidney's theoretical explanation of his craft. The question follows, of course, what Sidney meant by his "pictures" and "notable images"; this question I shall reserve for discussion in a later chapter.

The Renaissance association of thinking with seeing, and the constant recourse to visual and pictorial explanations for what is only possibly, and certainly not exclusively, a visual and pictorial activity may not strike the modern reader as particularly unusual. We are accustomed to the metaphor — so accustomed, in fact, that we may not recognize it as a metaphor. While most people would probably concede that not all thinking involves internally visible images, they would also follow Sidney and his contemporaries in using visual metaphors if asked to explain their own mental operations. The facts of the matter are simple enough. In spite of the extraordinary advances of modern science, we have very little more definite knowledge about the mystery of thought than Sidney did. It is almost true to say that the more we think about thought, the less we think we know. In the absence of a more adequate explanation, it remains almost as true today as it was four hundred years ago that most attempts to describe thought take recourse to analogies with the sense of sight.[8] Our ways of "looking" at the mental processes have not changed that much.

It is difficult, perhaps even useless, to take issue with the general voice of man as it makes itself heard through centuries of established tradition. In recent decades, however, as scholars have turned more and more attention to the ways of thinking about thinking, it has become increasingly clear that the traditional visual analogies for thought are not only misleading but also deeply entrenched stumbling blocks to the advancement of more sophisticated theories. Gilbert Ryle has included this problem in his well-known "dogma of the Ghost in the Machine." He argues, quite plausibly, that visual analogies used to describe the theoretical processes are superstitions that fail to account for the unclear and unexpected patterns of ordinary thought.[9] Benjamin Lee Whorf makes a similar point, though he prefers to speak in terms of imaginary space and its relationship to language. We live, he points out, in a "linguistically determined thought world" that began to take shape in ancient Latin, where the use of spatial terms to describe nonspatial phenomena (*educo, religio, com-*

8. Cf. Walter J. Ong, "System, Space, and Intellect in Renaissance Symbolism," *Bibliothèque d'Humanisme et Renaissance*, 18 (1956), 231.
9. Gilbert Ryle, *The Concept of Mind* (London, Hutchinson & Co., 1949), p. 303. Cf. also p. 306.

prehendo) was widespread. Such verbal habits were given a new dimension in the later Middle Ages, when flourishing trade, standardization of weights and measures, the need to keep records, scientific advances, increased use of mathematics, the invention of clocks, along with numerous other cultural and technological changes, contributed to the development of the highly quantified and spatialized vocabulary of modern man.[10] In indirect confirmation of Whorf's view, Walter Ong has argued that the tendency to describe mental operations by spatial analogies is a late scholastic legacy to the contemporary world.[11]

There can be little debate, then, that the late Middle Ages and Renaissance were periods critical to the development of visual epistemology. It was a time when science and technology made

10. *Language, Thought, and Reality: Selected Writings of Benjamin Lee Whorf*, ed. John B. Carroll (Cambridge, Mass., The MIT Press, 1956), pp. 154–157.

11. Walter J. Ong, "From Allegory to Diagram in the Renaissance Mind," *The Journal of Aesthetics and Art Criticism*, 17 (1959), 435. Johan Huizinga, in *The Waning of the Middle Ages* (London, Edward Arnold & Co., 1924), p. 182, noted a related tendency in the later Middle Ages: "The religious emotion always tended to be transmuted into images. Mystery seemed to become graspable by the mind when invested with perceptible form. The needing of adoring the ineffable in visible shapes was continually creating ever new figures. In the fourteenth century, the cross and the lamb no longer sufficed for the effusions of overflowing love offered to Jesus." Although the bibliography on this subject is far too large to be included here, a few titles may be found useful. Marshall McLuhan's *The Gutenberg Galaxy* (Toronto, University of Toronto Press, 1962) has been the most provocative of modern works on this problem. See also *Explorations in Communication*, ed. Edmund Carpenter and Marshall McLuhan (Boston, Beacon Press, 1960). J. F. Soltis has recently published a summary of the most important contemporary views: *Seeing, Knowing, and Believing* (London, George Allen & Unwin, 1966). John W. M. Verhaar presents the phenomenological position in *Some Relations between Perception, Speech, and Thought* (Assen, Van Gorcum, 1963). More historical studies include: Walter J. Ong, *Ramus, Method, and the Decay of Dialogue* (Cambridge, Mass., Harvard University Press, 1958); H. J. Chaytor, *From Script to Print* (Cambridge, England, W. Heffer & Sons, Ltd., 1950); Sister Joan Marie Lechner, *Renaissance Concepts of the Commonplaces* (New York, Pageant Press, 1962); and several useful monographs by William M. Ivins, Jr. For a fuller summary of recent opinion, see Soltis's bibliography.

great strides by replacing logic with mathematics as the language of nature. This shift, along with many others, involved a more subtle transition from hearing to seeing as the appropriate sense for investigating and finally explaining the natural world. The order of the macrocosm was no longer explicable in traditional categories; as Galileo well knew, the key to nature's secrets was measurement, and measurements could be reduced to graphs, diagrams, and charts with complete precision. At the same time it was discovered that diagrams, or visual abstractions, could be viewed within the mind as well as without; that the understanding of nature involved no more than the observation of patterns in internal space; and that thought itself could be understood as the silent deployment of mental objects across the internally visible interstices of the mind. From this point of view, it is not surprising that it was also an age when conscience began to replace the confessional as the appropriate place for meeting God.

Vision is, of all the senses, the most objective. Sight gives us access to most of the mensurables in nature: we see heights, distances, spatial relationships between objects, a broad variety of colors and textures. It is primarily because of our eyes that we can distinguish forms and structures. Visual metaphors provide much of the vocabulary of objectivity: we "see" what someone means, we take a dim "view" of a proposition, we "focus" on a problem, we draw a question into "perspective." And it is because of our profound submergence in this highly quantified, objectified, and visualized intellectual environment that we fail to be surprised by Sidney's persistent association of thinking with seeing. In an age when concordances, footnotes, graphic analyses of texts, and a rigorously structural approach to literature prevail, when oral recitation is deemed impractical, and when poetry is described in terms of an "objective correlative," there is indeed nothing very striking about the "speaking picture" of poetry.

Sidney's equation of thought with sight and his numerous comparisons of the verbal art of poetry with the pictorial art of painting are indications of his profound (if only partly conscious) submergence in the tendencies of his age. But, as previously remarked, the Renaissance penchant for spatial and visual habits of thought represents a concentration and intensification of many older attitudes. Sidney, along with his educated contemporaries, was immersed in a philosophical tradition that dated from ancient Greece and in more general cultural patterns that had begun to emerge in the Middle Ages. It is to these traditions that I shall now turn, in part to outline more completely the traditions themselves and in part to provide the foundations for a deeper understanding of this important feature of Renaissance culture.

1

The Tradition of
Visual Epistemology

THE DISCOVERY OF MIND

The modern world view is replete with acquired attitudes and thoroughly conditioned approaches to experience. By the time we are intellectually mature enough to objectify our methods of objectification, those methods are already so subjective that we find them difficult to isolate and analyze. One of the most common of such approaches, as I have mentioned, is the notion that thinking ought to be described as a kind of seeing. Certainly this idea was current, in various formulations, long before the twentieth century, but it would be a mistake to suppose that it amounted to anything more than a convenient hypothesis about the real nature of things. The idea was nascent with many of the pre-Socratics, but it was not until the early decades of the fourth century B.C. that it emerged completely in the Platonic dialogues.

Plato's philosophical predecessors were far too numerous to receive adequate treatment here. In general, however, we may concur with Aristotle that for the pre-Socratics there was nothing except the sensible contents of the visible universe.[1] Their

1. Aristotle, *Metaphysics*, 987ª.

11

materialism was accompanied by, and perhaps had its source in, a failure to make a clear distinction between thought and sensation. An eminent psychologist has pointed out[2] that the feeling of self-consciousness shared by most modern adults — the assurance that one has thoughts distinguishable from both the external world and the body itself — is an acquired attitude that develops late in childhood. In his early years a child believes that he thinks by making words and that his words are external things. Like children, the pre-Socratics had not fully interiorized — indeed, they had not fully localized — the objects of their thought and so lacked the awareness of a strict separation of thought and sensation that we take for granted today. This tendency is clear, for example, in the philosophy of the Pythagoreans, who were preoccupied with principles of form and structure that seemed to them to underlie the flux of the natural world. By generalizing from mathematical observations about harmonics, they arrived at the question (to borrow Burnet's reconstruction): "If musical sounds can be reduced to numbers, why not everything else?"[3] The resulting cosmology gives the appearance of distinguishing the mathematical principles that explain the phenomenal world, the objects of thought, from the phenomenal world itself, the object of sensation. But as Aristotle seems to have recognized, the division of matter and thought was in fact only an illusion. Like most of their predecessors, the Pythagoreans believed that the rational structure of nature is coextensive with the material that conforms to that structure. Numbers were not abstract things of the mind but spatially extended units; and as long as numbers and the material things they enumerated were thought of as being the same, there could be no absolute division between thought and sensation.

2. Jean Piaget, *The Child's Conception of Physical Causality* (New York, Harcourt, Brace and Company, 1930), pp. 242–243.

3. John Burnet, *Early Greek Philosophy*, 4th ed. (London, A. & C. Black, 1930), p. 107.

In general, then, the pre-Socratics illustrate the commonplace that the domain of any philosophical enterprise is circumscribed by its own implicit or explicit assumptions. Since the modern dualism of matter and spirit had not yet been conceived, *res cogitantes* were simply submerged in the monolithic continuum of *res extensae*. The mind was understood by analogy with the physical organs: *psyche* was the breath of life; *nous* was the mind as an absorber of images; and, most important for present purposes, knowledge was a form of seeing or having seen.[4] Like the rest of the material cosmos, the pre-Socratic mind was displayed on the outside of an as yet undiscovered inside. Only when the processes of thought were distinguished from those of sensation could the center of philosophical inquiry shift from the "what" to the "how" of knowledge. This shift was first fully realized in the Platonic dialogues, but its evolution can be most clearly understood as an adaptation of the formulations of Parmenides.

The extant fragment of Parmenides' poem opens with a description of the philosopher being carried in a chariot to the Gates of Day and Night. Here he is greeted by a goddess who relates to him what she calls the three "Ways": the Way of Notbeing, the Way of Mortal Opinion, and the Way of Truth. Once the first two methods have been disposed of, the goddess concludes: "One path only is left for us to speak of, namely that It is" (Frag. 8).[5] The one true premise from which all deductions follow is merely the simplest affirmative assertion of existence, and that which is said to exist in the statement "It is" is called the One. Like the Platonic Good, the One seems to have represented a point of philosophical departure, a principle from which all true statements would follow. But while he was prob-

4. Bruno Snell, *The Discovery of the Mind* (Cambridge, Mass., Harvard University Press, 1953), pp. 244–245.

5. I have used the Burnet translation (*Early Greek Philosophy*, pp. 172 ff.), though selections from Parmenides' poem are available in several different versions.

ably verging toward what we call an abstraction, Parmenides' description of the One makes it clear that he was not entirely successful. In addition to being uncreated, indivisible, and eternal, the One also has a distinctive spatial quality: it has sides equidistant from a center, like a gigantic sphere, with the result that it reaches out equally in every direction (Frag. 8).

At first glance Parmenides seems to have clarified the confusions that beset the Pythagoreans. His poem is evidence that he had rescued the mind from the not-self and given it a special object in the One, thus separating the subject from the object of knowledge. But his description of the One as a gigantic, in some sense extended, sphere is the crucial flaw in Parmenides' insistence that there be a strict separation between thought and sensation. In fact, the model for his implicit theory of knowledge was the sense of sight. Whereas the objects of normal vision are the transient phenomena of nature, the supreme object of thought is an immaterial, yet visible, geometrical form stretching in pristine perfection before the gaze of the mind. Thus the distinction between thought and sensation is blurred by the fact that in describing cogitation Parmenides simply moved the space of the external world into the interior and described thinking as a special kind of seeing. The goddess is being completely literal when she describes the One as "well-rounded truth," and it is not at all inconsistent that the Way of Mortal Opinion should fall into error because of its "wandering eye."

While Parmenides' most important contribution to the history of philosophy may well be the discovery that reason and sense have radically different operations, it is equally important that, owing to ontological assumptions implicit in the Greek world view, his division between thought and sensation was more nominal than real. The natural priority of the sense of sight and the inherited association of thinking and seeing were thoroughly reinforced by the verbal tradition from which Parmenides drew the language for his poem. As W. K. C. Guthrie has remarked, the Greek verb *noein*, which we translate "to think," connoted an act of vision, a seeing with the mind.[6] Given his intellectual milieu, it was to be expected that Parmenides' One, inscribed with perfect circularity through the reaches of mental space, should have been visible to the eyes of the mind. Therefore, in spite of his insistence that the powers of reason were completely different from those of sensation, Parmenides had almost no alternative to the equation of thought and sight that he passed on to his philosophical successors.

Initially there are several obvious points of comparison between Plato and Parmenides. Most important perhaps, both believed that the known, in order to be known, must be fixed and unchanging. In both systems there is an overlapping of epistemology and ontology, for the objects of knowledge are also the truest forms of existence. Accordingly, concepts have real objective referents: for Parmenides in the One, for Plato in the Ideas or Forms. Unlike his predecessor, however, Plato attempted to bridge the worlds of Being and Becoming with the doctrine of participation, which provides that the eternal Forms are reflected in the temporal manifold. Knowledge is acquired through recollection, the perception and recognition of the Forms as they are observed in the shifting apparitions of external flux. This process rests on a foundation of psychological principles set forth in the *Timaeus*. The soul is divided into three parts: the appetitive part, appropriately situated in the belly; the spirited part, located in the heart; and the reason, "which is the divinest part of us and lord over all the rest." This third part, located in the head and distinguished by its immortality, was originally formed from the

6. W. K. C. Guthrie, *A History of Greek Philosophy*, 3 vols. (Cambridge, England, Cambridge University Press, 1962–1969), II, 17–18.

same ingredients as the intelligible universe, "only no longer so pure as before, but second or third in degree of purity." [7] Because of this fundamental similarity between knower and known, the rational soul has access to the order of the cosmos; knowledge is of like by like, intelligible Ideas by the intellectual soul.

Plato almost invariably describes recollection as an act of vision. The Forms are "in" nature in such a way that the sight of them is enough to awaken the soul with an intimation of their being. For obvious reasons, Plato therefore considered sight the most important of the senses; only because he sees the divine pattern stretching through physical nature can man ultimately gaze upon the Forms. The primacy of vision manifests itself not only in the recollection of the Forms from visual particulars but also in the very act of knowing. In the *Sophist*, for example, the expert dialectician is the man "that discerns clearly *one* Form everywhere extended throughout many." [8] The most sustained instance of the association of thinking with seeing, and undoubtedly the most important in the subsequent history of the conception, appears in the *Republic*. The philosopher-king is one who has a passionate desire to see the truth, and whose clarity of vision provides him with an infallible pattern for the ordering of society.

Socrates describes the Good as the final goal of the philosopher's study — that from which everything good and right derives its value. When pressed to be more explicit, he admits that a full description of the Good is beyond his powers, but he offers as an alternative to relate what seems to him the thing that most nearly resembles it. It is, he argues, the sun, the offspring of the Good, which has been created "in the same relation to vision and visible things as that which the Good itself bears in the

7. Plato, *Timaeus*, 44ᵈ and 41ᵉ in *Plato's Cosmology*, trans. F. M. Cornford (New York, The Library of Liberal Arts, 1937), pp. 142 and 150.

8. Plato, *Sophist*, 253ᵈ in *Plato's Theory of Knowledge*, trans. F. M. Cornford (London, Routledge & Kegan Paul, 1935), p. 262. Cf. 254ᵃ.

intelligible world to intelligence and to intelligible objects." [9] Just as the sun illuminates all sensible things, the Good sheds its light on all intelligible things. Once the vision of the Good has been achieved, the entire structure of truth lies revealed before the mind's eye. Ultimate knowledge, therefore, is a kind of understanding, a nondiscursive, nonverbal contemplation of radiant Forms. With such an approach to knowledge, the description of understanding as a visual process was as literal as it was inevitable, for no other phenomenon in the limited range of human communication with the not-self seemed to offer the immediacy and clarity of vision.

Plato also made a place for discursive thought in his epistemology, and, like the other mental processes, it is usually represented as a form of internal vision. The distinction between thought and understanding is illustrated in the section of the *Republic* that immediately follows the comparison of the Good with the sun. Here, by the use of a line divided into two unequal sections, Socrates proposes to distinguish the four levels of human cognition. The lower section of the line, which symbolizes the visible order, is again divided into two additional parts. The lower portion represents the range of reflected images in the visible world, and the perceiver's state of mind is characterized as imagining. The second level in the lower section has visible things as its objects, and the perceiver's state of mind is belief. Socrates quickly dismisses the lower section of the line and turns his attention to the upper, which stands for the intelligible order. This is also divided into two parts. The lower division is appointed to the study of arithmetic and geometry, disciplines limited by the fact that they proceed deductively from unproved assumptions and that they employ images as an aid to reasoning. As a consequence of these limitations, the third level has thinking as

9. Plato, *Republic*, 508^{a-b}, trans. F. M. Cornford (London, Oxford University Press, 1941), p. 219.

its state of mind. The supreme level is reached when the first principle of all has been discerned, and the result is knowledge or intelligence. This highest mode of cognition, which abandons images for Forms, is that nondiscursive contemplation of truth which I have just described as understanding.

The divisions of the line perfectly illustrate the role that vision plays in Plato's understanding of human cognition. At all four levels the knower's comprehension of the known hinges on his ability to see. At the lower division both the reflections of things and the things themselves are the objects of normal vision. At the upper level the imperfect geometrical "images" are substituted for the Forms; we are constantly reminded that these ideal configurations are most appropriately viewed by the eyes of the mind. Complete knowledge of the Forms is achieved when they are illuminated by the Good, which is itself apprehensible only by an act of immediate mental vision.

In a subsequent section Plato outlines the curriculum that the young philosophers will follow in their approach to the Good. The program reaches its conclusion with training in "Dialectic, which is the same thing as the ability to see the connexions of things." [10] The entire course leading up to dialectic consists of mathematical studies, selected because the properties of number seemed to have the power of leading the student to the contemplation of numerical Forms. But, like his predecessors Parmenides and Pythagoras, Plato failed to disengage his Forms from their extended and visually perceptible attributes. Abstract mathematical quantities are described as though they were materially extended objects. Good mathematicians, we are told, have nothing but scorn for those who would divide numerical units into parts.[11] The straight line is defined, not abstractly as the shortest distance

10. Ibid., 537^c (Cornford, p. 259).
11. Ibid., 525^d (Cornford, p. 242). Cf. Tobias Dantzig, *Number: The Language of Science*, 4th ed. (New York, The Macmillan Company, 1954), pp. 25–26.

between two points, but as "that of which the middle is in front of both extremities" "(i.e., to an eye placed at one end and looking along the line)." [12] Just as Parmenides thought of the One as a perfect sphere, so Plato thinks of his mathematical Forms as objects perfectly visible to the eyes of the mind.

It was undoubtedly the impression of simultaneous purity and visibility that explains the prominence of mathematics in Plato's later dialogues. Imperfect geometrical shapes in nature could be surveyed in their ideal proportions within the mind, thus providing an apparent conjunction of two worlds. In the *Timaeus*, Plato adapts the principles of Euclidean geometry to the structure of the universe, thus making it clear that the intelligibility of the world is explicitly mathematical. From the disorderly movements of the dancer we can cull the fixed pattern of the cosmic dance. Philosophy has its beginning in the rational product of human vision, which establishes a link between the visible architecture of the world and the eternally fixed objects of thought. Through his sight man perceives the one in the many, the Forms of things visible to the eye within. The mind, in turn, finishes the cycle by comprehending the geometrical principles upon which the creation was organized.

The Greek equation of mind and matter and the related association of knowledge with mental vision reach an important plateau in the Platonic dialogues. Plato was the first major European philosopher to distinguish reason from extramental flux, and he may therefore be said to have initiated an important modern dualism. But science cannot progress beyond the boundaries that language imposes upon it. Since Plato had no way of verbally differentiating his internal world of Forms from the external universe of change, he proceeded by way of analogy and

12. *Parmenides*, 137°, trans. F. M. Cornford in *Plato and Parmenides* (London, Routledge & Kegan Paul, 1939), p. 118. The parenthetical explanation is from T. L. Heath, *A History of Greek Mathematics* (Oxford, The Clarendon Press, 1921), p. 216.

described the mental processes as an act of seeing with the mind. That Plato's analogy should have become a staple of Western thought is merely a reminder of the breadth of his influence.

Even Aristotle, in many ways Plato's most profound antagonist, retained the association of thinking with seeing, though in a form suited to his particular philosophical ends. In general, it may be said that whereas Plato's conception of the universe was dualistic, Aristotle's was unified. The Platonic division between sensible flux and intelligible Form was accompanied by concomitant distinctions between thought and sensation, knowledge and opinion. Aristotle's philosophy, by comparison, allows for an infinite variation of reality along a single, graduated continuum. Between the lowest level of potentiality (primary matter) and the summit of actuality (pure form) stretches the richly variegated hierarchy of modifications upon the two extremes. The human body, no longer the prison house of reason, is joined with the soul in mutual interdependence. Plato's dichotomies are replaced by a broad spectrum of numerically indefinite shades and modulations; sensation overlaps with thought, and change is informed by fixity. But lest the contrast between the two thinkers appear too extreme, we should remember (with Jaeger) that "Aristotle made himself out of the Platonic philosophy." [13] The vestiges of the early days in the Academy are perhaps nowhere clearer than in the Stagirite's description of the mind. The mind is divided into two parts on the principle that every natural class involves matter, which is potentially all the particulars included in the class, and a cause, which is productive in the sense that it makes them all. The passive intellect is characterized by its capacity for becoming all things. The active intellect is described in terms reminiscent of the Platonic Good; it "is what it is by virtue of mak-

13. Werner Jaeger, *Aristotle: Fundamentals of the History of His Development*, trans. Richard Robinson, 2nd ed. (London, Oxford University Press, 1948), p. 13.

ing all things: this is a sort of positive state like light; for in a sense light makes potential colours into actual colours." [14]

The traces of Platonism are also clear in Aristotle's distinction between discursive reason and intuitive reason, which are in many ways comparable with Plato's thought and understanding. Intuitive reason is superior to discursive reason because it has access to pure forms, the indemonstrable first principles of science. Like the Platonic understanding, intuitive reason is described by analogy with sensation — the person in contemplation has the pure forms clearly before his mind.[15] Jaeger explains intuitive reason as a kind of mental vision and adds that it is the only vestige of Platonic contemplation to appear in Aristotle's metaphysics.[16] The verb used to describe intuition (*theorein*) is literally translated "to inspect" or "to keep one's gaze fixed on." The visual analogy is perfectly fitting, for as Aristotle understood it, vision is similar to intuition in its nondiscursive and fully comprehensive immediacy.

The critical differences between Platonic and Aristotelian epistemology occur at the level of discursive reason. As previously noted, Plato insisted upon a radical distinction between the objects of thought and the objects of sensation. But the efficacy of this division is diminished by Plato's repeated equation of seeing with thinking. This confusion arises, at least in part, because the Ideas are often conceived of as principles of organization, the underlying shape or structure of things. As Eric Havelock has remarked, "the trouble with the word Form is precisely that as it seeks to objectify and separate knowledge from opinion it also

14. Aristotle, *De Anima*, 430[a]14–17. Except where otherwise indicated, citations from Aristotle are from *The Works of Aristotle*, ed. W. D. Ross, 12 vols. (Oxford, The Clarendon Press, 1908–1952).
15. Aristotle, *De Memoria*, 449[b]18.
16. Jaeger, *Aristotle*, p. 205. Cf. also H. H. Joachim, *Aristotle: The Nicomachean Ethics* (Oxford, The Clarendon Press, 1951), p. 198.

tends to make knowledge visual again." [17] Without discussing the concept of form, Aristotle recognized the deficiences of the theory of Ideas and ultimately abandoned it. As an alternative he brought Plato's Forms down to earth, stripped them of their transcendence, and joined them with matter as the actualizing constituents of all Being. In spite of significant modifications, however, Aristotle's conception of form retains one important Platonic characteristic. In the same way that Plato's purportedly abstract Ideas have a tendency to become visible (or visualizable), Aristotle's forms vacillate between distinct cognitive levels. At times form is an abstract definition, at others it is a visible outline, and at others the visible and the abstract overlap.[18] This overlapping of shape and definition in form was in no way a confusion on Aristotles' part. According to the psychology of *De Anima*, discursive thought is never completely free from its roots in sensation. Intellection proceeds through the senses, where sight is far and away the most important source of knowledge, revealing the differences between things. The objects of thought, once abstracted from the visible forms of sensation, enter the mind as disembodied shapes or outlines. Accordingly, "when the mind is actively aware of anything it is necessarily aware of it along with an image; for images are like sensuous contents except in that they contain no matter." [19] We stamp thought images upon the memory, just as we create impressions with a seal. The imagination has access to the intelligible forms and acts as a kind of messenger between memory and mind. Judgments occur when the soul is able to fuse a number of images into a unified picture.

Both Plato and Aristotle recognized that philosophy must proceed from a definite theory of knowledge. Their epistemological quarrel, which hinges on the distinction between transcendent

17. Eric A. Havelock, *Preface to Plato* (Cambridge, Mass., The Belknap Press of Harvard University Press, 1963), p. 268.

18. Cf. Aristotle, *Metaphysics*, 983^{a}26–27; 996^{b}5–8; 1033^{a}33–34; and *Physics*, 193^{a}28–^{b}5.

19. Aristotle, *De Anima*, 432^{a}6–8.

22

and immanent form, was to provide the poles for subsequent philosophical debate. But the similarities between their systems were as important for posterity as the differences. For both philosophers knowledge always involves an object, and that object is nearly always something seen, submerged either in natural flux or within the mind itself. It was this predominantly visual explanation for the mental processes that Aristotle inherited from Plato and then modified to suit his own purposes. From the most primary visual perceptions to the highest level of contemplation the human soul never thinks without an image. Form as shape and form as idea are merged in the visible presentations of intellection, which function both as initial percepts and subsequent abstract concepts. Knowledge and reality are thus joined in the common conception of visual form, which unifies multiplicity at its very root.

Despite modifications and new developments, all of the important philosophical systems of antiquity maintained that thinking is a form of seeing. From its very beginnings, for example, Atomism was characterized by the habit of describing thought as a form of visualization. Epicurus (b. 342 B.C.) was the most influential thinker within the school, though his theory of knowledge was later popularized in the poetry of Lucretius. He argued that thought occurs when "idols" enter through the pores of the body and form images in the heart, just as vision occurs when "idols" from external objects enter the eyes. Scientific knowledge is achieved through concepts — what Diogenes Laertius describes as "preconceptions" — pictorial genera and species that can be recalled from the memory for comparison with new images and that provide the basis for making judgments. The memory is the receptacle for a variety of composite photographs that form the standards for all scientific knowledge.[20] Thinking is literally the internal viewing of images derived and refined from sensation.

20. R. D. Hicks, *Stoic and Epicurean* (New York, Charles Scribner's Sons, 1910), p. 217.

What it is that actually sees within the mind goes unexplained, though we may assume that Epicurus imagined a sort of inward eye fixed on the shifting images of the heart.

The Stoics were similar to the Atomists in their description of the mental processes in terms of images or presentations but took a course of their own in conceiving of the presentation as a mental fiction, a reflection of reality, and not in any sense material.[21] To arrive at a criterion for judging the truth of the images was a major problem. Since sensation was not deemed absolutely trustworthy, and since Stoic empiricism and material-ism precluded the possibility of a priori standards for such judgments, the solutions chosen presented obvious loopholes for later critics. Zeno (336–264 B.C.) argued (rather unsatisfac-torily) that a presentation could be judged trustworthy because of its "intrinsic nature," which made it "graspable" to the mind.[22] Chrysippus (281–205 B.C.) took recourse to a doctrine of preconception, which prescribed "a general notion which comes by the gift of nature (an innate conception of universals or general concepts)." [23] Based on the assumptions of the Stoic epistemology, however, the philosophical justification for the attainment of truth could not be established without triggering internal contradictions. As a result, the dilemma seems to have persisted without any adequate resolution. But for our purposes

21. Cf. Diogenes Laertius, *Lives of Eminent Philosophers*, VII, 45–46, trans. R. D. Hicks (New York, G. P. Putnam's Sons, 1925), 2 vols., II, 155–157: "A presentation (or mental impression) is an imprint on the soul: the name having been appropriately borrowed from the imprint made by the seal upon the wax. There are two species of presentation, the one apprehending a real object, the other not. The former, which they take to be the test of reality, is defined as that which proceeds from a real object, agrees with that object itself, and has been imprinted seal-fashion and stamped upon the mind: the latter, or non-apprehending, that which does not proceed from any real object, or, if it does, fails to agree with the reality itself, not being clear or distinct."

22. Cicero, *Academia*, I, xi.

23. Diogenes Laertius, *Lives*, VI, 54 (II, 163).

it is enough to note that the Stoics were at one with most of their contemporaries in the association of thought with sight.

The later Roman Stoics turned their attention from explicitly epistemological problems to the relationship between knowledge and ethical action. Because of their new interests and the significant gap in time separating them from the predecessors, they borrowed many ideas that fell beyond the traditional lines of their school. Seneca (d. A.D. 65), for example, had read Plato as well as Zeno and Cleanthes. He argues that the philosophically initiated have access to Wisdom's true "apparitions," but adds that such a sight is not for dull eyes.[24] The Platonic Ideas, which he calls "shapes" (*figuris*), are transcendent and eternal objects of thought to which the best artists direct their gaze.[25] It is significant that Plato's tendency to convert abstractions into visible shapes has become, with the passage of time, a more explicit feature of the theory of Ideas. This habit of making the merely implicit more obvious and dogmatic is characteristic and becomes increasingly pronounced as the tradition continues to develop.

The philosophers of the Middle and New Academies agreed with the Stoics that the *visa* were presented visually, but they dissented from the notion that true images could be distinguished from false ones. While accepting the basic assumptions of Stoic epistemology, the Academics argued that absolute certitude is impossible, thereby sidestepping the contradictions that beset Zeno and Chrysippus. This is the position taken by Cicero in the *Academia*, where he warms to the Socratic argument that nothing can be known except that we know nothing.[26] But other sources reveal that Cicero wavered in his theory of knowledge, and it seems likely that he never reached a final position on the nature

24. Seneca, *Ad Lucilium Epistulae Morales*, XC, 29, trans. R. M. Gummere, 3 vols. (New York, G. P. Putnam's Sons, 1917–1925), II, 417.
25. Ibid., LXV, 7–8 (Gummere, I, 449).
26. Cicero, *Academia*, II, xxiii.

of the mind. In a sense he adopted both halves of Plato's dualistic psychology without coordinating them in a single system. For example, in an optimistic mood he held out great hope to those who longed to penetrate into the heart of truth "by the keenness of mental vision." [27]

There was no wavering in the mind of Plotinus (ca. A.D. 203–269), whose philosophical system perfectly illustrates the extremes of visual epistemology. Indeed, he rarely discusses knowledge without mentioning vision at the same time, so intimately were those phenomena associated in his mind. The universe, as he conceived of it, consists of a series of graduated emanations of light from a central point. In the middle is the One, the indivisible, eternally brilliant source of all creation; at the circumference is matter, described as the privation of light. The first emanation is *nous,* the receptacle of the Ideas, the unified exemplar in which every part is the whole, and the whole is every part. Next is the world soul, the intellectual principle, which represents the unity of all individual souls, the link between the sensual and the supersensual. Beneath the individual soul is the material world, where the light is most dim.

The human soul is suspended in the very middle of this hierarchical structure. Below it is the phenomenal world, and above it the higher gradations of intellect, *nous,* and the One. The mind, almost like an eye on an axis, communicates with these worlds by seeing them, by looking up or down. The equation of thinking and seeing appealed to Plotinus in part because the two processes, as he understood them, entailed identical relationships with their objects. In the activity of seeing, the eye remains unchanged, just as the soul, in the act of knowing or seeing, suffers no alteration. All that enters is the object of mental vision, but it is possessed without affecting the essence of the

27. Cicero, *Tusculan Disputations,* I, xix, trans. J. E. King (New York, G. P. Putnam's Sons, 1927), pp. 53–55. Cf. also I, xvi.

soul. This mobility between a variety of cognitive states is guaranteed only by stressing the soul's absolute independence of its objects. And this independence is ensured by the equation of thought with sight, for among the senses the eye alone bridges the chasm between subject and object without apparently suffering any change. Knowledge is of like by like, but only in the sense that the soul has a kinship with the objects of its vision (whether below or above), and not in the Aristotelian sense that it "becomes" any of them. The distinction between sensation and intellection is therefore merely a question of degree, for in both it is the eye of the soul that sees; "sensations are dim spiritual perceptions, spiritual perceptions are clear sensations." [28]

In the lower forms of cognition the soul sees images or pictures, and the task of knowledge is to bring these into clearer focus with the truths they mirror. But before it can turn from the world of merely reflected truths, the soul must be purified; it must retire from the observation of external images to the contemplation of itself. Upon entering this stage the soul is at first aware only of the object of its vision and does not distinguish itself as subject; "it knows the phase seen but not the seeing phase." Self-consciousness comes when the soul is finally able to "bring over from itself the knowing phase as well: seeing subject and seen objects must be present as one thing." [29] Purification at the level of the intellectual principle prepares the soul for the higher vision of *nous,* the exemplar of all beauty. Now, "when you are self-gathered in the purity of your being, . . . now call up all your confidence, strike forward yet a step — you need a guide no longer — strain, and see." [30] This stage achieved,

28. William Ralph Inge, *The Philosophy of Plotinus,* 3rd ed., 2 vols. (London, Longmans, Green and Co., 1929), I, 227. Cf. also Plotinus, *The Enneads,* VI, vii, 7.

29. Plotinus, *The Enneads,* V, iii, 5, trans. Stephen MacKenna, 5 vols. (London, The Medici Society, 1917–1930), II, 74.

30. Ibid., I, vi, 9 (MacKenna, I, 88).

the indefatigable soul moves onward toward the final ecstatic vision of the One, where the distinction between knower and known, as well as between seer and seen, is lost in an indescribable flood of light. In the moment of vision the subject and the object of knowledge join in perfect, radiant union.

Plotinus clarified and systematized much that was only implicit in the philosophy he inherited. As I have argued, the association of thinking with seeing was almost inevitable in early Greek thought. The force of the verbal tradition, the absence of objectivity, and the natural primacy of vision among the senses left few if any alternatives. If they had alternatives, Plato and Aristotle ignored them and thus transformed habit into tradition. With *The Enneads* this traditional formula became the critical link between the human soul and the surrounding universe. The sharp Platonic dichotomies of thought and sensation, and of knowledge and opinion, are rendered less distinct by virtue of the mind's participation in all cognition. The gap between heaven and earth is diminished by a procession of hierarchial gradations, and a bridge is constructed along the lines of inward vision. Hereafter the transit between the two regions may be accomplished with greater ease, for the same eye that surveys the images of nature can penetrate into the realm of eternal beauty. We are more than ever impressed with the dignity of the human mind, with its participation in the intellectual principle, and with the unlimited sweep of its vision. No longer is the soul a processing plant for floods of impressions, seals, images, lights, and myriad sensations. Rather, it retains its purity and agility, moving actively and with brilliant speed through a broad range of cognitive states. Plotinus agreed with his predecessors that the known, in order to be known, must be seen. But he surpassed them in his optimism: there was nothing, to his mind at least, that could not be seen.

THE CHRISTIAN VIEW

Even before the time of Plotinus the whole of Western culture was adapting itself, however unwillingly, to the powerful influence of Christianity. Pagan philosophy, like Roman politics, was acceptable only to the degree that it could be integrated into the ideology of the new movement. One of Plotinus's most important contributions to the progress, indeed to the preservation, of Platonism was to cast that philosophy into a form that appealed to subsequent Christian thinkers. His universe of luminous emanations was designed, probably unwittingly, to accommodate a God of light. And as Augustine was to discover, the Christian deity, like the Plotinian One, could be approached best along the illuminated paths of mental vision.

Christianity entered the world as the revealed Word of God, and not as an abstract philosophical system. The question of knowledge, particularly the knowledge of God, had been settled for Christians by the teachings of Christ as preserved in Scripture. Here, most notably in the fourth Gospel and in the influential Epistles of Paul, Christ's presence in the world is described over and over as a flood of divine light. There was, of course, considerable precedent in the Old Testament for such a metaphor: the creation was initiated with light (Genesis 1:3), the Psalms are suffused with the divine brilliance (27:1; 97:11; 119:105), and Isaiah laments (59:9) that the Jews "wait for light, but behold obscurity." But in the memorable first chapter of John we are confronted with a series of more or less philosophical equations that were to become a standard point of departure for Christians in all ages. God, we are told, is the Word, or *logos*, the informing principle of all creation. The significance of the Word is made comprehensible in Christ, for "In him was life; and the life was the light of men. And the light shineth in darkness; and the darkness comprehended it not" (1:4–5). The love of light, which amounts to faith in Christ, is the key to personal salvation. "And this is the condemnation, that light is come into the world, and men loved darkness rather than light, because their deeds were evil. For every one that doeth evil hateth the light . . . But he that doeth truth cometh to the light, that his deeds may be made manifest, that they are wrought in God" (3:19–21). Truth, which is God, Christ, or the *logos,* is grasped by Christians in their love of the light. Upon the assertion that He is "the light of the world" (9:5), Christ brings sight to the eyes of a blind man. Metaphor and fact are united in the man's first hesitant vision of the living truth, for the literal sight of Christ results almost immediately in perfect spiritual vision, or faith (9:35–39).

Christ's rebuke to Thomas — "blessed are they that have not seen, and yet have believed" (20:29) — suggests that, once Christ has retreated from the earth, faith will be a kind of spiritual myopia, "blind belief." But we are not many pages into Paul's epistle before it becomes clear that the sight of the truth in the man Jesus Christ has been replaced by other kinds of seeing. Almost from the outset there is the assurance that "the invisible things of him from the creation of the world are clearly seen, being understood by the things that are made" (Romans 1:20). This association of understanding with the sight of things in the phenomenal world is augmented by a divine light burning in the hearts of believers. "For God, who commanded the light to shine out of darkness, hath shined in our hearts, to give the light of the knowledge of the glory of God in the face of Jesus Christ" (II Corinthians 4:6). Paul's persistent reminder that "we walk by faith, not by sight" (II Corinthians 5:7) is really a distinction between the objects of the spirit (which belong to faith) and the things seen in the external world, for he is also persistent in reminding his readers that "The eyes of your understanding" have been "enlightened" (Ephesians 1:18) and that "ye were sometimes darkness, but now are ye light in the Lord: walk as children of light" (Ephesians 5:8). To be sure, Paul was careful to make it clear that the gap between revealed truth and rational knowledge could be bridged only by faith. But it is also important that by "blindness" he usually means an un-Christian preoccupation with things seen by the carnal eye or else the clouded but compelling vision of the faithful. In the latter, paradoxical sense, the eye of Christian wisdom must fix its gaze on the unseen, on the mysterious, whose meaning will be unveiled to believers alone, to those illuminated through willing blindness.

Many of the early Christian fathers were learned men, thoroughly grounded in the traditions of pagan thought. Because there was no clear distinction between philosophy and theology, and as a result of numerous religious controversies, the language of pagan learning slowly worked its way into the fabric of revelation. Platonism was the prevailing system in the early Christian period, and by a happy coincidence it was found that an alliance between philosophy and faith could be effected without serious embarrassment to either. Plato's great wisdom, like the wisdom of the Church, was commonly thought to have been gathered from the teachings of Moses. Plato had written of a single, creative Good, a brilliant being accessible only to the eyes of the mind. The remarkable affinities between contemplation and the internal light of faith were too obvious to be ignored. Philo of Alexandria (25 B.C.–A.D. 40), who influenced later Christians by bringing philosophy to the Old Testament, describes the mind as "the sight of the soul" and argues that belief is the result of visual intuition, not verbal demonstration.[31] Like Philo, the

31. Philo of Alexandria, *Quod Deus Immutabilis Sit,* 45–46, in *Works,* trans. F. H. Colson and G. H. Whitaker, 12 vols., The Loeb Classical Library (Cambridge, Mass., Harvard University Press, 1962), III, 33. Cf. *De Posteritate Caini,* 166–167 (*Works,* II, 427).

Christian fathers explained the operations of faith in the same way that Plato had explained intuition, as a seeing with the mind. Tertullian (b. 160), for example, believed that Paul saw and heard the Lord only because his soul had eyes and ears of its own.[32]

Of course, understanding was not simply a matter of reading the Bible. Not everyone who read the Word had faith; and the absence of faith, it was maintained, guaranteed that the reading would be imperfect. Many of the church fathers explained this phenomenon by reverting to the psychological notion *simile simili cognoscitur*, which Plato had employed to account for human knowledge of the Forms. The letter of Scripture is material, to be seen by the eye of sense; but the inward meaning is spiritual and must be surveyed by man's spiritual vision.

More than any of his contemporaries, Augustine channeled a knowledge of Platonism into the mainstream of Christianity. In the Neoplatonic circles that he frequented at Rome and Milan, he found a rationale that made it possible to reconcile his passionate disposition with his chosen religion. Augustine proceeded in the spirit of *fides quaerens intellectum*, convinced, like his predecessors, that the light of faith must precede the vision of truth. We begin "in faith, to be made perfect in sight. This also is the sum total of the whole of what is laid down." [33] Augustine's spiritual growth, as recorded in *The Confessions*, was accompanied by a series of modifications on his fundamentally visual habits of thought. His conversion to Christianity was in one sense a conversion to a new way of looking at God. As a youth he could imagine no more than he saw with his carnal eye, and so he thought of God as a vast corporeal object, stretching to

32. Tertullian, *De Anima*, trans. Peter Holmes, 4 vols. (Edinburgh, T. and T. Clark, 1869–1870), II, 429.

33. Augustine, *Enchiridion ad Laurentium de Fide, Spe, Caritate*, V, trans. Ernest Evans (London, Society for Promoting Christian Knowledge, 1953), p. 3.

the limits of the universe. In time, however, his reading of Plato and his conversion to Christianity opened the eyes of his soul to the eternal light of the Lord.[34] This was one of the discoveries that later developed into the Augustinian doctrine of illumination. A metaphysical dualism of matter and spirit underlies this doctrine and forms the basis for Augustine's distinction between two kinds of vision: one for perception and the other for thought. The second level is further divided between *scientia*, the rational knowledge of temporal things, and *sapientia*, the intellectual knowledge of eternal things. This trinity of mental states operates through three separate varieties of vision; one for sensation, one for discursive reason, and one for intuition.[35] Vision, by far the most important of the senses, occurs when the soul exercises its capacity for receiving visual stimuli. Like Plotinus, and unlike Aristotle, Augustine considers sensation an activity of the soul: the inner eye looks out; the images do not rush in.[36] The second level of vision accompanies knowledge, which involves the internal observation of images retained in the memory. This process is only partially comparable to Aristotle's formulations, for although the images originate in sensation, Augustine gives no account of abstraction. The images are visible because of an inner light of truth that illuminates the mind.[37] Like the Plotinian One, which is the sun of the intellect, the inner light is the lamp of all understanding, God Himself, and the primary object of Christian wisdom.

The Augustinian doctrine of wisdom has been the subject of considerable debate. In brief, the theory involves a world of Ideas (borrowed from Neoplatonism) contained in the Christian *nous*, Christ, and united within the mind of God. These

34. Augustine, *Confessions*, VII, 10.
35. Augustine, *De Trinitate*, XI, ix, 16; XII, xv, 25. The three levels of vision are discussed at length in *De Genesi ad Litteram*, XII, vi, 15.
36. Augustine, *De Trinitate*, XI, i, 1.
37. Augustine, *De Magistro*, XII, 40; and *De Trinitate*, XII, xv, 24.

divine conceptions are the exemplars of all creation and the standards according to which all human judgments are made. The crux of the matter rests in Augustine's assertion that those with "a strong and vigorous mental vision" are able to view the Ideas "all together in the truth." [38] If the mind sees the Ideas and if the Ideas are contained within the divine essence, then it would appear that the human mind has the capacity to behold the essence of God. While this is not the place to rehearse the controversy, it is noteworthy that most commentators have been hesitant to interpret Augustine's statements as an ontologism. Their reluctance has been due in no small part to Augustine's own saving inconsistencies. In a Pauline mood, for example, he could argue that "faith has eyes by which it sees that that is somehow true which it does not yet see; it certainly sees that it does not yet see what it believes." [39] At the least we may be certain that Christian wisdom, as Augustine understood it, consists in the mental vision of exemplar Ideas illuminated by God. Whether or not the mind actually sees God must remain an open question. But regardless of modern interpretations, the doctrine of illumination and the related doctrine of divine exemplarism were an important part of Augustine's legacy to the Middle Ages. His Christian Platonism rendered God and God's universe intelligible and equipped man with a precise — and emphatically visual — method for apprehending that intelligibility.

38. Augustine, *De Libero Arbitrio*, II, xiii, 36, in *Earlier Writings*, trans. J. H. S. Burleigh (Philadelphia, The Westminster Press, 1953), p. 158.

39. Augustine, *Epistolae*, CXX, ii, 8, cited by Eugène Portalié, *A Guide to the Thought of Saint Augustine*, trans. R. J. Bastian (London, Burns & Oates Ltd., 1960), pp. 116–117. Cf. also *Epistolae*, CXLVII, iii, 8; *De Genesi*, XII, xxxi, 59; *Soliloquia*, I, viii, 15; and *De Peccatorum Meritis*, I, xxv, 38. Some discussions of the problem are: Portalié, pp. 110 ff., with a useful summary of recent opinion; Copleston, II, 60 ff.; and Richard McKeon's preface to Augustine in *Selections from Medieval Philosophers*, 2 vols. (New York, Charles Scribner's Sons, 1929), I, 3 ff.

The five or six centuries that followed Augustine's death were not remarkable for the quantity or originality of philosophy produced. It was not until the twelfth and thirteenth centuries, which saw the rediscovery and translation of Aristotle's logical and scientific writings, that large numbers of thinkers began to revise older traditions. During the interim Platonism remained the dominant influence; Christian truth resided in transcendent Ideas that filled the mind of God and were accessible to human thought through an inner vision that functioned in complete independence of the lower forms of cognition.

Plotinus's supremely intelligible universe and his tendency to turn inward and upward made a deep impression in the mind of the Pseudo-Dionysius (fl. ca. 500). Indeed, were one to remove all the Plotinian elements from his philosophy, there would be little left but trinal triplicities and the darkness of unknowing. The universe of the Pseudo-Dionysius descends in orderly emanations from the indivisible and eternal unity of God. The divine essence — which far exceeds the content of human conceptions — manifests itself in a brilliant flood of light, which is received and reflected according to the dignity of the recipient. Above man are the angelic hierarchies that, because of their close proximity to God, have an especially clear insight into the nature of things. The light then descends into the human soul, its purity diminished by passing through the corrupting veil of the flesh. The ascent to divine wisdom may follow either of two routes, both of which equate knowing with seeing (or with a sight so intense that it results in blindness). The *via negativa* strips away the veil by negating the material content of images applied to God, "like as men who, carving a statue out of marble, remove all the impediments that hinder the clear perceptive of the latent image." [40] The positive way affirms the contents of ma-

40. *The Mystical Theology*, II, trans. C. E. Rolt (London, Society for Promoting Christian Knowledge, 1920), p. 195.

terial images with the qualification that they be understood "superessentially," that is, when the term "Good" is applied to God, we mean that he is the "superessential" Good. At the conclusion of this process we should have a supernatural vision of all things united within the first cause.[41]

The most important departure from the general predominance of Platonism during this transitional period occurs in the writing of Boethius (480–524). In addition to translating the *Organon*, he completed several commentaries on Aristotle, thereby introducing both the materials and the method that were to characterize scholastic philosophy. In his commentary on Porphyry's *Isagoge* (which he also translated), Boethius outlines the psychology of *De Anima* in great detail and with impressive accuracy. He maintains the tripartite division of the soul, though the visual component in abstraction is presented more emphatically than in Aristotle. Sensible form enters in the images of sensation, and "when the mind receives these incorporeals intermixed with bodies, separating them, it looks upon them and contemplates them." [42] Universals are therefore not transcendent Platonic Ideas but forms only psychologically separable from sensible objects.

But Boethius was not consistent in his allegiance to the principles of Aristotle's epistemology. In the commentary on Porphyry he makes it clear that he recognizes a difference between Plato and Aristotle and that his role as expositor does not commit him to the latter's position.[43] In other words, Boethius was undecided, or at least unwilling to align himself with either philosopher while borrowing extensively from both. In this regard his example is instructive, for such a fusion of the two

41. *The Divine Names*, V, 7, trans. C. E. Rolt (London, Society for Promoting Christian Knowledge, 1920), p. 138.

42. Boethius, *In Isagogen Porphyrii Commenta*, I, 11, trans. Richard McKeon, in *Selections*, I, 96.

43. Ibid., I, 11 (McKeon, I, 98).

36

main traditions of visual epistemology was to become the norm in medieval philosophy, particularly after the distinction between philosophy and theology had been fixed. With the revival of Aristotle, Christianity had to become more tolerant of natural science and therefore of knowledge derived from the senses. The debate over universals is only one reflection of the tensions implicit in this collision of old and new. Aristotle's psychology gained preference among philosophers and logicians because it defined the limits of certitude that could be achieved in the absence of an overriding illumination. The theologians, however, were preoccupied with spiritual knowledge and generally gravitated to the Augustinian position, with its emphasis on understanding. Such an obvious division of interests, with its attendant division in theory, was an important aspect of medieval Scholasticism at its height. During the twelfth and thirteenth centuries the crux of the debate became increasingly clear: while everyone agreed that thinking is a kind of seeing, there was considerable disagreement as to the nature and status of the objects seen.

The Christian Platonism of Augustine, as I have noted, emphasizes that the objects seen within the mind are real, while natural particulars are cut off from, and merely dim reflections of, that higher inward reality. God, the pinnacle of the ontological order, is thus also the summit of Christian knowledge. In line with such Augustinian assumptions, Anselm (1033–1109) equates highest truth with the supreme object of internal vision. The human soul, by its natural participation in the spiritual order, reflects that order more perfectly than any of the objects of external flux. It is its own mirror, wherein it contemplates "the image of what it cannot see face to face." [44] The believer has the assurance that by straining mental vision to its absolute maximum he will achieve a conception that approximates God

44. Anselm, *Monologium*, LXVII, trans. S. N. Deane (London, Kegan Paul, Trench, Trübner & Co., Ltd., 1903), p. 132.

— which is the assurance that underlies the famous ontological argument.

The comparison of Anselm and Peter Abelard (1079–1142) casts light on one of the deepest fissures in the "seamless" robe of medieval thought. Unlike Anselm, who built upon a firm Augustinian foundation, Abelard was the bête noire of philosophical realism. By ignoring traditional theological imperatives and by following the assumptions of empirical psychology to strictly logical conclusions, he exposed many of the weaknesses in the current Christian epistemology. According to Abelard, thought occurs when the understanding turns its attention to an image that derives from sensation. Before it reaches the understanding, however, the image must first pass through the imagination. The result, like an architect's conception of a building, is "a certain imaginary and fictive thing, which the mind constructs for itself when it wishes and as it wishes." [45] The picture before the mind has none of the ontological significance of Aristotle's intelligible forms. Rather, the images are universal only in the sense that they are generalized and confused representations of several individual objects. The effect of Abelard's dialectic is twofold. First, he implies that the order of being consists of individual material objects, and that Platonic Ideas and Aristotelian forms have no substantial existence. Second, since mental images are mere likenesses of the things thought about, the orders of being and knowledge are effectively separated. The Platonic formula has been exactly reversed: by looking within we see the imperfect reflections of things actually existing in natural flux.

While still a student, John of Salisbury (1115–1180) heard Abelard lecture in Paris; thus it is probable that the moderate quality of his realism first took shape during his years at univer-

45. Abelard, *Glosses on Porphyry*, trans. Richard McKeon, in *Selections*, I, 239. For a summary of the realist-nominalist struggle, see Meyrick H. Carré, *Realists and Nominalists* (London, Oxford University Press, 1946), passim.

sity. John's psychology springs from Aristotle in that the universals pictured in the mind have a foundation in extramental reality. Genera and species are "mental representations of actual, natural things, intellectual images of the mutual likenesses of real things." [46] But John also makes a place for wisdom, which is distinguished from science because it has to do with divine knowledge. Wisdom is rooted in sensation, for the intuitive understanding (which produces wisdom) is capable of gleaning divine truths from the prior disquisitions of reason. The distinction between science and wisdom and the connection of the latter with spiritual knowledge are indications that John had read some Augustine along with his Aristotle. Intuition is possible because of the soul's innate participation in the "divine wisdom," which "embraces the nature, development, and ultimate end of all things." The object of knowledge in this supreme mode is "an image, as well as an idea of the world," [47] and we have access to it, at least in part, because the mind can see.

In a way similar to Boethius, John of Salisbury borrows from both of the main epistemological traditions. The Christian philosopher with an interest in logic could hardly fault Aristotle's psychology; but the Stagirite did little to account for spiritual knowledge, while Augustine did a great deal. Therefore it is not uncommon to find the two traditions, as it were, back to back. The eye of reason scrutinizes the images from without, while the eye of the understanding gazes at the luminous regions of metaphysical truth within. With John of Salisbury the eye of reason predominates, and Augustine enters only when there is no obvious alternative.

With the Victorines, on the other hand, the balance of influence takes exactly opposite proportions. Hugh of St. Victor

46. John of Salisbury, *The Metalogicon*, II, 20, trans. Daniel D. McGarry (Berkeley, University of California Press, 1962), p. 121. Cf. also IV, 9 (p. 217).
47. Ibid., IV, 31 (McGarry, p. 250).

(1096–1141) constructed his theory of knowledge on a broad Augustinian base, beginning with the division of the soul's faculties according to three kinds of vision. Originally all three forms of sight were clear. Since the Fall, however, the eye of contemplation (*oculus contemplationis*) has been blind, the eye of reason (*oculus rationis*) has been blurred, and only the eye of the flesh (*oculus carnis*) has retained its original clarity.[48] By the determined study of philosophy, however, man may regain the sight of reason and thence proceed to the contemplation of God and the primordial exemplars. Aristotle's only appearance in this predominantly Augustinian framework occurs in Hugh's description of abstraction. The eye of reason is directed to images drawn through sensation and imagination, or to those retained in the memory. But discursive reason is described as a kind of searching through concepts and is sharply distinguished from the highest exercise of the mind, contemplation, the final vision of that which is sought. The ascent to divine knowledge (to Hugh's mind the end of all learning) is a typically Augustinian kind of seeing and generally characteristic of the Victorine theory of knowledge.

Aristotle's way of looking at things was perhaps better known to early medieval philosophers than is generally recognized. Nevertheless, it is true that his full weight was not felt until the thirteenth century, particularly among such Dominicans as Albert the Great and Thomas Aquinas. This is not to suggest, however, that Aristotle's mounting influence brought about a decline in the authority of Augustine. To the contrary, a long line of Franciscans preserved the traditions of Christian Platonism, although very often preservation involved significant alteration. In short, the philosophers of the thirteenth century made

48. Hugh of St. Victor, *De Sacramentis Christianae Fidei*, I, x, 2, cited by John P. Kleinz, *The Theory of Knowledge of Hugh of Saint Victor* (Washington, D. C., The Catholic University of America Press, 1944), pp. 19–20, to whom I am indebted throughout this section.

the paradoxical discoveries that Aristotle could be brought to the service of natural theology and that Augustine could be adapted to the purposes of natural philosophy.

Scholastic interpretations of Aristotle's psychology were colored, to an important degree, by the influence of the philosophers of Islam. The *intellectus agens,* of brief and uncertain import in *De Anima,* becomes a crucial feature in the Arabian redactions of peripatetic epistemology. According to Avicenna (980–1037), the active intellect is a separate agency that confers actuality on the human mind. Initially the individual intellect is a mere potential. Because it is naturally endowed with first notions, however, the soul is able to actualize its potential by converting the images of sensation into universals. When this preparation is completed, the mind is *in habitu,* prepared for and passively awaiting the intervention of the *intellectus agens.* The final step occurs when the active intellect, like a sudden blaze of sunlight, illuminates the formerly potential images and renders them actually intelligible to contemplation. Thus the role of the individual soul in the acquisition of knowledge (in becoming the *intellectus adeptus*) is emphatically passive. According to Avicenna's own analogy, the soul has two faces, one directed to sensible objects, the other to intellectual objects. While taking care to ignore the objects below, the soul must also keep a clear eye turned to the principles that flow in from above.[49]

By emphasizing the eternal independence of the active intellect, by setting it high in the ontological order, and by stressing the dualism of active and passive, the Arab commentators created a Platonic Aristotle who had obvious attractions for Christian philosophers. Except for the fact that the source of Augustinian illumination was God, there was little to distinguish its opera-

49. My summary is a condensation of materials in F. Rahman's *Avicenna's Psychology* (London, Oxford University Press, 1952), a translation with extensive notes. Averroes's psychology, though different in detail, follows essentially the same pattern as Avicenna's.

tions and effects from the Arab version of the active intellect. The obvious step, taken most notably by Robert Grosseteste (ca. 1170–1253) and most of the Franciscans who followed him, was to identify the *intellectus agens* with God, thereby bringing *sapientia* and *scientia* under the same banner. Grosseteste argues that divine light is shed upon intelligible images and the eye of the mind (*oculus mentis*) in the same way that the sun illuminates the physical eye and visible things.[50] The analogy between corporal and spiritual *lux* is critical to Grosseteste's metaphysics as well as to his epistemology. The creation of the universe occurred when God dispersed shafts of light, all regulated by geometrical laws, through uninformed matter. For this reason Grosseteste was convinced that the study of optics and geometry were essential to an understanding of the phenomenal world.[51] In addition to its function as a *principia essendi*, however, light is also a *principia cognoscendi*, for the luminous geometrical forms constituting the structure of the universe derive their existence from the same exemplary brilliance that illuminates the intelligible forms before the eyes of the mind. God causes being, and God causes knowledge; and he causes them in accordance with the same visible laws.

Roger Bacon (1212–1292), Grosseteste's disciple at Oxford, followed his master's psychology in almost every detail. The changes that he did make were more in name than in principle; for while Grosseteste had considered himself a follower of Augustine, Bacon expounds almost identical doctrines in the names of Aristotle and Avicenna. These are the supreme philosophers, who argued that the active intellect is a separate, illuminating substance to be indentified with God himself.[52] According to

50. Robert Grosseteste, *On Truth*, trans. Richard McKeon, in *Selections*, I, 274.
51. A. C. Crombie, *Robert Grosseteste and the Origins of Experimental Science, 1100–1700* (Oxford, The Clarendon Press, 1953), p. 104.
52. Roger Bacon, *Opus Maius*, II, 5.

Bacon, the external object produces an immutation in the sense organ, which in turn produces an image in the imagination. The phantasm is then illuminated by the active intellect, thus producing the actual *species intelligibilis.* "Species" is, of course, a logical term, a universal, and Bacon sometimes uses the word in this sense. But he also uses it in connection with light — in the sense, for example, that species of light are essential to vision.[53] In fact, Bacon's division of species is identical to Grosseteste's division of light. The sensible species that accumulate in the imagination are converted into intelligible species by the active intellect in the same way that Grosseteste's corporeal light is rendered intelligible.[54] And in the same way that Grosseteste's ontology and epistemology hinge on geometrical principles inherent in light (corporeal and immaterial), Bacon's visible species function according to mathematical laws governing both the order of being and the order of knowledge. The numerical principles that regulate the alterations of the physical universe enter the mind as sensible species and in being rendered intelligible become the (still visible) species of logic. Building upon such assumptions, Bacon is quite confident in the assertion that the terms of logical discourse are intimately bound up with the metaphysical structure of the universe — which is to say, with mathematical forms borne into the mind along the rays of visible light.[55]

The extreme realism of Franciscan epistemology arises from a foundation in Augustinian Platonism only occasionally modified by the more or less Platonic Aristotle of the Arabs. Many of the same philosophical ingredients run through the texture of Dominican epistemology, though the relative proportions are al-

53. Ibid., V, v, 1.
54. Ibid., V, i, 4.
55. Ibid., IV, i, 2. Bacon recognized formal logic as a science but distinguished it (*Opus Maius,* II, vi) from his own metalogic, in which terms, by their ontological significance, bear more than formal weight.

most exactly inverted. The rediscovery and translation of Aristotle's writings stimulated a general revision of Arab interpretations and a much more selective appropriation of Augustianian doctrines. Albert the Great (1206–1280), a spark to even greater lights, adopted the theories and terminology of the Platonic tradition but interpreted them in accordance with the orginal Aristotle. Most significantly, perhaps, Albert generally adheres to the Aristotelian theory of abstraction, recognizing the active intellect as an illuminating agent within the individual soul, and not in separation. In this divergence from tradition Albert had a follower in his student Thomas Aquinas (1225–1274), who also makes a distinction between the active intellect and God.

According to Thomas, the light of human reason is sufficient for the acquisition of natural truth, and the special illumination of divine grace is essential only for divine truths. When the impressions received by the senses are converted into images by the internal senses, the resulting phantasms have the same relationships to the intellect as color does to sight. The active intellect, working from within the soul, illuminates the phantasm and abstracts the universal element, producing the *species impressa* in the passive intellect, which reacts to this immutation by forming the *species expressa* or *verbum mentis*, the concept itself.[56] Unlike Augustine, whose psychology provides for the apprehension of forms apart from matter, Thomas, in concurrence with Aristotle, regards all cognition as a cooperation of body and soul in which knowledge is according to the mode of the knower, not the thing known. While knowledge is a form of mental vision, the intelligible species before the mind's eye derive from sensible species, and not divine exemplars.[57] In addition, Aquinas emphasizes that the proper object of knowledge is the external particular and that the concepts in the passive intellect are merely

56. Thomas Aquinas, *Summa Theologica*, I, 85, art. 1.
57. Thomas Aquinas, *Summa Contra Gentiles*, III, 41.

the means by which such knowledge is made accessible. All thought is accompanied by phantasms, but the images before the mind are no more than likenesses of the things actually known.[58] Accordingly, the eye of the human mind has a special and limited range of vision. Suspended between the material and the spiritual, it is blind to the objects of those regions as they are in themselves and must bring them into focus by converting them to intelligible species.

This important separation between the order of being and the order of knowledge points up a crucial difference between Thomas's epistemology and that of the Franciscans. Bacon and Grosseteste assume that the contents of the mind exactly reproduce the structure of the extramental world, whether in the direct vision of divine exemplars or in the geometrical forms that enter through sensation. The identification of knowing with seeing, according to such assumptions, implies an exact and unimpeded visual contact with the structure of all being. Aquinas, on the other hand, assumes a certain disparity between the contents of the mind and the things that those contents represent. This spirit of moderation is characteristically Aristotelian, and it helps to explain Thomas's tendency to describe concepts as verbal constructions rather than images. The final stage in abstraction involves, as I have already mentioned, the formation of the *species expressa* in the passive intellect. *Expressa* has a strong tactile thrust and connotes both the molding of visual form and the expression of ideas in words. The alternative phrase for the intelligible species in *verbum mentis*, which suggests that Aquinas used *expressa* in the latter sense. Thus the final concept may be understood as an internally "expressed" word that, although related to the images required in all thought, is itself explicitly verbal. The categories of logic were, for Thomas, the categories of extramental reality; but the adequa-

58. Aquinas, *Summa Theologica*, I, 85, art. 2.

tion of the intellect to that reality, though invariably dependent on images, seemed to be most precisely expressed in the terms of logical predication. In short, since the known cannot be seen as it exists per se, it could be better characterized in words than in images.

Thomas's tendency to identify the intelligible species with words is in marked contrast to the position taken by his contemporary Bonaventure (1221–1274). The Franciscan master would have agreed with Thomas that we have no direct knowledge of God's essence or of the divine exemplars, but Bonaventure looked upon the sensible and intelligible worlds as a graduated hierarchy of visible symbols that reflect, with varying degrees of precision, their origin in God. Such reflections are visible in three different forms: by shadows in external nature; by traces within the mind; and by images above the mind. To this arrangement of the objects of knowledge there correspond three modes of vision: the outward, sensual vision of the body; the inward vision of the spirit; and the upward vision of the mind. This division of the intellectual and real orders provides the structure for Bonaventure's well-known *Itinerarium Mentis in Deum*, a description of the soul's ascent through the various *vestigia Dei*, culminating in an ecstatic and indescribable vision of God.[59]

Bonaventure describes sensation and the process of abstraction in terms more or less consistent with *De Anima*. The soul is originally a tabula rasa; external objects produce likenesses in the sense organs which proceed to the interior senses, where they are judged; judgment takes place when the light of the active intellect stimulates the passive intellect to extract the universal from the phantasm. The intelligible species that results, as Bonaventure understood it, consists of a visual form transmitted from the object to the mind. At the highest levels of cognition God is also reflected in the intellect, though the forms that appear are

59. Bonaventure, *Itinerarium Mentis in Deum*, I, 4.

spiritual, devoid of material attributes. The objects seen in these different phases of knowledge are similar in that their contents are ultimately reducible to numerical relationships. Since number is the preeminent exemplar in the mind of God and also the most important vestige of the maker's hand in nature,[60] Bonaventure's universe, like Bacon's, is shot through with intelligible forms. The ontological and epistemological orders intersect in the numerical substructure of the traces and images before the mind's eye, which express themselves and are ultimately known by being seen.

The condemnations of 1277 stimulated an increased confidence in Augustinianism, and predictably a number of Franciscans, in oppostion to Thomism, took shelter in the traditional theory of knowledge. At the same time, however, the end of the thirteenth century brought a more important division of interests within the ranks of the Franciscans. Duns Scotus (1266–1308), for example, while constantly pronouncing himself a follower of Augustine, expounds doctrines that reflect more than a passing acquaintance with Aristotle. The subtle doctor has more in common with Aquinas than Bonaventure in his denial of Augustinian illumination,[61] and like Aquinas he joins an interest in logic with a tendency to identify intelligible species with logical terms. William of Ockham (1295–1349) moved even further than Scotus from the intellectual mainstream of the Franciscan order. He adopted and considerably modified the terminist logic that had begun to develop during the thirteenth century. Peter of Spain (d. 1277) was the most popular exponent of this highly quantified approach to dialectic, though his extreme realism is to be distinguished from Ockham's so-called nominalism. Peter

60. Bonaventure, *Itinerarium*, II, 10. For a full discussion of the contents of Bonaventure's images, see Étienne Gilson, *The Philosophy of St. Bonaventure*, trans. Dom Illtyd Trethowan and F. J. Sheed (New York, Sheed & Ward, Inc., 1938), p. 220.
61. Duns Scotus, *Opus Oxoniense*, I, iii, 4, art. 5.

assumes that every predicable corresponds to a universal in the real order, with the result that his logic can be appropriately described as a dialectical metaphysics, or metalogic.[62] By plugging logical terms into his (implicit) ontology, Peter gives them the same status as mental images in the systems of Bacon and Grosseteste.

Although he retained an interest in terms, William of Ockham rejected what he thought of as the confusion of logic and metaphysics. Unlike Aquinas, whose moderate realism results from the belief that the categories of knowledge have an imperfect resemblance to divine ideas as they manifest themselves in nature, Ockham discards exemplarism and maintains that God has ideas of individual things alone. Universals therefore have no foundation in extramental reality but function as mental pictures or patterns that merely stand for a variety of discrete things.[63] As an alternative to the theory of abstraction, Ockham argues that we have true knowledge of the external world through intuition. This is usually described as a form of intellectual vision, but as a vision in which the object of thought is the individual thing itself, not an image viewed internally.[64] Ockham's visual epistemology, then, almost exactly contradicts that of his Franciscan predecessors. For him the eye of the mind has penetrated the medium of abstraction and sees the particulars of nature as they exist in themselves. Internal images, on the other hand, are emptied of ontological significance and function primarily as predicates in a strictly formal logic.

The more traditionally characteristic features of Franciscan

62. Peter of Spain, *Summulae Logicales*, trans. Joseph P. Mullally (Notre Dame, Ind., The University of Notre Dame, 1945), from Mullally's introduction, p. xxxii.

63. William of Ockham, *Ordinatio*, II, viii, *prima redactio*.

64. Ibid., I, Prologue. In his introduction to Ockham's *Philosophical Writings* (London, Thomas Nelson & Sons Ltd., 1957), p. xxix, Philotheus Boehner points out that Ockham also held an "intellection theory" in which the universal is identical with the act of abstraction.

epistemology — dualist psychology, the doctrine of illumination, the identification of the *intellectus agens* with God, extreme realism, and a preoccupation with the mathematical sciences — were carried on into the fourteenth century by philosophers such as Roger Marston (d. 1303) and Matthew of Aquasparta (ca. 1240–1302).[65] But the importance of Franciscan philosophy, particularly in its mathematical phase at Oxford, does not become fully appreciable until the Renaissance. Highly visualized modes of thought, coupled with the predominance of quantity among the categories of science,[66] led to a peculiarly diagrammatic conception of mental space. The natural order was more and more understood as a function of mathematical relationships that, when plotted out on the graphs of the mind, might be viewed in their timeless aspect as exemplar patterns in the divine intelligence. This tendency reached its fullest medieval expression in the works of Ramón Lull (ca. 1235–1315), who proposed to set forth the divine hierarchy in elaborate logic charts. Since he conceived of the logical and metaphysical orders as conforming to the same abstract patterns, Lull's trees and disks also represent the basic divisions of the human mind. The structure of thought, as he understood it, like the structure of the universe, is reducible to a series of spatial relationships that may be reproduced in abstract pictures. This same tendency, in a more sophisticated and productive form, reappears in the Renaissance, when scientists like Galileo and Kepler discover that Nature's book is replete with geometrical diagrams and equations. For them, as for Bacon and Grosseteste, the order of being and the order of knowledge are governed by identical mathematical laws: laws imperfectly visible in nature, more perfectly visible in the

65. For summaries, see D. E. Sharp, *Franciscan Philosophy at Oxford in the Thirteenth Century*, passim, and Carré, *Realists and Nominalists*, pp. 104–105.
66. Cf. A. C. Crombie, *Medieval and Early Modern Science*, 2 vols. (Garden City, N.Y., Doubleday & Company, Inc., 1959), I, 182.

mind, and most perfectly visible in the fixed patterns of God's eternal plan.

THE RENAISSANCE

I shall reserve extensive commentary on the Renaissance for Chapter 2, where the extraphilosophical ramifications of visual epistemology will be my subject. The need for such a shift in emphasis is instructive, for it underlines the fact that while men of the Renaissance were more than ever concerned with ideas, their concern was more varied and, strictly speaking, less philosophical than it had been for men of the past. Renaissance philosophers contributed little that was completely new to the wealth of ideas inherited from pagan and Christian antiquity. Their preoccupation with nature as a developing system, for example, and their interest in the question of infinity were problems with numerous antecedents in the traditions of the past. But Renaissance thought was characterized by a tendency to emphasize the relationship between man and his world as an end in itself rather than as a means to the knowledge of God. Nominalism sharpened the distinction between nature and grace, philosophy and theology, and generally stimulated the development of science and the empirical method. The revival of Platonism in some ways dulled the effects of Ockham's razor, but the Neoplatonic coloring of the revival encouraged the view that inaccessible transcendent forms were immanent in external and human nature. Platonism precipitated the gradual replacement of logic by mathematics, with the result that nature came to be understood as a self-complete and precisely quantifiable network of numerical relationships rather than a series of logical categories. Mathematics also gave support to the notion that knowledge has to do with structures reducible to a visible medium, and not with strictly verbal classifications. In general, then, it was the emphasis rather than the originality of Renaissance thought that made it distinctive, and a paramount feature of this emphasis was an intensification of the visual elements already present in the inherited epistemological tradition.

Whether Nicholas of Cusa (1401–1464) was the last great philosopher of the Middle Ages or the first of the Renaissance is a disputable point. It is hardly open to question, however, that by rejecting medieval cosmology and asserting an infinite universe, he initiated an idea that attracted a considerable following in the latter period. The effect of Nicholas's conception of infinity is similar to that of nominalism, for it creates an almost unbridgeable gap between the finite mind of man and the infinite mind of God. The epistemological leap from the oppositions and distinctions of discursive reason to God, the *coincidentia oppositorum*, is effected only through intellectual vision, through an inward sight that bears the beholder to a point beyond mere conceptual divisions. This mental ascent is possible because the human mind is the image of the divine, and because by reflecting upon itself it apprehends the likenesses of truths that are actually present in the intellect of God.[67]

Nicholas colored his basically Platonic theory of knowledge with an Aristotelian account of abstraction and the fundamentals of medieval faculty psychology. Sense impressions are converted to images on a fine spiritual film in the front cavity of the brain, the imagination. These images, along with those stored in the memory, pass to the midbrain, where reason has a confused vision of forms still imperfectly separated from matter. In the rear cavity is mind, an independent and incorporeal image of God, the exemplar of all things. By turning inward the mind conceives the point, the line, and the surface, and then applies them to the images abstracted from nature.[68] Since God employed number

67. Nicholas of Cusa, *Idiota*, III, 3 ("*De Mente*"). Cf. Ernst Cassirer, *The Individual and the Cosmos in Renaissance Philosophy*, trans. Mario Domandi (New York, Harper & Row, 1964), pp. 13–14.
68. Ibid., III, 8–9.

when He created the world, and since human thought is naturally equipped with a vision of perfect numerical forms, the highest powers of the human intellect are capable of extracting the intelligible contents from the images before the mind's eye.

As a Christian, Nicholas naturally subordinated the claims of natural philosophy to the higher knowledge of God. Accordingly, he valued the exactness of mathematics only secondarily as a foundation for scientific inquiry, while its primary function was to deepen man's capacity for understanding God. Since all knowledge necessarily involves the use of images to represent invisible truths, the alliance between mathematics and visible symbols at least guaranteed that the objects of mental vision would contain nothing uncertain or imprecise.[69] According to *De Docta Ignorantia*, perfect geometrical forms, conceivable only in the mind, are the exemplar patterns for similar forms imperfectly manifested in nature. By ascending through these various forms, the mind arrives at an apprehension of absolute simplicity, the divine coincidence of opposites in which all forms are comprehended simultaneously. The result of this intuition cannot be stated in words, but it can be accurately symbolized (as it is conceived) in geometrical images. For example, if one side of a triangle is extended to infinity, it will coincide with the other two sides. Thus an infinite straight line, by containing the sides of all triangles, is analogous in its simplicity to God.[70] While he is careful not to confuse the image with the object it represents, Nicholas is firm in the conviction that mathematical symbols accommodate the invisible essence of God to the visual mode of human cognition with absolute precision.

Nicholas of Cusa borrowed many of the principal features of his epistemology from the traditions of the Middle Ages. His

69. Cf. Cassirer, *The Individual and the Cosmos*, pp. 52–53, to whom I am indebted throughout this section.

70. Nicholas of Cusa, *De Docta Ignorantia*, I, 12. Cf. also *Idiota*, III, 7.

habit of associating knowing with seeing, moreover with seeing mathematical forms, may have derived from a similar practice among thirteenth-century Franciscans. He also expressed agreement with Ramón Lull in a note to the *Ars Magna*, a work that no doubt, confirmed his own highly visualized exemplarism.[71] But Nicholas broke with the past by emphasizing the soul's independence in acquiring knowledge. Although the mind is God's image, it requires no special illumination in order to function; and while it abstracts intelligible forms from sensible images, the soul contains within itself the perfect examplar patterns. The mind attains knowledge, not when it reproduces extramental reality, but when it generates the mathematical forms within its own nature. The soul is thus internally complete, a free and creative microcosm in which the numerical structure of the great world may be viewed with unflawed clarity.

Nicholas of Cusa gathered his Platonism from the inherited Christian tradition; but Marsilio Ficino (1433–1499) and the members of Cosimo de' Medici's Florentine Academy had access to the original dialogues. Like Nicholas, Ficino stressed the independence and hence near divinity of the human mind. Man is a composition of soul and body, with a *tertium quid*, a fine spiritual vapor that serves as a medium between the other two. The images of sensation are carried by the spirit to the imagination, where new and purer images are conceived. Through these the eye of the soul is stirred to the recollection of universal ideas it holds within itself.[72] The soul, because of this natural ability to look upward to the divine archetypes and downward to the sensible world, has an almost unlimited range of vision. Such assumed

71. Paolo Rossi, "The Legacy of Ramón Lull in Sixteenth-Century Thought," *Medieval and Renaissance Studies*, V (1961), pp. 188–189.

72. Marsilio Ficino, *Commentarium in Convivium Platonis*, VI, 6. For a discussion of pneumatic psychology, see George Sidney Brett, *Psychology, Ancient and Modern* (New York, Longmans, Green and Co., 1928), pp. 25–26.

scope goes far to account for Ficino's immense optimism, his assurance that because it sees all things, the soul is "the center of nature, the middle point of all that is, the chain of the world, the face of all, and the knot and bond of the universe." [73]

Ficino complemented the dignity of the soul by weaving his theory of knowledge into the fabric of his metaphysics. Following Plotinus, he describes the structure of the cosmos as a series of emanations; God created and illuminated the Angelic Mind, which in turn devolved upon the World Soul, the essence of all rational souls and the principle of form animating material creation. God, who is equated with the Platonic Good and identified with the sun, radiates an incorporeal brilliance that fills the universe. This divine light manifests itself in different images at each level of the cosmic order: in the Divine Mind as Ideas, in the Soul as concepts, in nature as seeds (seminal ideas), and in matter as shapes. The universe is thus permeated with visible forms that are at once the principles of being and of knowledge. These are comprehended in the third emanation, the World Soul, which informs the natural order, mirrors the intelligible order, and provides the link between the two by illuminating the human mind.[74]

Ficino thus enhanced human dignity by moving the Plotinian emanations into the mind itself, thereby binding the temporal and the eternal through the mediation of the spiritual *tertium quid*.[75] His habit of describing thought as vision, while central to his conception of the soul's mobility, was also a model for his discussion of the will. The universe, in its aspect of being and truth, is the object of knowledge; but in the aspect of goodness it is the object of love — and "all love begins with sight" (*amor*

---

73. Ficino, *Platonic Theology*, III, 2, trans. Josephine L. Burroughs, *Journal of the History of Ideas*, 5 (1944), 231.

74. Ficino, *Commentarium*, I, 3; II, 3–5; and *Platonic Theology*, III, 2.

75. Nesca A. Robb, *Neoplatonism of the Italian Renaissance* (New York, Octagon Books, 1968), p. 67.

itaque omnis incipit ab aspectu).[76] The forms of external things
enter the soul and meet corresponding Ideas painted within. If
the shapes conform, the will is activated positively with love; if
they disagree, the result is repulsion and hatred. It was partly
owing to Ficino's influence that this familiar doctrine came into
close alliance with the central features of visual epistemology as
they passed into the later Renaissance. Indeed, the work of the
Florentine Academy was a critical stage in the development of
the equation of thinking and seeing, for Ficino not only produced
translations of the main documents of Platonism and Neoplatonism but, through his commentaries, presented the tradition in
a way that encouraged visualist interpretations of Plato's theory
of knowledge.

Giovanni Pico della Mirandola (1463–1494) was the most important of Ficino's early followers. Like his master's, Pico's
theory of knowledge provides that the images abstracted from
sensation merely present an occasion for the recollection and
contemplation of Ideas that the soul contains within itself. And,
again like Ficino, his epistemology is closely bound up with his
theory of love, for love is the function of a single intellectual
faculty, the sight. In his commentary on Benivieni's *Canzone
d'amore*, a sonnet sequence inspired by Ficino's commentary on
the *Symposium*, Pico asserts that "sight is twofold, corporeal, and
spiritual; the first is that of Sense, the other of the Intellectual
faculty, by which we agree with Angels." [77] God's intelligible
light, which informs the entire universe, is also the source of
beauty in all of its graduated manifestations. External objects are
known by being seen, first in the images of sensation and then
by comparison with Ideas in the mind. Such vision also produces

76. Text and translation from Ficino, *Commentarium*, VI, 8, trans. Sears
Reynolds Jayne (Columbia, Mo., University of Missouri Press, 1944), p. 193.
77. John Pico della Mirandola, *A Platonick Discourse Upon Love*, trans.
Thomas Stanley, ed. E. G. Gardner (Boston, The Merrymount Press, 1914),
p. 27.

love: in carnal men for the beauty of the material object seen through the corporeal eye and in men of intellect for ideal beauty seen only by the eye of the mind.[78] Although Pico was following Ficino, he expanded and elaborated the Platonic doctrine of love into a form that had considerable influence during the sixteenth century. By connecting vision with the operations of the will and by maintaining the older associations of seeing with knowing, Pico's exposition of Benivieni's poetry rendered visual epistemology accessible to writers outside of the strictly philosophical tradition.

Ficino's influence, along with that of Augustine and the Pseudo-Dionysius, is discernible in the theological writings of John Colet (ca. 1467–1519), one of the earliest English Platonists. Colet adjusted the Christian trinity of faith, hope, and charity to suit his conception of the pilgrim's pathway to God. Following Augustine, he regarded hope as the first step, a purification of spirit resulting in the willingness to follow God's beckoning. The second step progresses to faith and the vision of Christian truth (*secunda fides revelatorumque*) as it is parceled out in Scripture.[79] Colet identifies truth with the light of Christ, the bearer of the divine *logos*, whose sunlike radiance is accommodated to human vision through the medium of the apostles. In the manner of Ficino and Pico, Colet's third step represents the fruition of knowledge through vision in a positive disposition of the will toward that which is loved.

As Colet's example well illustrates, the influence of Italian Neoplatonism was crucial to the spread of visual epistemology among Renaissance philosophers. But even where Ficino's impression was apparently not very deep, the tendency to construe thought as a kind of vision was common. Philip Melanchthon (1497–1560), for example, while generally an enthusiastic Aris-

78. Ibid., pp. 30, 41–42.
79. The Latin is from *Ioannis Coleti Enarratio in Epistolam S. Pauli ad Romanos*, trans. J. H. Lupton (London, Bell, 1873), p. 182.

totelian, anchored his thought in a doctrine of *lumen naturale*, which accounts for the innate intuition of moral principles and the idea of God.[80] And Pietro Pomponazzi (1462–1525), an integral Aristotelian, regarded imaginative presentations as essential in all cognition, thus emphasizing the visual character of thought. But he also insisted that the images before the mind, however far abstracted, retain their connection with matter.[81] Like most Aristotelians, Pomponazzi was at one with the Platonists in equating thought with sight but in complete disagreement as to the nature of the objects seen. His argument with Platonic epistemology was one side of what had for centuries been an almost exclusively two-sided battle. But in the present context it is what he affirmed that finally matters. He believed that to think was to see. That belief, almost as old as thought itself, had found an extremely fertile field in the minds of the men of Pomponazzi's generation; in fact, it was the common property of every Renaissance philosopher who put pen to paper and the unquestioned assumption of every literate person during the same period.

SUMMARY

The backward glance of intellectual history is perhaps over-prone to dwell on the obvious differences between men and ideas, too ready to dismiss prominent similarities as self-evident, and therefore somehow irrelevant. We are constantly reminded, for example, that Plato and Aristotle were the founders of easily distinguishable philosophical traditions. Yet we should remember that all philosophers share the urgent desire to bring order

80. Frederick Copleston, *A History of Philosophy*, 6 vols. (Westminster, Md., The Newman Press, 1946–1953), III, 227.
81. Cf. Andrew Halliday Douglas, *The Philosophy and Psychology of Pietro Pomponazzi* (Cambridge, England, Cambridge University Press, 1910), p. 202.

to apparent chaos and that beneath broad differences of doctrine they are joined in a common enterprise. To a certain degree each so-called system of philosophy can be understood as an individual rationalization of the same primary impulse.

Plato and Aristotle claim our attention because they were immensely successful at organizing and articulating this characteristic philosophical preoccupation. They proceeded from the common assumption that the universe is thoroughly reasonable in its organization, and that this intelligible structure is accessible to the human intellect. For both philosophers the truth was necessarily objective; and in order to be fixed it had to weave itself into the determinate structure of the not-self. The gap between the human mind and the external world therefore had to be bridged. Sight, of all the forms of cognition, seemed most adequate for transporting the data of the outside into the mental regions of the inside. Furthermore, by unanimous decision the most perfect of the senses and in the absence of a better analogy, sight served both philosophers as a model for the mechanism of thought itself. By their consent to this explanation for human intellection, Plato and Aristotle generated a tradition that persisted long after the decay of Greek civilization.

The development of visual epistemology during and after the decline of Rome may be accounted for in at least two ways. First, of course, there was the sheer momentum of the Greek and Latin philosophical traditions. Second, and perhaps more important, was the grounding of Christian faith in revelation, in truths beyond proof that had to be seen in some mysterious way before they could be believed. The truth of Christ was something revealed, something discovered at the end of a passage from darkness to light, or from blindness to vision. Platonism attracted Christian philosophers because it laid claim to a world of transcendent knowledge and because it offered a rationale sufficient to account for the acquisition of that knowledge. The believer had to see more than could be sketched out on a tabula rasa by a willing soul. In one sense the medieval reliance on Plato, even in so hesitant and partial a Platonist as Thomas, may be understood as the alternative to an admission of blindness.

The philosophers of the Renaissance, while adopting the traditions of visual epistemology, turned their eyes from the divine itself to the divine as they found it in nature, or in the human soul. The widespread distinction between microcosm and macrocosm proceeded from the confident assumption that the study of man and man's world would lead to the knowledge of God and that although the divine essence exceeded human vision, the *vestigia Dei* were eminently visible throughout the phenomenal world. With the growth of experimental science and the revival of mathematics came the spirit of analysis, a general unwillingness to view nature as a procession of vague symbols, and a tendency to equate truth with a precisely quantifiable structure to be extracted from beneath superficial disorder. There were still sermons in stones, but they could not be understood until the stones had been weighed, measured, tabulated, and compared. Plato saw the Good in the sun, and Bonaventure saw a good God. The Renaissance philosopher also saw God in the sun, but as often as not he saw him through a matrix of velocities and weights reduced to a visual medium — a form that had no actual resemblance to the sun itself.

2

The Renaissance Spectrum

As I have argued in the preceding pages, the rise of humanism resulted in what most historians of philosophy consider a period of decline — at least, when assessed from a purely philosophical point of view. The intellectual historian, on the other hand, is likely to find the Renaissance of special interest. Such a division of enthusiasms suggests that it is probably a mistake to measure the Renaissance by the same rule that we apply to the Middle Ages. If the so-called medieval synthesis is rooted in a preoccupation with philosophy, then Renaissance philosophy is rooted in what I shall call, for lack of a better term, culture. Renaissance humanism was a credo geared to the temper of its age, a period of two or three centuries in which political change and religious upheaval formed a social background to revolutions in science, technology, art, and literature. The humanist was impatient with what he considered scholastic quibbling, and he was prone to associate profundity with more than mental activity. Renaissance thinkers tended to subordinate metaphysics to practical considerations: the philosopher was very often also a scientist, an artist, or a statesman. In general, then, although philosophy was central to the intellectual milieu of the Renaissance, it was the center of a much larger circle than it had been during the Middle Ages.

Along with this general expansion of culture, and as one of its major effects, the Renaissance experienced a kind of media explosion — an enlargement of the literate public and a multiplication of channels through which old ideas might take new expression. Humanism, with its emphasis on the relation of man to the world, brought the intellectual forms into the laboratory, the studio, and the marketplace. The thoughts of men, traditionally viewed within the minds of an educated minority, broke from their mental moorings and drifted into the space of the extramental world, where they became visible in a revolutionary new way. Accordingly, during the Renaissance the established conventions of visual epistemology became an important social and cultural phenomenon. They provided authority and a rationale for the notion that thoughts could be seen within, and a model for the increasingly common assumption that they could be seen without, the mind.

THE GUTENBERG REVOLUTION

Although the Greeks were able to standardize an alphabet and thus record their thoughts, they had no form of mass written communication. Reading for the ancients meant reading out loud, so that composition and delivery were geared to auditory standards of excellence. Conditions were largely similar during the Middle Ages, when cumbersome manuscripts provided the sole means for storing written information. For the small educated minority even individual reading and writing were not the silent and essentially visual procedures that they are today. The medieval scholar or cleric read as much with his lips as with his eyes, pronouncing the words and listening to them as his eyes

61

moved slowly across the page. *Legere* was the correlative of *audire;* reading was acoustical, and mental comprehension was accordingly associated with hearing. Writing was a similarly oral process: the author would pronounce his thoughts as his hand recorded them on paper, catching and weighing the meaning through the medium of words heard rather than seen.[1] A composition would be judged more by its immediate auditory impact than by standards of logical consistency, since the latter implies a textual scrutiny on the part of the audience which was impossible in manuscript culture. The *quaestiones,* oral debates in the schools, were rambling dialogues in which the educational emphasis was placed more on the process of dialectic itself than on the products that might result. The shortage of books and the scarcity of copies must have encouraged a high degree of memorization and a concomitant premium on ready-made arguments garnered from *auctoritas.* Knowledge was often retained by being capsulized in runes of proverbial wisdom. Chaucer, we may recall, is much given to *sententiae;* even Pertelote can recite the formulas of ancient wisdom, though in her case it is as much for our "myrth" as for Chaunticleer's "solace."

Oral communication is an essentially subjective experience in which mental activity is almost wholly absorbed in the physical process of speaking or of listening. Spoken language is spatially vague, ephemeral, and expressive by tone and gesture as well as by explicit content. Exact meaning is therefore difficult to distinguish from the medium of articulation. In the same way, word definition is to some extent arbitrary in a culture of manuscripts, where the same authors are not read by many people at the same time and where individual writers develop their own terms as they proceed. But the invention of the letterpress revolutionized

1. Dom Jean Leclerq, *The Love of Learning and the Desire for God,* trans. Catherine Misrahi (New York, Fordham University Press, 1961), pp. 19, 214–215.

the psychology of communication. The transition from script to print resulted in the gradual substitution of visual for auditory methods of transmitting and receiving ideas.[2] At the same time it facilitated the proliferation of printed materials in a world of increasing literacy, thus inducing a widespread association of knowledge with words seen on a page rather than heard in dialogue. Language fixed in a book is no longer vague or transient but may be referred to and reexamined; it gives to knowledge the qualities of objectivity and detachment that we associate with the sense of sight. To borrow an analogy, if the spoken word is a moving picture of thought, one frame passing imperceptibly into the next, then the printed word is a snapshot in which the same thing may be seen over and over. Ideas were seemingly rescued from auditory flux by being cemented to a page.

Printing also stimulated the idea that words could stand for things with a precision impossible during the Middle Ages. Printed words are all the same height and evenly reproduced, suggestive of order and permanence. The mass production of books forced the standardization of spelling and thereby fixed the "look" of language once and for all. At the same time the definitions of words had to become more rigid in order that the same meaning would be conveyed to a man in Kent as to a man in Cornwall. Terms were thus linked to definite meanings and arranged within the pages of a lexicon. As such they were objectified, unitized, and could be manipulated like objects laid out in space.

Along with the shift to visual symbols of communication the printing press also brought a radical increase in the quantity of

2. Cf. Marshall McLuhan, "The Effect of the Printed Book on Language in the 16th Century," in *Explorations in Communication* (Boston, Beacon Press, 1960), p. 29; and H. J. Chaytor, *From Script to Print* (Cambridge, England, W. Heffer & Sons, Ltd., 1950), p. 4. On the distinction between chirographic and typographic visualism, see Walter J. Ong, *The Presence of the Word* (New Haven, Conn., Yale University Press, 1967), pp. 47–49, 85–87.

information available to the literate population. The value of printing lay in the possibility of quick and almost unlimited repetition of written materials. But the realization of this value required that books be accommodated to a public largely unacquainted with the classical languages. Therefore the translation of ancient texts became a major occupation of the humanists, stimulating the development of modern European languages. At the same time the shift from Latin to the vernaculars introduced subtly different bases for verbal conceptualization, for while Latin generally expresses concept relations by the use of inflection, the vernacular languages perform the same operation through prepositions. This aspect of modern grammars, which has been described as "the most sweeping and radical change in the history of the Indo-European languages," [3] is important because it indicates a firmer grasp of concept relations than is possible in Latin and because it implies that Renaissance men, more than their forefathers, viewed the relation between two concepts as a distinct, third concept. Such developments in the vernaculars are similar in their implications to those of the Gutenberg revolution taken as a whole. Just as the visualization of words encourages their association with objective things, so the modern languages have a tendency to isolate meaning into separate verbal units. All of these changes contributed to the evolution of language from a continuous flow of interwoven sounds to a linear disposition of distinct visual symbols. In short, by increasing the visual component in communication printing reinforced the traditional equation of thinking with seeing, and indirectly encouraged the notion that cogitation involves the arranging of conceptual units into significant spatial relationships, whether in the mind or in a book. An important effect of this advance in technology was

3. Edward P. Morris, *On Principles and Methods in Latin Syntax* (New York, Charles Scribner's Sons, 1902), p. 102. Cited by McLuhan, *The Gutenberg Galaxy* (Toronto, University of Toronto Press, 1962), p. 233.

that it supported, and in some cases even stimulated, similar effects in otherwise unrelated areas of human endeavor.

THE RENAISSANCE THEORY OF LOVE

The connection between visual epistemology and theories of love has already been discussed in relation to Ficino and Pico. But the Italian Platonists inherited the doctrines from an earlier poetic and philosophic tradition generated by the artists of the *dolce stil nuovo*. Guido Cavalcanti (ca. 1255–1300) helped to initiate the movement by combining the conventions of troubadour love poetry with the main doctrines of scholastic psychology. As Maurice Valency has remarked, "the stilnovist was interested less in the conduct of love than in its phenomenology; he developed a science of love." [4] Cavalcanti and his contemporaries were ignorant of the *Symposium*, and so they naturally took recourse to Aristotle's psychology, though it was the Neoplatonic Aristotle of the Arab commentators. Love begins when the forms of women enter the senses as images (*phantasmata*). These are combined and separated by the imagination and stored in memory. The active intellect then illuminates the image, abstracts the ideal form, and imprints it on the possible intellect. This new impression enables the soul to contemplate the exemplar of feminine beauty and thus provides a basis for comparing and judging individual women.[5] The Neoplatonic coloring of the theory is evident in Cavalcanti's conception of the active intellect as a force linked to the spheres, a source of illumination independent of the mind itself.

4. Maurice Valency, *In Praise of Love* (New York, The Macmillan Company, 1958), p. 218.
5. See J. E. Shaw's detailed discussion in *Guido Cavalcanti's Theory of Love* (Toronto, Toronto University Press, 1949), p. 38 and passim. Cf. also Valency, *In Praise of Love*, pp. 223–224. The clearest exposition of this theory occurs in "Donna mi prega," particularly in lines 8–14.

The second stage in love begins when desire is aroused for a woman who matches the ideal image before the mind's eye. She is the lady whose visage enters through the eyes and prints itself so fixedly on the heart (the seat of the imagination) that it causes love to appear. Love is said to have celestial "virtues," potencies that are transmitted to the soul from the spheres through the agency of the active intellect.[6] Thus the stilnovist often compares his beloved to a star in human form or to an angel inhabiting a star, whose light causes knowledge and whose visible shape stirs desire. Such poetry is obviously not the result of an ambition to describe actual amorous encounters; nor is it complimentary or courtly in tone. The lady, at least as an object of the poet's love, exists within the mind, and the torments of passion are those experienced by the lover in his relations with an object seen within, and not with an actual woman.

Although Cavalcanti and the stilnovisti removed the affairs of love from the external world to the regions of mental vision, it remained for Dante Alighieri to spiritualize amorous theory by aligning it with the moral and religious doctrines of Christianity. Cavalcanti thought of the lover's vision as a purely psychological event and took a generally dim view of its results — an enslavement to passion and the debilitation of reason. Dante, on the other hand, regarded the vision of God as the most exalted human experience and felt that the love of a woman (also a predominantly visual experience) could ultimately lead to this pinnacle of the religious life.

In one of his letters Dante writes that "since every causative force is in the nature of a ray emanating from the first cause, which is God, it is manifest that that heaven which is in the highest degree causative receives most of the divine light."[7] But

6. Guido Cavalcanti, "Donna mi prega," l. 11.
7. *Dantis Aligherii Epistolae*, X, 25, trans. Paget Toynbee (Oxford, The Clarendon Press, 1920), p. 207.

God the creator is also God the illuminator of the human soul, with the result that the causative light is at the same time an intelligible brilliance. This radiance is dispersed through the agency of nine angelic hierarchies, which contemplate God with a clarity that "exceeds the eyes of the human mind" (*la quale soverchia gli occhi de la mente umana*) and which transmit His creative and intellectual light to the sublunar world.[8] Mortal beings participate in the divine influence according to their spiritual dignity; plants by vegetative spirits, animals by sensitive spirits, and humans, endowed with rational souls, in the same fashion as the angels.[9] But while the absolute source of mental activity resides in God, Dante (abandoning the Pseudo-Dionysius for the Aristotle of the Arabs) also holds that actual knowledge derives from sensation. Accordingly, the soul is equipped with two kinds of vision: sensitive sight for distinguishing colors and rational sight for apprehending the ends of things.[10] Incorporeal spirits of light travel between the eye and its object, carrying the forms to the imagination, where they are illuminated from within and rendered intelligible.

Many of these principles, which appear in the *Convivio*, take a more imaginative expression in the "book of memory," *La Vita Nuova*. Here the glance of Beatrice is the "beginning of love," for "from her eyes, as she moves them, come flaming spirits of love which strike the eyes of him who watches her, and penetrate so that they reach the heart." [11] Dante's first meeting with Beatrice takes place when he is nine years old, "when for the first time the glorious lady of my mind appeared to my eyes."

8. Dante, *Convivio*, II, iv, 16–v, 8 (pp. 173–174). All citations are from *Le Opere di Dante*, 2nd ed., ed. M. Barbi, et al. (Firenze, Società Dantesca Italiana, 1960), and the translations are my own unless otherwise noted. At *Convivio*, III, xii, 7 (p. 220), Dante compares God to the sun, giver of life and intellectual light.

9. Ibid., III, ii, 14–15 (pp. 198–199).

10. Ibid., I, xi, 3 (p. 160).

11. Dante, *Vita Nuova*, XIX, First Canzone, 51–54 (*Opere*, p. 21).

The sight of Beatrice triggers a series of reactions that progress from the poet's vital spirit to his animal spirit, which "began to marvel greatly, and addressing the visual spirits especially, it pronounced these words: 'Your beatitude has now appeared.'" [12] The second encounter, which occurs some nine years later, is also an important visual experience, for Dante again seems to see his beatitude in Beatrice. But since he still looks upon Beatrice as a mortal woman, the poet's love is similar to the spiritual myopia of the stilnovisti. This error is hinted at in a dream in which Christ appears to Dante and tells him to sweep aside the false conception of love which he views in his imagination. His blindness persists, however, until after Beatrice's death, when he recognizes her as divine among women and finally as a spiritual influence bearing the gift of beatitude directly from God. Her departure from external view forces Dante's vision inward, with the result that he sees Beatrice as "a great spiritual beauty, which spreads the light of love through heaven." [13]

In a well-known study of the *Vita Nuova*, Charles Singleton argues that Dante found the structure for his theory of love in the mystical traditions of Christian Neoplatonism.[14] For both Augustine and Bonaventure the mind's road to God begins with objects seen *extra nos*, proceeds to objects *intra nos*, and terminates with objects *supra nos*. The pattern of love is therefore circular: God's love descends through the medium of Beatrice, and by the same medium (viewed without, within, and finally above) Dante's love returns to God. The final ascent to a vision of God does not occur in the *Vita Nuova*, though it is foreshadowed in the poet's prayer that he may ascend to a vision of Beatrice's glory.[15] It is not until the *Paradiso* that Dante can claim: "I was

12. Ibid., II (p. 3).
13. Ibid., XXXIII, Fifth Canzone, 22–24 (p. 41).
14. Charles Singleton, *An Essay on the Vita Nuova* (Cambridge, Mass., Harvard University Press, 1949), pp. 105 ff.
15. Dante, *Vita Nuova*, XLII (*Opere*, p. 49).

in the heaven that most receives His light and I saw things which he that descends from it has not the knowledge or the power to tell again." [16]

The bold fusion of Christian philosophy with the conventions of the stilnovisti was one of Dante's most influential innovations. By transporting the themes of romantic and religious love onto an inner stage of the mind and by incorporating the main traditions of visual epistemology into the scheme of his drama, he set an important precedent for the poets who were to succeed him. Furthermore, the appearance of Neoplatonism in his poetry is an early instance of a tendency that grew much more pronounced as the theory of love continued to develop. Beatrice was the model for many a *bella donna*, though with the passage of time her successors become more and more difficult to distinguish from the Platonic Idea of perfect beauty.

Petrarch's Laura bears many similarities to Beatrice. "It was she," writes the poet, "who turned my youthful soul away from all that was base, who drew me as it were by a grappling chain, and forced me to look upwards." [17] Laura has the influence of "a celestial spirit, a living sun," and within her eyes Petrarch sees "a sweet light which shows the way that leads to heaven." [18]

16. Dante, *Paradiso*, I, 4–6, trans. John D. Sinclair (New York, Oxford University Press, 1948), p. 19. A discussion of *The Divine Comedy* is here foregone because it would entail needless repetition of materials already sufficiently elaborated. The *Paradiso* is, of course, one of the most sun-drenched documents in European literature and in some ways as much a visual as a purely literary experience. Dante reaches the end of his spiritual journey in a final vision of the eternal light of God (XXXIII, 85–90 [Sinclair, p. 483]). "In its depth I saw that it contained, bound by love in one volume, that which is scattered in leaves through the universe, substances and accidents and their relations as it were fused together in such a way that what I tell of is a simple light." For an interesting commentary on the place of visual epistemology in *The Divine Comedy*, cf. Joseph Anthony Mazzeo, "Dante and the Pauline Modes of Vision," *Harvard Theological Review*, 50 (1957), 275–306.

17. Petrarch, *Secretum*, trans. William H. Draper (London, Chatto & Windus, Ltd., 1911), p. 121.

18. Petrarch, *Rime*, XC, 12 (p. 129); and LXXII, 2–3 (p. 105). All

Like Beatrice, Laura dies; and, like Dante, Petrarch retains the vision of his lady's lovely eyes long after her passing. Her image blazes within his mind, and although it makes life turbulent with unfulfilled longing, it also provokes lofty speculation.[19]

Although he was to some extent a follower of Dante, Petrarch brought much that was distinctively new to Italian poetry. The sight of Laura leaves him with none of the assured resignation that Beatrice brought to Dante. As one of the earliest humanists, Petrarch reflects a preoccupation (both in his life and in his art) with moral and religious conflict. While *The Divine Comedy* moves from earth to heaven along the orderly lines of Christian doctrine, Petrarch's poetry runs through a dizzy course of unresolved tensions between romantic and religious love. Moreover, where Dante's vision of Beatrice is almost always the motive for religious thoughts, Petrarch very often regards Laura as a purely poetic inspiration. (His unwearying repetition of the Laura/laurel pun is well known.) He thinks of her lovely eyes as a book, his source for what he knows and writes of love. And her image, which he bears reflected in his heart, pervades visible nature and makes it possible to see Laura in all things.[20]

But Petrarch's most important contribution to visual epistemology was his replacement of Aristotelian dialectic (to which he was openly hostile) with a more or less Platonic theory of knowledge. Although deficient in Greek, he acquired his Plato secondhand through deep reading of Cicero. His position is clear enough in his handling of a passage from *De Natura Deorum* (I, viii, 19), where Cicero inquires about the "kind of eyes of the soul," that Plato must have had to observe the construction of

---

selections are from *Rime, Trionfi e Poesie Latine*, ed. F. Neri et al. (Milan, Ricciardi, 1951). The translations are my own. Cf. also *Rime*, CCCXXXVI, 1–8 (p. 434), where Petrarch has a vision of Laura which he likens to the radiance of the celestial spirits.

19. Ibid., CVII (p. 149). Cf. also CCXLVIII, 1–4 (p. 322).
20. Ibid., CLI, 13–14 (p. 217); and CXXVII, 7–14 (p. 178).

the universe. To Petrarch's mind, at least, the answer is implicit in the question itself. Plato saw the creation with the eyes of his soul, the same eyes that men have always used to see invisible things.[21] Given such assumptions about the nature of knowledge, we can understand Petrarch's glorification of poetry as a manifestation of his general tendency to locate the roots of knowledge in the subjective vision of the individual soul.

From Petrarch the main lines of Renaissance love theory moved to Ficino and Pico, with whom, as I have remarked, visual epistemology is submerged in an almost completely Neoplatonic approach to knowledge. Ficino's commentary on the *Symposium* provided the intellectual background for Benivieni's poetry and for the sonnets and commentary of Lorenzo de' Medici, and his translations and commentaries were enormously influential in the establishment of Plato as the primary source for subsequent developments of the love tradition.

Plato's impress is clearly discernible in the *Dialoghi d'amore* of Leone Ebreo (ca. 1460–1530). Leone's is one of the most philosophical of the love treatises, primarily because the author insists that knowledge must always precede love, "for nothing may be loved that is not first known under the aspect of the good." [22] Vision is the primary source of knowledge; normal sight gives perceptual knowledge to the external world, and mental vision (*vedere intellettuale*) gazes upon the transcendent and incorporeal truths.[23] Leone leans to the Aristotelian description of abstraction but identifies the *intellectus agens* with God, the luminous receptacle of Platonic Forms. The objects of both sensitive and intellectual vision are illuminated by the eternal spe-

21. Petrarch, *On His Own Ignorance,* trans. Hans Nachod, in *The Renaissance Philosophy of Man,* ed. Ernst Cassirer, Paul Oskar Kristeller, and John Herman Randall, Jr. (Chicago, University of Chicago Press, 1948), pp. 97–98.

22. Leone Ebreo, *Dialoghi d'amore,* ed. Santino Caramella (Bari, G. Laterza & Figli, 1929), p. 8. The translations are my own.

23. Ibid., p. 179.

cies in the mind of God. These Forms, the eternal exemplars of all created things, illuminate both the intellectual vision and the species in the imagination (from which the mind abstracts universals). Thus the soul, according to Leone, has two faces: one, which is understanding, looking toward the intellect and above it, and the second turned toward sense and corporeal things. Each view provides a cognitional basis for love, one spiritual and the other sensual. In keeping with his intellectualism, however, Leone accorded the feminine graces a relatively minor place in the hierarchy of beauty. The supreme beauty is found in the active intellect; a divine unity manifests itself in the forms of the arts, sciences, and moral virtues, viewed individually in the possible intellect. It is therefore completely appropriate that Filone (the lover in the *Dialoghi d'amore*) is enamored of Sofia, beauty in the sense of wisdom. Not only is love an intellectual vision, but it is also a vision of intellectual objects in strict separation from the delights, however divine, of the feminine form.

Although it is probably better known than most of the *trattati d'amore*, there is little of striking originality in Baldassare Castiglione's *Il Libro del Cortegiano*. Castiglione generally adheres to the main lines of tradition: knowledge precedes love; the lady's image must conform to the ideal in the lover's mind; and the lover should progress from the vision of individual women to a universal beauty seen only with the eyes of the mind. He also rehearses the conventional six steps to ideal form (as contrived by Pico), beginning with "the shadow of sensuall beautie," and concluding with perfect beauty, "which lyeth hidden in the innermost secretes of God, lest unhalowed eyes shoulde come to the sight of it." [24] In spite of its eclecticism, however, *The Book of the Courtier* has retained a special interest for students of English literature because of Hoby's influential translation in

24. Baldassare Castiglione, *The Book of the Courtier*, trans. Sir Thomas Hoby (London, J. M. Dent & Sons, Ltd., 1928), pp. 303, 312–313, 318–321.

1561 — a translation that made the Italian theory of love, with all of its epistemological implications, readily available to English poets.

Amorous theory also came to England in Giordano Bruno's *De Gli Eroici Furori*, which was published in London in 1585, complete with a long and elegant dedication to Sir Philip Sidney. Although it was the last of the important love treatises, *De Gli Eroici Furori* is in some ways the most original. Like Leone Ebreo, Bruno reduces the role of women to near insignificance and concentrates on the theoretical and intellectual aspects of love. He is more literal and more persistent than any of his predecessors in asserting the equation of thinking and seeing; indeed, along with the doctrine of infinity (which he adapted from the Copernican "hypothesis"), visual epistemology occupies a central position in Bruno's overall philosophical system. All love, according to Bruno, begins with sight: sensible love from the eyes of the senses and intellectual love from the eye of the mind. Owing to a radical disproportion between the mode of the human intellect and divine things, all higher cognition involves the viewing of symbols, "called by the philosopher a speculation of phantasms, and by the theologian, a vision only by similitude, mirror and enigma." [25] But these are not images derived from sensation. Once it has ascended through sense, imagination, and reason, the soul becomes intellect or mind and reflects upon divine similitudes within itself. The highest form of love is not born until the soul has made this retreat from external images and purified its vision by a recognition of its link with God, the light of the mind and spark of the will. Since God is infinite, the concept of God seen within can be refined and perfected innumerable times without ever containing his essence. Heroic love therefore progresses through a potentially infinite series of refine-

25. Giordano Bruno, *The Heroic Frenzies*, trans. Paul Eugene Memmo, Jr. (Chapel Hill, N.C., University of North Carolina Press, 1964), p. 253.

ments upon images contained within the soul. The intensity of love is commensurate with the dignity of the objects before the mind's eye, with the result that the will burns more fiercely as the intellect sees more clearly. In brief, "the soul always desires to love more than it loves and to see more than it sees." [26]

Bruno illustrates his theory in a poetic adaptation of the Actaeon myth. The young hunter releases his mastiffs and greyhounds in the woods and then sees the naked beauty of Diana (who represents, for Bruno, the image of God's absolute light reflected in nature). As soon as he has seen her, Actaeon's dogs turn upon him, and the hunter becomes the hunted. Bruno explains that Actaeon represents the human soul in search of divine wisdom and beauty. The dogs are intellect and will, and they pursue their master because by seeing (understanding) Diana, he has assimilated her beauty into himself. The result in Actaeon is heroic frenzy, a rapture in which the will is inflamed by the "intellectual perception of the good and the beautiful." [27] This is an eminently rational madness — a distraction from earthly things in which the objects loved are necessarily known and, since known, necessarily seen.

If Cavalcanti's doctrine of romantic love, vaguely linked to Peripatetic psychology and ending in the submission to irrational passion, represents one extreme of Renaissance amorous theory, then certainly Bruno's formulations represent the other. Bruno dwells persistently on the spiritual and intellectual aspects of love and proceeds from a position of frank Platonic subjectivism. His introduction of the concept of infinity and his emphasis on the divine creativity of the individual soul are in marked contrast to the doctrines held by the theorists of the Middle Ages. In spite of these important differences, however, Bruno, Cavalcanti, and the others are linked by the common notion that all love involves

26. Ibid., p. 133. Cf. also p. 237.
27. Ibid., p. 108.

knowledge and that all knowledge involves vision. Whether the beloved is a woman, an idea, or God, there is universal agreement that it cannot be loved without being seen. The gradual shift from Aristotelian to Platonic epistemology, which coincides roughly with the temporal transition from the Middle Ages to the Renaissance, brought an increased importance to the place of vision in the love treatises and greater dignity to the nature of the objects seen. This is consistent with the general tendency in Renaissance philosophy to emphasize the role of vision and mentally visible objects in explaining cognition. Moreover, and equally important, during and after the revival of Platonism in Florence, the *trattati d'amore* came into close association with aesthetics, and thus provided a channel through which visual epistemology might flow into theories of painting and poetry. Indeed, Bruno's treatise perfectly illustrates this multiplication of cultural channels; *De Gli Eroici Furori* is at once a philosophical tract, an emblem book, and a sonnet sequence.

MATHEMATICS

Although the study of numbers was encouraged by the medieval Franciscans at Oxford, the full revival of mathematics did not occur until the fifteenth and sixteenth centuries, when it accompanied the rise of Neoplatonism and the emergence of new attitudes toward science. The mind of Leonardo da Vinci, like that of his predecessor Nicholas of Cusa, could not be satisfied with the seemingly arbitrary verbiage of medieval science. Mathematics offered precision, guaranteed a clean division between the subject and object of inquiry, and provided a grammar of symbols by which sense impressions could be translated into pure intellectual vision.[28] Neoplatonism and mathematics were the

28. Cf. Ernst Cassirer, *Individual and the Cosmos in Renaissance Philosophy*, trans. M. Domandi (New York, Harper & Row), p. 173.

primary ingredients in the hypotheses of Copernicus, whose *De Revolutionibus* (1543) revolutionized the scientific conception of space by rendering it absolutely geometrical. Under such a system it was the normal practice to think of the universe as a gigantic network of related spatial units that were best understood by visual analogies. For the Renaissance scientist, however, mathematics was not the impersonal tool of pure abstraction that it is today. Kepler, for example, followed Copernicus in the conviction that mathematical laws underlie all natural phenomena; but he also believed that those laws were regulated through the quasi-divine agency of the sun.

Although the revival of mathematics began in Italy, it quickly spread into other European countries. England was particularly receptive to the new method, producing several major mathematicians before the close of Elizabeth's reign. As early as 1533 Sir Thomas Elyot, in his Platonic dialogue *Of the Knowledge which Maketh a Wise Man*, distinguished two levels of reason in the human soul. "In the fyrste is that portion of divinitie, whiche is in man, whereby he is made to the image and similitude of god. In the other be noumbres and figures." [29] By associating abstract numbers with visible figures, Elyot gives early expression to a tendency that was to become more pronounced with later English scientists.

In 1542 Robert Recorde published *The Grounde of Artes*, the first complete arithmetic textbook produced in England. An able teacher, Recorde placed great emphasis on fundamental principles, practical application, and the constant use of visual aids to illustrate proofs. His characteristically Platonic approach to knowledge is betrayed by his habit of explaining everything — including even Aristotle's logic and *Ethics* — in geometrical

29. Sir Thomas Elyot, *Of the Knowledge which Maketh a Wise Man*, ed. Edwin Johnston Howard (Oxford, Ohio, The Anchor Press, 1946), p. 80. Cf. also pp. 81–82.

terms.[30] Recorde's techniques clearly influenced William Cunningham, who recommended the former's mathematical works as an introduction to his own *Cosmographical Glasse* (1559). This catchall of astronomy and applied mathematics is laid out in a luxurious profusion of diagrams, maps, charts, pictures of astronomical instruments, and illustrations of the phases of the moon. The contents perfectly illustrate the happy marriage of numerical science and a visual medium within the abstract, nonverbal, pictorial space of a book. The strong, but subtle, impression that this attractive volume creates is that the space and the objects of the not-self are stretched on a scaffolding of numerical relationships that are best represented as something to be seen. Lines, angles, charts, diagrams — all of these contribute to the suggestion that abstract quantities, by the use of which we understand the external world, actually and visibly inhere in that world. It is as though space thinks, or at least has meaning, in a graphically obvious way.

Perhaps the most notable of the English mathematicians was John Dee, who was notable in part, we shall have occasion to recall, because he was Sir Philip Sidney's teacher. In his preface to Henry Billingsley's translation of Euclid's *Elements* (1570), Dee gives clear expression to the way in which scientists of his age viewed the universe. All things are formed according to a numerical law, "For this was the principall example or patterne in the minde of the Creator." [31] Beneath the divine archetypes Dee describes two subordinate stages that reflect the plan in the mind of God: an intermediate level in the minds of angels and the souls of men and a base level in the constitution of all creatures. This numerical trinity, which derives from the traditions of Neoplatonism, has a profound significance in the overlapping

30. Robert Recorde, *Pathway to knowledg* (1551), Sig. 3iᵛ–3iiᵛ.
31. John Dee in his preface to Euclid's *Elements*, trans. Henry Billingsley (1570), Sig. iʳ.

orders of Dee's ontology and epistemology. Things supernatural are eternal, immaterial, indivisible, accessible to the mind alone, and the implements of scientific demonstration. Material things, on the other hand, are divisible, corruptible, the objects of sense perception, and the bases of probable conjecture. Between the Ideas and sensible particulars are "Thynges Mathematicall." Immaterial yet perceptible in matter, immutable yet divisible by art, inaccessible to sensation yet prior to all human conceptions, these "generall Formes" are the object of the inner eye of the mind.[32] For Dee and for many men of his generation, such perfect geometrical images, clearly visible only across the reaches of mental space, were the patterns of truth, linked to first mathematical causes in the plan of a numerically minded God.

Dee's works were contemporary with those of Thomas Digges, the first and most outspoken advocate of the Copernican theory in England before the arrival of Bruno. Digges explains the infinite universe with graphic clarity in A *Perfit Description of the Caelestiall Orbes* (1576). The book contains a large folding diagram that portrays a heliocentric system of spheres; but it also includes a number of stars bordering on the outside of the eighth sphere and a legend stating that these stars are stretched throughout infinite space. The diagram is of interest here because it points up the fact that a simple picture could make the sophisticated concept of infinity clear and plausible before the eyes of its viewers — something, one imagines, that Digges realized would have been impossible through words alone.

Like most Renaissance mathematicians, Digges was on the threshold of modern science; but at the same time he drew inspiration and doctrine from an abundant tradition. Contemptuous of strict empiricism, he took recourse to a doctrine of Platonic illumination that provided him with what he calls "the rule of Reason," a corrective to the uncertain ways of sense. "The rule

32. Ibid., Sig. i^r.

of Reason," as Digges construes it, is a God-given "Lampe" shedding light on geometrical forms pictured within the mind.[33] Even such emphatically nonvisual phenomena as moral abstractions may be seen, argues Digges, in Aristotle's *Ethics,* where "with geometricall figures [he] most beautifully paynteth out Justice, discerning and severally comparing sundrie partes thereof with Geometricall and Arithmeticall proportions." [34] Obviously, Baconian induction was still a thing of the future. This fact, in conjunction with their typically Platonic distrust of physical nature as a source for accurate demonstration, made it perfectly reasonable for Elizabethan scientists to turn their eyes upon truths subsisting *ante rem* in the divine mind, to be discovered and contemplated only within. God's laws were still accessible to human vision, but for the Renaissance mathematician the *logos* as seen in the New Testament gave way to principles of harmony and proportion more literally seen across the geometrical interstices of mental space.

PICTURES AND EMBLEMS

Perhaps in no way did printing facilitate the visualization of concepts so much as in the illustration of books. At first, of course, the block prints were crude, just as most of the medieval hand-drawn pictures had been crude.[35] But with time the idea that an illustration could do more than accurately represent an individual object became increasingly common. As Digges seems to have recognized, a picture could condense otherwise awkward

33. Thomas Digges, A *Perfit Description,* "To the Reader," cited by Francis R. Johnson, "Thomas Digges, the Copernican System, and the Idea of the Infinity of the Universe in 1576," *The Huntington Library Bulletin,* 5 (1934), 80.

34. Thomas Digges, A *Geometrical Practice, named Pantometria* (1571), Sig. Ai^v.

35. William M. Ivins, Jr., *The Artist and the Fifteenth-Century Printer* (New York, The Typophiles, 1940), p. 17.

and complicated verbal statements into a form graspable at a glance. Printing also made it possible to repeat the same pictures innumerable times, thus expanding the content of each individual's shared visual experience. Whereas verbal formulas, no matter how familiar, drift away almost as they are uttered, exactly repeatable pictures are objects readily distinguishable from the organs by which they are perceived, and they have all the permanence of real things. Furthermore, illustrations greatly simplified the process of natural classification. In a famous herbal by Leonhard Fuchs, published in 1542, the author's woodcut illustrations do not represent particular plants but are visible schemata of what were thought to be the generic forms.[36] Such illustrations can, as it were, "boil down" the multiplicity of natural things into a single visual form, which then stands for numerous related but less perfect objects. The visible diagram can be like many things without being any of them, just as geometrical figures can be said to contain an infinite variety of similar figures.

At about the same time that printing was invented, a critical development was occurring in the aesthetics of painting. Just as Renaissance mathematicians became increasingly preoccupied with proportion as embodied in visible form, so the theorists of painting brought geometrical principles to the artist's canvas. In his *Della Pittura*, Leon Battista Alberti asserts that the artist must understand geometry in order to paint. As a humanist he felt it his mission to prove that painting was an intellectual process, not merely a craft. His revolutionary scheme of perspective effected the complete rationalization of visual space and brought the painter and the observer into a static "point of view" with respect to the artifact. Perspective cemented visual objects into fixed spatial relationships by arranging them along the coordi-

36. William M. Ivins, Jr., *Prints and Visual Communication* (Cambridge, Mass., Harvard University Press, 1953), p. 44.

nates of unified space, in much the same way that checkers seem related to each other on a checkerboard, whereas they do not when laid out on a blank sheet of paper. According to Alberti's scheme, the content of a painting is largely indistinguishable from its form — a form accessible to sight and ultimately comprehensible by the eye of intellectual vision.

The notion that unity is a function of spatial organization is, no doubt, related to another of Alberti's innovations. He was one of a new breed of painters who wished to manifest the movements of the soul in the movements of the body. To achieve this objective, Alberti insists that artists should have a complete understanding of the fine points of the human body, which, when well portrayed, will give the observer more to think about than to look at.[37] In other words, Alberti wanted to make individual pictorial objects represent states of mind and ideas. This can be accomplished only by arranging the various components of a picture to a unified effect. But if this harmony of parts is achieved, then paintings can become visible symbols for things that are in themselves not visible at all — or not apparently visible. What is of central importance here is not so much that one thing can somehow precisely symbolize another but that the switchboard that converts the images into meanings is always the mind's eye. The assumption that mental states can be understood by being seen betrays the even more subtle assumption that ideas are themselves visible. Just as geometrical figures can stand for supernatural "Ideas" in Dee's formulations, so the spatial coordination of visual objects can stand for mental states in Alberti's. The transit from canvas to concept is thought to be a simple one because it is assumed that both painting and thinking consist in the orderly allocation of visible objects along the lines of geometrical space.

37. Cited from *Della Pittura* by William M. Ivins, Jr., *Art and Geometry: A Study in Space Intuitions* (Cambridge, Mass., Harvard University Press, 1946), p. 78.

By uniting artistic and scientific theory in the principle of exact form, Alberti established a precedent for succeeding theorists of painting. Following this example, Leonardo da Vinci erected his *Treatise on Painting* on a foundation of mathematical principles borrowed from Nicholas of Cusa. Leonardo argues that true science is both empirical and capable of mathematical demonstration — in other words, that scientific knowledge derives from sensation and that it is verifiable by mathematical laws also derived from sensation. Because it is by far the most reliable of the senses and because of its crucial role in mathematics, Leonardo persistently emphasizes the importance of vision. The loss of eyesight would be a kind of death to the world, for it would close out all beauty. Furthermore, without sight there would be no astronomy or cosmography, no mathematics, and, most important, no architecture or painting.[38] The motive behind this dwelling on sight is Leonardo's assurance, both as a scientist and as an artist, that form is visible — a conviction bearing with it the corollary that scientists and artists are bound to present those forms in full clarity to the inner and outer eye. Since the separation and reconstruction of accidental and essential qualities is a visual, not a verbal, process, it follows that poetry, like scholastic logic, is a game of hollow verbiage, while painting expresses the true essences of things. From Leonardo's point of view, then, the poet, along with any artist or scientist who works with words, is handicapped by the fact that his medium will always miss the precise — and precise, because visible — lineaments of truth.

In spite of their interest in mathematics, Alberti and Leonardo remained within the lines of empirical or Aristotelian psychology. The artist and the scientist are dependent upon sensation for knowledge and transcend the data of physical nature only to the degree that they uncover and give expression to the forms that

38. Leonardo da Vinci, *Treatise on Painting*, trans. A. Philip McMahon, 2 vols. (Princeton, N.J., Princeton University Press, 1956), I, 23.

nature is striving to attain. In accord with the general drift of Renaissance thought, however, the theory of art during the later sixteenth century reflects a revived interest in Platonic idealism and a concurrent decline in the influence of Aristotle. The doctrines of "mannerism," elaborated by such theorists as Frederico Zuccaro and Giovanni Lomazzo during the last two decades of the century, take their point of departure in the assumption that man has the power to fashion a world of Ideas within himself in complete independence of nature. Lomazzo, the more Platonic of the two writers, converted the philosophical doctrine of Ficino's commentary on the *Symposium* to the uses of art theory in his *Idea del Tempio della Pittura* (1590).[39] Following his source almost verbatim, Lomazzo argues that the divine light is reflected in a descending order of brilliance: in angels as exemplars and Ideas, in man as reasons and notions, and in matter as images and forms. Concerned primarily with artistic form, Lomazzo turns almost immediately to a discussion of that which delights us "by means of reason and sight" in material bodies.

That a physical, and hence visible, object should delight both reason and sight may seem paradoxical, but the enigma is dissolved in Lomazzo's assurance that Ideas are visibly manifest in the beauty of material things. Beauty, which shines within an object "from the infusion of its Idea," can be discerned in three qualities: order, mode, and form. Order is achieved through an appropriate disposition of the parts (ears equidistant from the nose) of the object; mode designates the proper size of each part in relation to the whole; and form is the "artful disposition" of lines, shadows, and colors. What strikes us about such qualities,

39. Lomazzo's debt to Ficino is made graphically clear in Appendix I of Erwin Panofsky's *Idea*, trans. Joseph J. S. Peake (Columbia, S.C., University of South Carolina Press, 1968), pp. 127–153, where parallel passages from the two authors have been translated by Victor A. Velen. The following quotations are all from pp. 143–145 of the Appendix. For a complete discussion of mannerism, see Anthony Blunt, *Artistic Theory in Italy 1450–1600* (Oxford, The Clarendon Press, 1940), chap. 9.

of course, is the fact that they are all separable from the thing itself. In contemplating the beauty of, say, a portrait, the final object of our attention would be a series of proportions that could be set forth quite as easily in numbers. Such reductionism, though, it may be possible, would miss a crucial feature of Lomazzo's position. While he does insist, with Ficino, that the trinity of qualities, as the reflections of a divine Idea, "cannot be any part of the body," it is also imperative that those qualities be visible in the body. Their theoretical separateness from material things guarantees that they are incorporeal and intelligible, thus delighting the reason; but their actual residence in bodies, particularly artifacts, ensures that they will also delight the sight. Numerical proportions would obviously fall short on the second count, for while they symbolize ideas, they cannot render those ideas visible in concrete things. It is hardly surprising, therefore, that Lomazzo found himself in a universe overflowing with visible forms, a place where the sight of beauty and the thought of beauty would amount to the same thing.

Liberated from externally derived norms of perfection, critics like Lomazzo turned to a higher nature viewed within the mind as the model for creation, and as a standard for aesthetic judgment. A somewhat similar tendency to Neoplatonism is clear in the poetry of Michelangelo, who agreed with his predecessors that the artist is initially inspired by nature, but added that the images of sensation must conform to an ideal viewed in the mind. Beauty is an incorporeal essence descending into the soul from the unified light of all essences in the divine mind. The beauty of an individual woman becomes more perfect when it ascends through the eyes into the intellect, where it becomes divine and pure. This essence, and not the external woman, is the beauty that is seen by the eyes of the mind.[40] The application of these

40. See, for example, "Dimmi, di grazia, Amor," and "Non vider gli occhi miei cosa mortale."

principles is evident in Michelangelo's painting and sculpture, where the grandeur and perfection of visible form provide an index to the artist's idealized conception of the human condition.

The expression of abstract ideas through a visual medium took an earlier and much more explicitly Platonic form in the Florentine Academy during the fifteenth century. Inspired by Ficino's translation of the *Corpus Hermeticum*, the Florentine Platonists discovered a new mode for expressing their thoughts in the hieroglyphic tradition stemming from ancient Egypt. The Renaissance interpretation of the hieroglyphs was essentially the same as that formulated by the Greeks and passed on to later ages in the writings of Plotinus. It was thought that the Egyptians had evolved a scheme of pictorial symbolism by which abstract ideas could be represented in the images of material objects. According to Plotinus, the pictures were invested with symbolic qualities through which the initiate, illuminated by a spontaneous influx of divine light, could achieve an intuitive understanding of the divine Ideas.[41] The abstract images served as a medium between the visual mode of human thought and the transcendent essences of things. The hieroglyphs were thus understood as externalized concepts, the images of highest contemplation transported from the subjective world of inner vision and reduced to complete visual objectivity. Of course, the meanings of the pictures were not visible to every eye, but for an illuminated minority the images provided a profound insight into the nature of reality.

Ficino and his followers agreed that sense perception and discursive reason were inferior to contemplation for attaining

41. Plotinus, *Enneads*, V, viii, 6. Cf. also Erik Iversen, *The Myth of Egypt and Its Hieroglyphs in European Tradition* (Copenhagen, Gad, 1961), pp. 45–46. Iversen emphasizes that the interpretations current in antiquity passed into the modern world without undergoing any significant changes (p. 64): "It is characteristic that the final formulation of that which until the eighteenth century should remain the almost undisputed conception of the hieroglyphs, is founded on Ficino's translation of Plotinus."

truth. In accord with the traditions of Platonism, they concerned themselves with the subjective aspects of knowledge, with Ideas not logically conceived and therefore not amenable to strictly logical or verbal exposition. The hieroglyphs had great appeal because they afforded a medium by which Ideas and complicated relationships could be expressed nondiscursively, according to the same visual mode by which they had been conceived. The truth of a picture, it seemed, could be grasped instantaneously, taken in at a glance. Ficino, for example, believed that the ancient symbol of a winged serpent biting its tail completely and perfectly represented the concept of time. The entire discursive argument could be contained, as it were, in a single image. The grotesque appearance of the symbol assured that the object contemplated could not be seen in the phenomenal world, that it was a transcendent essence invisible (incomprehensible) to the bodily eye. Furthermore, the numerical proportions embodied in the images linked them to the Ideas in the intellect of God.[42] In short, the hieroglyph made it possible to blur the old distinction between the *oculus mentis* and normal vision by joining intelligibility with objective and external visibility. The truths traditionally observed within could now be seen quite well without.

It was within this framework of assumptions that the emblem tradition took form. Ficino's hermetic translations were extremely popular, and in 1505 they were supplemented by the publication of *The Hieroglyphics of Horapollo*. This storehouse of ancient images, which remained popular for nearly two centuries, inspired a fashion for creating new hieroglyphic symbols — an intellectual craze that drew approval from so conservative a humanist as Erasmus. With time the emblems were incorporated into the broader current of decorative art or employed as illustra-

42. See E. H. Gombrich, "*Icones Symbolicae:* The Visual Image in Neo-Platonic Thought," *Journal of the Warburg and Courtauld Institutes,* 11 (1948), 170–171, 178.

tions of proverbs and maxims gathered together from ancient ethics. The ponderous religious and philosophical claims of the Florentines naturally lost some of their force as the form became more fashionable, but popularity did not always mean intellectual deflation. As late as 1626 Christoforo Giardi expressed the conviction that the knowledge and creation of symbolic images was supreme among the arts, for such images, devoid of matter and yet visible, could accommodate the forms of the moral and intellectual virtues to the mode of the human mind.[43]

The first emblem book in English was Geoffrey Whitney's *A Choice of Emblems* (1586), but Edmund Spenser's *Shepherd's Calendar* is clear evidence that Englishmen had earlier access to continental publications. In fact, there was considerable interest in emblem writing in England before 1580, and it will be useful to remember that this early enthusiasm revolved around Sir Philip Sidney and his circle of literary friends. Sidney himself wrote to Languet in 1573 of Ruscelli's *Imprese,* and Abraham Fraunce prepared a manuscript on emblems which he dedicated to his noble friend.[44] Bruno's *De Gli Eroici Furori,* as previously mentioned, was also dedicated to Sidney. It contains, in addition to long sections of strictly philosophical discourse, twenty-eight prose emblems (descriptions without pictures) with companion sonnets. Reserving discussion of Bruno's poetry for a later chapter, we may note that his prose emblems are aggregations of symbols, often very obscure in themselves but generally clarified in the verse and prose commentaries that follow. The absence of visible pictures in no way contradicts Bruno's contention that his tract is directed to both the eye and the ear, for the details

43. See the Introduction to Giarda's *Bibliothecae Alexandrinae Icones Symbolicae* (1626), trans. E. H. Gombrich, ibid., pp. 188–192.

44. Sidney mentions Ruscelli in a letter from Venice. Cf. *The Prose Works of Sir Philip Sidney,* ed. Albert Feuillerat, 4 vols. (Cambridge, England, Cambridge University Press, 1912–1926), III, 81. On Fraunce's MS, cf. Rosemary Freeman, *English Emblem Books* (London, Chatto & Windus, Ltd., 1948), p. 66.

in the emblems represent abstract ideas, concepts most appropriately viewed within the mind by the *oculus mentis*. In spite of the absence of actual illustrations, therefore, Bruno undoubtedly would have argued that there was much of great worth to be "seen" in his dialogue.

Samuel Daniel, another of Sidney's associates, published a translation of an Italian dialogue on the art of emblems, *The Worthy Tract of Paulus Iovius* (1585). Daniel rehearses the familiar equation of thought and sight in stressing the educational virtues of emblems. "To represent unto the sense of sight the forme or figure of anything, is more natural in act, and more common to al creatures then is hearing, and thereupon sayth Aristotle, that we love the sence of seeing, for that by it we are taught and made to learne more then by any other of our senses."[45] He adds that emblems may be employed to symbolize abstractions, "things incorporal," such as sorrow, purity, and so on. Along with the work of Bruno, Daniel's translation makes it clear that the dignity and utility of the emblem genre were still assumed with confidence in Sidney's generation. The emphasis on the fantastic and grotesque is retained, and it is repeatedly suggested that emblems are ideal vehicles for the transmission of well-defined concepts and abstractions. In brief, the Italian tradition of pictorial representation did reach England during the last three decades of the sixteenth century, and it arrived with the salient features of visual epistemology still intact.

METHOD

The widespread cultural influence of visual epistemology reached a climax in the writings of Peter Ramus (1515–1572), whose efforts to replace knotty scholastic pedagogical techniques with his doctrine of "method" made him famous throughout

45. *The Worthy Tract of Paulus Iovius* (1585), "To the Reader," Sig. Ai^r–Aii^r.

Europe. By the 1570's his textbooks on logic and rhetoric were well known in England. One scholar has even risked the statement that "whenever the word 'method' appears in the writings of the late sixteenth century in England, it amounts almost to a confession of the author's awareness of Ramus." [46] The *New English Dictionary* indicates that the word "method" began to appear in English during the later decades of the sixteenth century and that it was almost always used in connection with teaching. The philosophic concept of method, however, was evolved long before the Renaissance in Plato's *Phaedrus*. From the outset the basic metaphor was that of a *via*, or way leading somewhere — a metaphor that proved itself congenial to Christian philosophy, particularly when the acquisition of knowledge involved the movement through several intellectual levels. The notion of a mental pathway leading from one place to another also bore a strong spatial and visual component, and it was an obvious step to construe the *via* as something to be seen. In Bonaventure's *Itinerarium Mentis in Deum*, for example, the mind's route to God is mapped out in carefully graduated steps that lead upward to the creator through metaphorical space. The entire journey is described as an ascent through various levels of mental vision.

The humanists made extensive use of method in their reform of scholastic pedagogical techniques. Men like Vives, Sturm, and Melanchthon concerned themselves with the revision of outworn classroom procedures that slowed down learning. Neal W. Gilbert, describing method as a "party slogan . . . for the Renaissance," states that "an art is brought into method by being presented in short, easily memorized rules set forth in a clear manner so that the student may master the art in as short a time as possible." [47] By the time of the Renaissance, then, there

46. Wilbur Samuel Howell, *Logic and Rhetoric in England, 1500–1700* (Princeton, N.J., Princeton University Press, 1956), p. 263.
47. Neal W. Gilbert, *Renaissance Concepts of Method* (New York, Columbia University Press, 1960), p. 66, and passim.

had developed a close connection between method as a device for simplifying the presentation of school subjects and the concept of plan or system.

The education utility of method, however, was not its only importance. In association with the pedagogical reform there came an equally violent reaction against scholastic logic. The "dialecticians," as they were called — Valla, Agricola, Vives, Sturm, and Ramus — brought the late medieval movement toward quantification in logical procedures to its fulfillment.[48] The *loci* came to be understood as a comprehensive grouping of compartments in the mind, literally mental "places" where the full round of knowledge could be internally viewed. The old logic of oral disputation was gradually replaced by a concept of dialectic in which intellectual activity was thought of as the silent manipulation of mental units across internal space. It was through the writing of Peter Ramus that method, with its distinctively visual and spatial approach to the mental processes, reached its apex. Furthermore, as previously noted, it was primarily with him that method was identified.

The central difference between method as it appears in the formulations of Plato and Ramus is one of emphasis. In the Platonic scheme of things the use of the word "Form" to represent a transcendent "Idea" had implications that may not have been intended. The word suggests and even urges us to visualize or "image-ine" the Ideas as some sort of shape or outline. In-

48. "Quantification" is used here to describe the terminology of humanistic dialectic, but it is not to be understood in the sense that modern logic or logistic is quantified. Cf. Walter J. Ong, "System, Space, and Intellect in Renaissance Symbolism," *Bibliothèque d'Humanisme et Renaissance*, 18 (1956): "The 'way' of the methodologists . . . was free, or gradually freed itself, from auditory or oral commitments as it was elaborated in terms of ascent (*ascensus*) and descent (*descensus*), division, partition, distribution, induction, deduction, analysis, and the rest of the psycho-geometrical apparatus used to describe the intellectual processes" (p. 233). Though modern logic employs much of this terminology, the words bear none of the metaphysical overtones that they did in the Renaissance.

evitably our selection of examples will be of formal shapes that can be seen (triangles, squares) and that thereby establish a connection between the immutable Idea and geometrical patterns viewed within the mind. But the connection between contemplation (abstract thought) and the mental construction of highly pictorial systems (viewed by the mind's eye) remained implicit for Plato, a metaphor imperceptibly submerged in the word "Form" itself.

With Ramus, Plato's metaphor becomes a reality. His entire system rests on the explicit assumption that by merely thinking (the mind's eye in the act of "seeing") man can unfold the mystery of universal order. The floor plan of the cosmos is neatly contained in the orderly places of the human mind, and man has only to look within to understand. Although we may not have the knowledge of all things, we do have the power to know or to see them all (*puissance de les voir*). Man has this power naturally, "but when he shall have the art of invention before his eyes in its universal types, like a mirror representing the universal and general images of all things, it will be much easier for him (through these images) to recognize the subordinate species, and consequently to invent what he is looking for." [49] Taking such assumptions as his point of departure, Ramus sets out to reform the arts. He betrays his place in the ranks of the pedagogues by his assurance that the primary objects seen within the mind are the subjects of the curriculum; the same assurance that motivated Thomas Granger, an English Ramist, to assert that "the principles of all Arts, and Sciences, are naturall to the Soule, infused into it in the creation." [50]

Ramus began his reconstruction of the arts with the *trivium*, first of all with logic. Since he thought of logic, not as a specialized discipline, but as the mode for perceiving all things,

49. Ramus, *Dialectique* (1555), pp. 68–69. Translations, unless otherwise noted, are my own.
50. Thomas Granger, *Styntagma Grammaticum* (1616), A6ʳ.

it followed for Ramus that the structure of all the curriculum subjects conformed to the same logical pattern. Logical invention is reduced to strict science by the assumption that there are ten, and only ten, headings under which true statements can be made (cause, effect, subject, adjunct, opposites, analogues, name, division, definition, and authority). These places, or *loci*, are conceived of as ten slots on the mental switchboard that links the universal ideas in the mind of God with the world of discourse. By their connection with the *loci*, therefore, universals are considered self-evident, with the result that the most obviously true statement that can be made about an art is also the most general. In order to illustrate the structure of each art, Ramist textbooks exhibit large diagrams that look like a pyramid on its side. In the left margin the art is defined in the most general terms possible (logic is the art of reasoning well, rhetoric is the art of speaking well, and so on). This definition is divided again and again, until the art is dichotomized into its most indivisible constituents. The resulting diagram is literally a picture of the Ramist method. The operations of the mind, seen naturally by the eye within, have been transposed, with absolute precision, onto the pages of a book.

Ramus contended that method was the one way to truth, for arranging not only the arts but any subject of discourse. What emerges from this theory is the further contention that the truth of any subject, like one of Ramus's diagrams, consists of an orderly series of statements that progress from the most general to the most particular. Consistent with the pictorial conception of the *loci* and encouraged by the visual arrangement of mental processes on charts, this concept of discourse in no way involves speaking, the free exchange of ideas in dialogue. Rather, the attainment of truth is carried out on the silent and orderly diagrams within the mind. "At the heart of the Ramist enterprise," writes Walter Ong, "is the drive to tie down words themselves . . . in simple geometrical patterns." [51] Once this drive has been satisfied — when the nonspatial world of sounds has been reduced to the space of a graph and the subtle interplay of words heard has been converted to the silent manipulation of words seen — language has become mute, devoid of emotive value, and significant only because its terms can be viewed in relationships with other terms on a methodical chart.

Ramus owed his great popularity more to the prevailing intellectual climate in Europe than to anything distinctively original in his own system. His ideas on teaching were the fruition of humanistic anti-Scholasticism that had begun long before his birth in 1515, and his logical techniques were the climax of a long tradition of quantification that culminated in the topical logics of the dialecticians. His historical interest arises, therefore, not because of his contributions to any single branch of learning, but because his general approach illustrates many of the leading tendencies of his age. Central to this network of cultural tendencies was the gradual transition to an epistemology that assumed, implicitly or explicitly, that the known could be visualized in space, whether on charts, in geometrical shapes, or throughout the graphic regions of the mind. By committing words to visual space, Ramus gave great impetus to the notion that words, like thoughts, are best understood by being seen. The fact that words hang on Ramus's trees is nearly irrelevant, for the ultimate objects of knowledge are the formal shapes of the trees themselves.

SUMMARY

The implicit rationale for Ramus's mental graphs is similar to that of mathematicians such as John Dee, of the emblem writers

51. Walter J. Ong, *Ramus, Method, and the Decay of Dialogue* (Cambridge, Mass., Harvard University Press, 1958), p. 89. I am deeply in debt to Father Ong's book throughout this section.

following Ficino, or of poets like Bruno in that it proceeds from the belief that there is a direct relationship between an abstract pictorial construction (triangle, emblem, image) and a higher system of reality. The symbol somehow bridges the chasm that divides the mutable from the unchanging, the temporal from the eternal. The middle stage, the symbol or phantasm or triangle, is not so much a way of reconciling men to earth as it is a mental springboard into a higher realm. With Ficino and Dee, as with most Renaissance artists and poets, we are constantly reminded of this fundamental Platonic distrust of earthly things.

The ancient equation of thinking and seeing was first and foremost a philosophical concept, a convenient and at least ostensibly figurative way of explaining the mental processes. During the Renaissance, however, the metaphor became a reality through the literally visual expression of ideas in pictorial art and in emblems. The visual epistemology of the philosophical tradition was also swept into the conventions of Renaissance poetry, given definition by the poets of the *dolce stil nuovo*, and converted to science by the authors of the *trattati d'amore*. The revival of mathematics had the same effect, for the old analogy between thought and sight was realized in geometrical forms (the objects of thought) made actually visible. The Renaissance tendency to identify forms and Ideas with things literally seen was thus the massive cultural culmination of a similar, though much less pronounced, tendency in the inherited wisdom of antiquity. In a sense the Renaissance artist and scientist gave a local habitation to the airy nothingness of a predominantly verbal philosophical tradition. They incorporated forms into their pictures, made concepts into visible objects, and thought of Ideas as things easily converted to images and emblems. The characteristic dissatisfaction with things unseen resulted in the belief that everything, including the activity of the mind, could be represented to the sense of vision.

While the quantitative, pictorial, and generally visual aspects of communication flourished, words — particularly spoken words — were found inadequate to the demands of the age. This first complaint was shared by many Neoplatonists and most eloquently expressed by Augustine.

Which way soever the soul of man turns itself, unless towards thee, it is even rivetted into dolours: yea, though it settles itself upon beautiful objects without thee, and without itself: which beauties were no beauties at all, unless they were from thee. They rise, and set; and by rising, they begin to have being: they grow up, that they may attain perfection; which having attained, they wax old and wither: though all grow not old, yet all must wither . . . This is the law of them . . . Lo, even thus is our speech delivered by sounds significant: for it will never be a perfect sentence, unless one word gives way when it hath sounded his part, that another may succeed it.[52]

Speech is a composition of frail utterances following each other into silent oblivion. Even written words, although they give the impression of pinning ideas to a page, must be scanned one by one before they can be comprehended. As such, words are dim, discursive markers and seem a poor medium for symbolizing ideas whose content can be seen in a flash before the mind's eye and may be viewed there again and again without apparent change.

The second complaint is that words are vague and imprecise insofar as they refuse to be fixed to any strictly defined meaning. Concepts have all the objective clarity of things seen, but spoken words are a kind of conceptual putty that can be shaped and proportioned to the speaker's (or the auditor's) will. They are suggestive rather than definitive. They cannot stand as independent conceptual units but derive their signification from other words and from a context. It is thus difficult to make a word or series of words stand for an exact idea or class of ideas.

52. *St. Augustine's Confessions,* trans. William Watts, 2 vols. (New York, The Macmillan Company, 1912), I, 173–175.

They are clumsy in mathematics and untrustworthy in discourse. In short, words are imprecise, whereas images have definite limits.

In line with this suspicion of spoken words during the Renaissance came revolutionary changes in the methods and implications of verbal communication. The printing press and its immediate effects, along with the increased quantification of logic and the growing emphasis on simplicity and visual presentation in the teaching profession, radically altered the nature of words themselves. In a very real sense words functioned more and more as images. Stretched evenly on a page they became the well-ordered objects of sight. Meanings could be pinned down, and terms were made to stand for concepts in a way impossible before the invention of printing. The distance between the visible concept and the written word was decreased when language became standardized, when terms became dependable receptacles for concepts and systems of abstract ideas. In short, words, just as images, arranged along the lines of quantified geometrical space, had much the same conceptual potency as pictures. Visual epistemology had come full circle; at the same time that the old verbal equation of thinking with seeing became literal through visible forms, words themselves acquired many of the qualities of mental images.

The works of Sir Philip Sidney were written, and may be understood, against this background of traditions, assumptions, and implicit tendencies. Not surprisingly, Sidney's relationship to this intellectual milieu is clearest in *An Apology for Poetry*, his most direct and systematic statement about art. What did Sidney mean by defining poetry as "a speaking picture"? And after that question is answered, how does the definition work itself out in his prose and verse?

3

Sidney's Apology:
From Fore-conceit
to Ground-plot

Had Sidney had his own way, he would be ranked with men like Burghley and Leicester, and not with Spenser and Shakespeare. But early in his political career the young nobleman discovered that hardheaded idealism would not take him far in the court of Elizabeth, a queen who no doubt admired candor and high principle but who also saw their deficiencies in the real political world. In 1580 Sidney wrote an honorable but tactless letter to the Queen criticizing what he believed to be her forthcoming marriage to the Frenchman Alençon. While the letter had no apparent influence on Elizabeth's subsequent decision to abandon the marriage, it did result in its author's exile from court. The letter illustrates what any reader of Sidney's biography must recognize — the fact that he was never able to make his impressive ideals usefully operative in the Elizabethan political arena. Even his death, while celebrated by some as an example of great personal heroism, can be viewed as the result of unrealistic bravado in the face of overwhelming odds. In short, while it is hard not to admire Sidney's lofty principles, it is difficult to deny that they came to almost nothing in the world of cold, practical reality.

Though it is undeniable that Sidney's ideals had no place at court, we can be grateful that politics was not the only mode of expression open to him. In the period of enforced idleness that followed his exile from court he composed *An Apology for Poetry*, a document almost unique in its high claims for the literary art. The question has often arisen whether the aesthetic principles set forth in the *Apology*, eloquent as they are, were any more functional than Sidney's political ideals. In short, did his *gnosis* find its way into *praxis*? While I shall argue in the next chapter that it did, that discussion will follow most naturally from a preliminary excursus into the profoundly visual basis of Sidney's aesthetics.

The assumption that knowledge should inform action gives rise to the central argument of the *Apology* — that poetry is the best teacher of that which is most important in action, namely virtue. Sidney develops his case with simple logic. First he distinguishes between those disciplines that lead to a knowledge of things — medicine, rhetoric, and so on — and those that result in man's self-knowledge — history, philosophy, poetry. The three disciplines in the second category, which Sidney considers superior to those in the first, are then compared to determine which is supreme. The comparison has its basis in three crucial premises. First, following Aristotle and in line with his division between the disciplines, Sidney assumes that the highest learning is, broadly speaking, moral in content. In other words, it has to do with personal ethics and with public mores, the "ethic" and "politic" considerations. Second, again following Aristotle, Sidney argues that abstract knowledge is more effective in teaching than concrete knowledge, that the teacher should present universal ideas of virtues and vices. Third, Sidney was convinced that moral abstractions have the greatest pedagogical efficacy when they are made visible to the mind's eye, and not when set forth in verbal definitions. The third premise is the corner-stone of Sidney's theory, for it alone accounts for the supremacy of poetry. All three disciplines qualify according to the first premise. History is excluded by the second, for the historian is limited to the discussion of actual persons and events. Philosophy fails only with respect to the third, for while it is concerned with abstractions, it is also strictly verbal in method.

SIDNEY'S DEFINITION OF POETRY

Sidney's definition of poetry as a "speaking picture" (p. 18), therefore, and his constant reiteration that poetic imitation amounts to "feigning notable images of virtues, vices, or what else" (p. 21) were more than a nod to convention. It is pre-cisely his ability to make ideas visible to the mind that secures the poet's preeminence. The philosopher offers a verbal defini-tion "which doth neither strike, pierce, nor possess the sight of the soul" as much as the poet's picture does (p. 27). His logic notwithstanding, Sidney's notion that poetry should be described as a speaking picture is far from clear; we may wonder what it is precisely that we are intended to see in a poem. By the word "speaking" he means that poets necessarily create in a verbal medium — this is clear enough. But the word "picture" is not so easily explained. It could mean that poetry is a kind of rep-resentational painting in words, an art of language in which there is a premium on vivid descriptions of external nature. But such an interpretation goes sharply against the grain of the *Apology*, where moral abstractions, and not concrete objects, are the poet-teacher's primary subject. It is much more likely that by "picture" Sidney means an abstraction, a concept made visible to the reader's mind. "Picture" in this sense helps to explain the argument that poets, by coupling "the general notion

99

with the particular example," produce "an image of that whereof the philosopher bestoweth but a wordish description" (p. 27). To put it another way, the poet allows his reader to see a moral universal in action by submerging it in a specific character. The best poet is like "the more excellent" kind of painter, who "painteth not Lucretia whom he never saw, but painteth the outward beauty of such a virtue" (p. 20). By speaking picture, then, Sidney means the poetic fusion of moral abstractions with actual characters. If he is successful at this fusion, the poet will set "all virtues, vices, and passions so in their own natural seats laid to the view that we seem not to hear of them, but clearly to see through them" (p. 29).

It must be clear that while Sidney was dependent upon the traditions of visual epistemology for much of the theory of the *Apology*, he also made innovations of his own. That ideas could be seen was the standard assumption during the sixteenth century, but that they could be seen in a poem was something new. We can begin to understand this innovation, along with many of the others in the *Apology*, by recognizing that Sidney's conception of the end of poetry was, above all, pedagogical. The poet and the philosopher are similar in that they both fulfill this pedagogical objective, but the poet takes the laurel because he couples teaching with delight; he makes wordish moral philosophy palatable by presenting it in a pictorial form. In other words, the poet differs from the philosopher, not in the content of his lesson, but in his mode of presentation. Implicit in this argument is the assumption that moral abstractions are comprehended through a kind of mental vision and therefore most easily understood when set forth in pictures. Accordingly, poetry excels because it conforms to the fundamentally visual mode of human intellection.

The decidedly epistemological basis of Sidney's aesthetic has the virtue of confining the poet to themes that are accessible to the eye of human reason, but it also narrows the boundaries of the maker's domain. Most notably, it limits almost to exclusion the role of religious ideas in poetry. While there is room set aside in the *Apology* for poets who "imitate the inconceivable excellencies of God" (p. 18), it is noteworthy that that room is rather small. Like most Protestants of his time, Sidney drew a firm distinction between philosophy and theology, between the realms of nature and grace. Reason, though the gift of God, is the instrument of natural philosophy and concerns itself with ideas naturally conceivable, and therefore naturally visible, to the human mind. Divine philosophy also considers knowledge "to be seen by the eyes of the mind" (p. 12), but it is a supernatural vision that functions only in eyes cleared by faith. The very fact that he regarded divine truth as inconceivable explains the lip service Sidney pays to religious poets in his critical treatise and the general absence of explicitly religious themes in his poetry and prose. There could be no speaking picture, no delightful teaching, of wisdom received through grace but not learned, seen through the medium of faith but actually invisible to mortal eyes.

This dichotomy of nature and grace, with the concomitant division between poetry ("popular" philosophy) and theology, stems from an epistemological distinction current among many Renaissance Neoplatonists. The doctrines of religious Hermeticism, revived in Florence during the fifteenth century, had strong alliances with the dualistic psychology of Platonism and provided the highly visualized theory of knowledge which underpins the emblem tradition. During the sixteenth century these doctrines were influential in a variety of different forms. Sidney probably encountered magical Hermeticism in John Dee, who considered himself a Christian *magus*. He was also acquainted with the non-magical variety expounded by Philippe de Mornay in his *De la Vérité de la Religion Chrétienne* (1581). Sidney knew and respected Mornay during the 1570's and was later responsible for the translation of the early chapters of *De la Vérité*.

Sidney's translation of Mornay is concrete evidence that he was familiar with visual epistemology in its explicitly philosophical form. The Frenchman's sweet-tempered rationalism is suffused with the Platonic epistemology of double vision, one eye looking toward the phenomenal world and the other toward God's light within the soul. Since the tract was published in the year or so preceding the composition of the *Apology*, we may speculate that it afforded Sidney a timely confirmation of his own basically visual habits of thought. In Mornay he would have read that God (according to Trismegisthus) is visibly reflected in nature and that the divine image is engraved on the human soul. Furthermore, he would have found that God is the light of the intellect, just as the sun is the light of the world, and that God's causative beams correspond to man's vision of the arts and sciences. The essence of God is inconceivable to man, but the eye of the mind has the natural power to see God indirectly reflected in the external universe and within the intellect itself. Because of this natural vision, Mornay was confident that he could dispel the errors of atheism and stir men's faith "by painting out the true Religion lively before their eyes, with the joy, happines, and glorie which insue thereupon." [1]

Mornay's assurance that the sight of God's reflection will lure men to true religion bears a remarkable similarity to Sidney's confidence in the compelling power of poetic pictures. Not surprisingly, both authors have a distant source in Plato's *Phaedrus*, though Sidney almost certainly found his Plato in Cicero's *De*

1. A *Woorke concerning the trewnesse of the Christian Religion* (1587), in *The Prose Works of Sir Philip Sidney*, ed. Albert Feuillerat, 4 vols. (Cambridge, England, Cambridge University Press, 1912–1926), III, 191. Hereafter passages from these volumes will be cited as *Prose Works*. Mornay's French is from the first edition, published at Anvers, "Au Lecteur," Sig. 2ʳ. *Et ce seroit de leur repeindre au vif devant les yeux, la vraye Religion, & la ioye, l'heru & la gloire qui la suit.*

Officiis, where it is related that moral goodness would instill love in anyone who could actually see it.[2] Sidney identifies his sources at a crucial point in the argument of the *Apology:* "If the saying of Plato and Tully be true, that who could see virtue would be wonderfully ravished with the love of her beauty, this man [the Heroic poet] sets her out to make her more lovely in her holiday apparel, to the eye of any that will deign not to disdain until they understand . . . For as the image of each action stirreth and instructeth the mind, so the lofty image of such worthies most inflameth the mind with desire to be worthy, and informs with counsel how to be worthy."[3] The idealized images of heroic poetry both teach and delight, thus accomplishing Sidney's dual objectives. They teach by setting forth a moral abstraction that can be viewed by the mind's eye, and they delight ("inflameth the mind with desire to be worthy") by making the abstraction concrete in the lofty image of some worthy, also viewed by an inner eye. As such, poetic images serve exactly the same function as the internally visualized phantasms in the *trattati d'amore.* The idealized image of the *bella donna* is simultaneously the object of the intellect, producing knowledge, and an incitement to the will, resulting in love. Sidney retains the conventional alliance of image, intellect, and will but substitutes virtue for love as the end of the process. Images of virtue compel the will by moving "men to take that goodness in hand which without delight they would fly as from a stranger," and the same images "teach, to make them know that goodness whereunto they are moved" (p. 20). In effect, then, Sidney is only secondarily interested in the strictly verbal side of poetry and places the burden of emphasis on the simultaneously con-

2. Cicero, *De Officiis,* I, v, 15. Cf. also *De Finibus Bonorum et Malorum,* II, xvi, 52.
3. *Apology,* pp. 48–49. Cf. p. 40, where Sidney asserts that the poet must only make men "see the form of goodness (which seen they cannot but love) ere themselves be aware, as if they took a medicine of cherries."

crete and abstract pictures that those words produce in the reader's mind. The unquestioned assumption that mental seeing generates both knowledge and positive ethical action guarantees that the poet's audience will reap both *gnosis* and *praxis* from its reading.

Sidney was not entirely without precedent in linking moral doctrine to poetic pictures. At its inception the emblem tradition was associated almost exclusively with the arcane mysteries of ancient philosophy. By the middle of the sixteenth century, however, such writers as Andrea Alciati, Girolamo Ruscelli, and Théodore de Bèze turned the emblems from metaphysics to the more mundane purposes of ethics. This development took hold in Protestant England, where moral philosophy and the emblems were united in a long and fruitful partnership. In the earliest of the English emblem books the author, Geoffrey Whitney, declares that his work is designed to accommodate both "the eie, and the eare," with the result that "the minde maye reape double delight throughe holsome preceptes, shadowed with pleasant devises." [4]

The relationship between poetry and painting, which is central to the rationale of the *Apology* and which takes obvious expression in the emblem books, may have been suggested to Sidney by the theories of painting and poetry in vogue among his contemporaries and immediate predecessors. As previously noted, Leonardo drew a comparison between poetry and painting in praise of the latter. To his mind at least, scientific form was identical with externally visible form; the shapes seen by the physical eye and reproduced by the painter are things as they really are. The poet describes reality in words and therefore operates at one remove from scientific actuality. It is unlikely that Sidney knew Leonardo's *Treatise on Painting*. But he had his portrait painted by Veronese during his travels and pressed

4. Geoffrey Whitney, A *Choice of Emblems* (1586), title page.

Nicholas Hilliard with intelligent questions about art theory when in England.[5] Indeed, had Sidney been acquainted with Leonardo's tract, there is good reason to suppose he would have disagreed with its contents. Sidney considered external nature a "brazen" world and equated scientific knowledge with forms viewed in the poet's mind. The separation between natural and intellectual forms and the emphasis on ideal concepts rather than percepts as the models for imitation lend to Sidney's theory a Platonic coloring not to be found in Leonardo. The doctrines of the *Apology* have much more in common with contemporary mannerist theory, which accorded the artist a natural faculty for forming another nature within himself. The painter, like Sidney's poet, goes hand in hand with nature to the degree that all cognition begins with sensation; but he is also, like God, a maker, ultimately transcending physical reality through the formation of another, more perfect world seen within the intellect itself. It is this collection of transcendent concepts that the artist imitates — the same golden nature that the reader is expected to see in the writing of Sidney's hypothetical poet.[6]

5. On Sidney's portrait, cf. the correspondence in *Prose Works*, III, 84 and 87. Sidney's conversation with Hilliard is recorded in the latter's *The Arte of Limming*, The Walpole Society, I (1912), 27. Sidney asked a question on proportion: "Whether it weare possible in one scantling, as in the lenght of six inches of a littel or short man, and also of a mighty bige and taulle man in the same scantling, and that one might weel and apparently see which was the taule man, and which the littel, the picture being just of one lenght."

6. Geoffrey Shepherd, in his edition of the *Apology* (London, Thomas Nelson & Sons Ltd., 1965), discusses Sidney's acquaintance with mannerist theory in his introduction. "We must believe," he argues, "that Sidney is writing with a direct knowledge of advanced contemporary theorising on art, acquired, probably even formulated in part, by Sidney himself in eager discussion in courts and chambers rather than drawn from books" (p. 66). Shepherd (pp. 65–66) cites a long passage from Zuccaro's *L'Idea de'Pittori, Scultori et Architetti* as evidence of close similarities between Sidney's ideas on art and the mannerist program. Zuccaro asserts that God endowed man with "the faculty of forming within himself an intellectual Idea so that he might know all created forms and fashion (*formasse*) within himself a new world, and thus internally possess and enjoy in having spiritually what ex-

Horace's *ut pictura poesis* was a pronouncement that could be twisted to both the artist's and the poet's point of view. Leonardo was one among many spokesmen for the painters, but Sidney's celebration of poetic pictures would have received more immediate confirmation in the camp of the poets. There was, of course, a long and familiar tradition of picture writing in Italian love poetry and a science of amorous vision in the *trattati d'amore*. But explicit descriptions of the poet-painter were even closer at hand. Girolamo Fracastoro, for example, wrote that "the poet is like the painter who does not wish to represent this or that particular man as he is with many defects, but who, having contemplated the universal and supremely beautiful idea of his creator, makes things as they ought to be." [7] Bruno argued that "philosophers are in some ways painters and poets; poets are painters and philosophers; painters are philosophers and poets." [8] By conflating Horace's dictum with the Aristotelian doctrine that all thought requires phantasms, Bruno arrived at the conclusion that painters, poets, and philosophers deal with similar kinds of mental pictures.

Like Bruno and Fracastoro, Sidney proceeds from the assump-

---

ternally in nature he rejoices over and rules. Furthermore with this Idea, imitating God as it were, and rivalling nature, He gave him the ability to produce an infinite number of artefacts resembling nature's, and in pictures and carvings make a New Paradise appear on earth . . . But man forms many Ideas in himself because the things of which he forms the Ideas are distinct from himself, and thus his Ideas exist *accidenter*. Moreover, man's Ideas have low origins in the senses." Zuccaro's epistemology, like Sidney's, is a confusing mixture of Platonic idealism and Aristotelian empiricism.

7. Girolamo Fracastoro, *Naugerius, Sive de Poetica Dialogus*, trans. Ruth Kelso (Urbana, Ill., The University of Illinois, 1924), p. 60. Fracastoro is also similar to Sidney in the assertion that "the poet imitates not the particular but the simple idea clothed in its own beauties, which Aristotle calls the universal." The allusion to Aristotle is partially misleading, for the object of imitation is also identified with the "supremely beautiful Idea" of God.

8. Cited and translated from *Explicatio Triginta Sigillarum* by Frances A. Yates, *The Art of Memory* (Chicago, University of Chicago Press, 1966), p. 256.

tion that the objects of artistic imitation are not the individual impressions derived from sensation but concepts both formed and viewed within the mind. The poet represents ideas with words; the painter does the same thing with pictures. The similarity between the two approaches is not in the artifacts they produce but in the intellectual formulations that precede them. The word and line are merely the media through which more perfect truths may be seen. As John Hoskyns was to put it, "the conceipts of the minde are pictures of things and The tongue is Interpreter of those pictures." [9]

Sidney would have found it extremely difficult to understand or appreciate theories of poetry which gravitate toward subjectivism and which place a premium on effusions of powerful emotion. His rigorous intellectualism made it imperative that poets "know what they do, and how they do, and especially look themselves in an unflattering glass of reason, if they be inclinable unto it" (p. 72). The *Apology* makes ample provision for feeling; but emotion, like all mental phenomena, is adjudged susceptible to scientific analysis. In order to achieve its pedagogical ends, the finished poem must be perfectly clear; and such clarity, which makes teaching and delighting possible, will result only if the poet aligns his words with exactly conceived patterns of thought. Such is the sense of Sidney's argument that "the skill of the

9. *Direccõns for Speech and Style*, in Louise Brown Osborn, *The Life, Letters, and Writings of John Hoskyns*, Yale Studies in English, LXXXVII (New Haven, Conn., Yale University Press, 1937), p. 116. Abraham Fraunce, one of Sidney's closest followers, aped the doctrines of the *Apology* in *The Countesse of Pembrokes Ivychurch* (1591). In Part III, *Entituled, Amintas Dale* (p. 3), he describes poetry as "a speaking picture, and paynting, a dumbe poetry." Like his master, Fraunce emphasizes that the poem is not an end in itself but the occasion for purely conceptual activity. "The picturing, fashioning, figuring, or, as it were, personall representing of things in verse after this manner, is most effectuall and avayleable, to move mens mindes, to stirre up delight, to confirme memorie, and to allure and entice our cogitations by such familiar and sensible discourses, to matters of more divine and higher contemplation" (p. 4).

artificer standeth in that *Idea* or fore-conceit of the work, and not in the work itself" (p. 16).

IDEA AND CONCEIT

The words "idea" and "conceit" (as in "fore-conceit") came into Sidney's highly visualized intellectual world with a charge of psychic gunpowder not immediately obvious to the modern reader. "Idea" is defined in Thomas Cooper's *Thesaurus* (1565) as a "figure conceived in Imagination, as it were a substance perpetuall, beyng as paterne of all other sorte or kinde, as of one seale procedeth many printes so of one *Idea* of man procede many thousandes of men." A similarly pictorial tendency is clear in the writing of Thomas Blundeville, a Ramist, who defines "idea" as "a common shape conceyved in the mynde." [10] Sidney's own extreme predilection for visualizing the mental processes may be observed in his translations from Mornay's French. *Des Idées* is rendered "formes, shapes or Patternes," and *les formes intellectuelles* as "the myndly shapes." [11] The same or similar translation occurs with unfaltering regularity throughout the early chapters of *The trewnesse of the Christian Religion*. Sidney's first and only impulse upon being presented with the word "idea" was to think of a pattern or outline, something literally visible to the mind's eye.

The word "conceit," related to Italian *concetto* and frequently found in the emblem books, had a similar connotation. As early as 1569 Tasso compared the *concetti* of Petrarch and Pigna, finding the latter poet richer in the variety of his concepts and therefore the superior painter.[12] More than two decades later

10. Thomas Blundeville, *The Art of Logike* (1599), p. 5.
11. *Prose Works*, III, 237 and 279. Cf. also p. 284. The corresponding pages in the French edition of *De la Vérité* are 44, 97, and 103.
12. Bernard Weinberg, *A History of Literary Criticism in the Italian Renaissance*, 2 vols. (Chicago, University of Chicago Press, 1961), I, 184.

Giulio Cortese, in his *Avertimenti Nel Poetare* (1591), defined the conceit as a preliminary meditation on an object of written discourse. The *concetto* is to be drawn from sciences familiar to the learned reader in order "not to obfuscate or confuse the eye of the soul" (*tale che non offuschi, ò ingarbughli l'occhio dell'anima*).[13] The strong visual bias introduced by Tasso became a staple of sixteenth-century Italian views on the literary *concetto*. Applying Aristotle's dictum that all thought requires images, the Italians simply converted the ancient philosophical convention to the purposes of poetry.

Whether or not he was influenced from abroad, Sidney applied essentially the same formula as the Italians. A comparison of Mornay's French with Sidney's English is again instructive, for it provides an insight into the latter's sense of the relationship between the mentally visualized conceit and the subsequent work of art. Mornay writes: "Mais si tu eusses peu entrer en cest Esprit, lors qu'il a fait cest ouvrage, tu l'y eusses veu beaucoup plus beau: & quoy qu'il puisse faire, & que tu puisses dire, c'est tousiours trop moins que ce qu'il a pensé; & ceste pensee encore n'est qu'un rayon de cest Esprit dout toute ceste belongne est partie." And Sidney translates: "If thou couldest have entered into the mynde of that man at the making of his worke, thou shouldest have seene it farre more beautifull there: and all that ever he could do or say, is alwaies farre lesse than his Conceyt; and yet the same Conceyt of his is but as a sparke of the Mynd, whereof the same worke is a part." [14] Following Mornay in the notion that the artist has something to be "seene" (*veu*) in his mind, Sidney substitutes the noun "Conceyt" for

---

13. Cited and translated by Weinberg, *A History of Literary Criticism*, I, 235. Cf. also his discussion of Camillo Pellegrino (I, 243), who described the conceit as "a thought of the intellect, an image or resemblance of true things and of things which resemble the truth."

14. *Prose Works*, III, 253. Cf. also III, 255. The corresponding French pages are 63 and 66.

the verbal construction "has thought" (*a pensé*). In other words, a conceit is the equivalent of a thought and therefore something to be seen in the mind. Affective conceits function in exactly the same way. In the revised *Arcadia*, for example, Queen Helen's feelings are described when she discovers her beloved Amphialus wounded: "In which pittious plight when she saw him, though Sorow had set before her minde the pittifullest conceit thereof that it could paint, yet the present sight went beyonde all former apprehensions." [15] The artist's concept develops to different ends but according to the same means; the Arcadian shepherds are good poets because they "had theire fancyes opened to so highe Conceiptes." [16] The poet's conceit is a thought or idea, acquired through external vision and perfected within the mind. The concept that results is in turn visible to the eye of the intellect and provides the pattern or shape upon which the poem is modeled. In effect, then, the artificer looks at his Idea or fore-conceit as he composes his poem.

The absence of a clearly visualized fore-conceit in most English poetry is a primary cause of Sidney's scorn for his contemporaries. He insists that the majority of poems, when put into prose, lack a strong conceptual core and thus illustrate that most poets proceed "without ordering at the first what should be at the last" (p. 74). By reducing a poem to prose, it is suggested, we can determine whether or not it has what Sidney calls "meaning." This process, often associated with the Ramists, was a classroom technique for dissecting a text, known as "analysis." In its logical form analysis involves stripping the poetical crust from literature and then subjecting the remaining prose kernel to rigorous logical investigation. Obviously Sidney was not at all precious about separating poetic form from poetic matter. The

15. Ibid., I, 496. The revised *Arcadia* comprises vols. I–II of the *Prose Works*, while the original *Arcadia* is in vol. IV.
16. Ibid., IV, 1.

fact that the logic of a bad poem crumples under analysis implies not only that good poetry must be logical but also that the reason of a poem can be neatly severed from its rhetoric. This sharply dichotomous view of literature, with its heavy emphasis on concepts somehow visible beneath a surface of words, is borne out in Sidney's division of poetry into "two principal parts, matter to be expressed by words, and words to express the matter" (p. 73). The parts are appropriately deployed in a spatial relationship: the inside of a poem is the fore-conceit, while the outside is a verbal emblem of the interior. The conceptual interior must regulate the verbal exterior — as Gabriel Harvey puts it: "A pithie rule in Sir Philips *Apologie for Poetrie.* The Invention must guide & rule the Elocution: *non contra."* [17] Therefore, the external form that a work of literature takes is irrelevant except insofar as it reflects the logical structure beneath it. Accordingly, it should come as no surprise that Sidney thought of verse as a kind of apparel, "being but an ornament and no cause to poetry" (p. 21).

Sidney conceived of poetry more as an art of presentation than as an established body of knowledge or as a tradition with a definite history. The poet borrows his conceits from the philosopher, transforms them into speaking pictures, and thereby renders teaching delightful. Originally, however, the philosophers borrowed from the poets. Once they had stolen the "true points of knowledge" from poetry, they reduced them to what Sidney calls "method" and so made "a school-art of that which the poets did only teach by a divine delightfulness" (p. 64). "Method," as I have mentioned, was a word almost always associated with Ramus. The usage in the *Apology* is completely accurate, for putting a subject in method was Ramus's way of reducing it to a school art. Sidney's approval of the technique is

17. Gabriel Harvey, *Marginalia,* ed. G. C. Moore Smith (Stratford-upon-Avon, Shakespeare Head Press, 1913), p. 169.

implicit in his concession that the philosopher's methodical procedure is his one (if dubious) claim to pedagogical supremacy (p. 36).

Sidney's intimate acquaintance with method is equally evident in his other writings, where he consistently employs the term in the Ramist sense of reducing an art or a series of related ideas to simple order. In upbraiding Musidorus before the Arcadian court, Philanax was "so overgon with rage, that hee forgatt in his oration his precyse Methode of Oratory." [18] With a similar absence of order, Dametas attempts to explain the finer points of farming to Pyrocles: "He began with a wilde Methode to runne over all the art of husbandrie." [19] In a letter written to his brother, Robert, in October of 1580, Sidney outlines a course of study that might have come straight from one of Ramus's textbooks. He recommends Bodin's "method of writing Historie," undoubtedly referring to *Methodus ad Facilem Historiarum*

---

18. *Prose Works*, IV, 371. The incidence of the word "method" in the later decades of the sixteenth century was extremely high. William Cunningham, in his *Cosmographical glasse* (1559), remarks that many writers "observe no order or Methode in their teaching" (p. 3). Cunningham's usage is typically Ramist in that it links method with order and with teaching. William Lambarde writes in *Eirenarcha* (1588), II, vii: "To me, that am desirous to follow some order, and Methode of discourse, the generall must alwayes go before the particular." Thomas Morley commends his own pedagogical techniques in *A Plaine and Easie Introduction to Practicall Musicke* (1600), Shakespeare Association Facsimiles No. 14, ed. Edmund H. Fellowes (London, Oxford University Press, 1937), "To the curteous Reader": "As for the Methode of the booke, although it be not such as may in every point satisfie the curiositie of Dichotomistes: yet is it such as I thought most convenient for the capacitie of the learner." Shakespeare used the word on several occasions; see, for example, *I Henry VI*, III, i. 1–13; *Richard III*, I, ii, 114–116; *Twelfth Night*, I, v, 240–245; and *Antony and Cleopatra*, I, iii, 6–10:

> CHAR. Madam, methinks if you did love him dearly,
> You do not hold the method to enforce
> The like from him.
> CLEO. What should I do I do not?
> CHAR. In each thing give him way, cross him in nothing.
> CLEO. Thou teachest like a fool the way to lose him.

19. *Prose Works*, I, 166. Cf. also I, 437 and 481; IV, 53.

Cognitionem, which was composed under the direct influence of the French logician.[20] He also urges his brother to organize his reading with methodical, and emphatically visible, charts.

When yow reade any . . . thing . . . straite bring it to his heade, not only of what art, but by your logicall subdivisions, to the next member and parcell of the art. And so as in a table be it wittie word of which Tacitus is full, sentences, of which Livy, or similitudes wherof Plutarch, straite to lay it upp in the right place of his store-house, as either militarie, or more spetiallie defensive militarie, or more perticulerlie, defensive by fortification and so lay it upp. So likewise in politick matters, and such a little table yow may easelie make, wherwith I would have yow ever joyne the historicall part, which is only the example of some stratageme, or good cownsaile, or such like.

The notion that all arts, even those of war, can be divided into "logicall subdivisions" and thence committed to "a little table" is a habit of mind almost certainly acquired from Ramus's diagrammatic textbooks. Sidney concludes his instructions with an apology for writing in "great hast, of method without method" but promises "to write more largely" at another time.

The frequent appearance of Ramist doctrines in Sidney's works is hardly surprising, for the young courtier was exposed to the Frenchman's influence in a number of different ways. At the beginning of his Continental travels in 1572, Sidney stopped in Paris and probably met Ramus during his stay. Like all Protestant intellectuals, Sidney was undoubtedly shocked and disillusioned at Ramus's untimely death in the bloody Massacre of St. Bartholomew, which broke out during his sojourn in Paris. Four years later Theophilus Banosius published the posthumous *Petri Rami Commentariorum de Religione Christiana Libri Quatuor,* and dedicated it to Sidney with the assurance that the young

---

20. The full text of the letter will be found in the *Prose Works,* III, 130–133. Kenneth D. McRae has outlined the "Ramist Tendencies in the Thought of Jean Bodin," *Journal of the History of Ideas,* 16 (1955), 306–323.

Englishman had loved Ramus when he was alive and esteemed his memory now that he was dead.

Meanwhile, at home in England, Sidney's bumptious friend Gabriel Harvey was preaching the Ramist gospel at Cambridge. Harvey's two orations *Rhetor* and *Ciceronianus* were delivered to willing and eager undergraduates in 1575 and 1576. In witless youth, confesses Harvey, he "valued words more than content, language more than thought, the one art of speaking more than the thousand subjects of knowledge." [21] In the infinite wisdom of his reformed middle years, however, he addresses his gratitude to "most acute Ramus." In his *Ode Natalitia*, composed in Ramus's honor at about the same time as his orations, Harvey celebrates Method as "a heavenly virgin who directs the goddesses of the Arts," and he encourages all professors of philosophical eloquence to support the spread of Ramism in England.[22]

Harvey's enthusiasm was prophetic of Ramus's enormous popularity in England during the last two decades of the sixteenth century. Much of this growing interest was generated within Sidney's impressive circle of friends and literary associates. In 1584 William Temple dedicated his edition of Ramus's *Dialectic* to Sidney, and the poet replied with a letter of generous approval.[23] A few years before Temple's edition of the *Dialectic*, at about the time of (or shortly before) the composition of the

21. Cf. *Gabriel Harvey's Ciceronianus*, ed. Harold S. Wilson, trans. Clarence A. Forbes (Lincoln, Neb., The University, 1945), p. 10.

22. Warren B. Austin, "Gabriel Harvey's 'Lost' Ode on Ramus," *Modern Language Notes*, 61 (1946), 245–246. Cf. also Harvey's discussion of method in *Fowre Letters*, in *Elizabethan Critical Essays*, ed. G. Gregory Smith, 2 vols. (London, Oxford University Press, 1904), II, 235–236. For an outline of Ramus's implication in the Nashe-Harvey controversy of the 1590's, cf. Chauncey Sanders, *Robert Greene and the Harveys* (Bloomington, Ind., Indiana University, 1931).

23. *Prose Works*, III, 145. Temple also wrote a critique of the *Apology*, which is discussed in J. P. Thorne's essay "A Ramistical Commentary of Sidney's 'An Apologie for Poetry,'" *Modern Philology*, 54 (1957), 158–164. For a further example of Temple's Ramism, cf. *A Logicall Analysis of Twentie Psalmes* (1605).

Apology, Abraham Fraunce was at work on the *Sheapheardes Logike*, which was subsequently dedicated to Sidney's close friend Edward Dyer. The British Museum copy of this Ramist treatise is accompanied by two shorter works (also by Fraunce): *Of the nature and use of Logike* and *A bryef and general comparison of Ramus his Logike wth that of Aristotle, to ye ryghte worshypful his verye good Mr and Patron Mr P: Sidney.*[24] In the later and more familiar *Lawiers Logike* (1588), Fraunce notes that the shorter treatises were written before the *Sheapheardes Logike* when he "first came in presence of that right noble and most renowmed knight sir Philip Sydney." He adds that "these small and trifling beginnings drewe both him [Sidney] to a greater liking of, and my selfe to a further travayling in, the easie explication of Ramus his Logike." [25] A *bryef and general comparison* consists of a lively dialogue between "a methodical Ramyst" and "an obstinate Aristotelian," the latter of whom blusters his contempt for the fact that "Ramus rules abroad, Ramus at home, and who but Ramus?" [26]

The *Sheapheardes Logike* is a slim summary of Ramus's *Dialectic*, with a heavy emphasis on "natural" logic as it is found in literature — found, according to Fraunce, in Spenser's recently published *Shepherd's Calendar. Of the nature and use of Logike*, also an outline of the Ramist system, may have been of special interest to Sidney. Fraunce argues that the natural "gyfte of dialectica" is perfectly exemplified in the famous oration of Menenius Agrippa.[27] Sidney uses the same example in the *Apology* as an illustration of "poetical invention." Agrippa approached the Romans, not with "figurative speeches or cunning

24. *British Museum Add. MS* 34361.
25. Abraham Fraunce, *Lawiers Logike*, Sig. qi^r. Cited by Wilbur Samuel Howell, *Logic and Rhetoric in England, 1500–1700* (Princeton, N.J., Princeton University Press, 1956), p. 223.
26. Fraunce, *A bryef and general comparison*, 32^r.
27. Fraunce, *Of the nature and use of Logike*, 30^v.

insinuations, and much less with far fet maxims of philosophy."
Rather, "like a homely and familiar poet," he offered "them a
tale" (p. 40). Fraunce and Sidney understand the tale in the
same way but interpret it to different ends. Fraunce, the would-be
logician, sees a dialectical core within a literary shell. He uncov-
ers the argument of the oration through logical analysis, just as
Sidney exposes the absence of "meaning" in a bad poem. Sidney,
speaking as a poet, sees a delightful tale encompassing a fore-
conceit. The logician, like the reader of Sidney's hypothetical
poet, is expected to see the logical form within the poetic fiction.
Conversely, Sidney's poet is expected to "figure forth" the mentally visible form in a poetic fiction, thus making knowledge delightful. The two points of view are complementary rather than
contradictory; they represent alternative ways of looking at exactly the same thing.

Sidneys' debt to Ramus, or at least to the highly visualized
intellectual milieu that culminated in Ramism, was far more
extensive than is generally recognized. The appropriation of
method, along with the pictorial machinery of the Ramist logic,
though the most obvious and perhaps the most important, is by
no means the only trace of the French logician in the *Apology*.
Sidney's penchant for *usus* — that is, for defining the arts in
terms of their practical ends — is in line with the Ramist position, as is his conception of poetry as an art of visual presentation. Furthermore, the poet and the logician share the assumption that the assent to truth arises, not as a result of propositions
leading to a clearly defined proof, but because the human mind
has a natural insight into the nature of truth itself. It was because of this natural insight, "imprinted," as Fraunce describes
it, "in the inward power of mans soule," [28] that the Ramists could

28. Fraunce, *Lawiers Logike*, Sig. Gii^r. Cf. also *Of the nature and use of
Logike*, 29^v. "That therefore is true Logike, wch is agreable to reason im-
prynted in man, and apparant in ye very things, arguments, and disputations
of ye most excellent in everye kynde."

claim to discover their logic in all sorts of ostensibly nonlogical texts. Like Fraunce, Sidney insists that "the inward light each mind hath in itself is as good as a philosopher's book," adding that the philosophers originally distilled their wisdom "out of natural conceit" (p. 37).

The specific details of Ramus's influence upon Sidney will undoubtedly remain matters for conjecture. Those that I have listed are but a few that might be mentioned, and none of them should be considered beyond question. But with the help of several educated guesses there begins to emerge, between the two men, a general similarity centering around a common set of opinions about the nature of the human mind. For Ramus, each of these branching trees is rooted in the bold — and naïve — assumption that the visible shape of the diagram corresponds to an identical shape viewed by the internal eye. The definitions and divisions of the arts and sciences are artificial and must be learned; but the structure of each subject, the pattern that the definitions and divisions will follow once they have been discovered, is naturally and innately visible in every rational soul. According to the Ramists, therefore, the "natural conceit" is not a faculty subject to development but the "paterne & foundation of all true Logike, wch eyther god hathe drawne or nature layed downe in mans mynde." [29] What we see in the mind is, quite literally, a Ramist diagram without any words on it.

Sidney was apparently familiar with Ramus's notion that innate knowledge is graphic and diagrammatic rather than verbal. To the argument that the natural conceit is innate to the soul, for example, he adds that it resides there "not in the words of art which philosophers bestow upon us." He would have concurred with Ramus that the words in which an art is set forth are secondary and derive their meaning from a prior conceptual frame upon which they are arranged. This concurrence is per-

29. Fraunce, *Of the nature and use of Logike,* Sig. 29^r.

haps clearest in a speech of Pyrocles, who, while excusing his own intellectual laxity, offers us an insight into his author's point of view.

> I must needes saye thus muche (my Deare Cossyn) that I fynde not my self wholly to bee Condempned, bycause I doo not with a Continuall vehemency followe those knowlledges wch yow calle ye betteringes of my mynde. For, bothe the mynde yt self must, (like other thinges) some tymes bee unbent, or else yt will bee eyther weykened or broken, and these knowlledges, as they are of good use, so are they not all the mynde may stretche yt self unto: who knowes whether I feede my myndes [sic] with higher thoughtes?, truely, as I knowe not all the particularityes, so yet, see I the boundes of all these knowlledges.[30]

Each of the "knowlledges," according to Pyrocles, is a composition of "particularityes" arranged within a definite structure. While the details of each art have been forgotten, he is still able to see the pattern ("the boundes") of all knowledge with the eye of his mind. The words are gone, but the picture remains.

Clearly, then, the poet's Idea or fore-conceit is not a word or a verbal definition, nor is it an image of a phenomenal object. Rather, it is a diagrammatic concept, a mental chart upon which the "reasons" of a poem are organized. Once this basic structure is clearly visualized, it must be filled out with the logical divisions of the poem's subject. When the "universal consideration" is fully divided and stretched in precise detail before his mind, the poet has only to submerge it in an individual verbal fiction (a person or an incident). The resulting fusion of the particular with the general is the speaking picture of poetry. Since a good poem will imitate this diagrammatic concept and since the conceit is by definition natural to all men, it is theoretically certain that every reader will see the meaning in the poem and will accede to its universal truth. In the details of Pyrocles' description of his life, for example, we are expected to discern the diagram-

30. *Prose Works*, IV, 11–12.

matic structure of tragedy: "Receyve here not onely an Example of those straunge Tragedyes, but one, that in hym self hathe conteyned all the particularityes of theyre mysfortune: And from henceforthe beleeve yt may bee, synce yo^w shall see yt ys, yo^w shall see I say, a Living Image and a present Story of the best Paterne, Love hathe ever shewed of his worckmanship." [31] We are being alerted to a speaking picture of tragedy. Pyrocles contains within himself, within the "particularityes" of his narration, a "Living Image" of tragedy, in which "Example" we are expected to see the "Paterne" upon which all tragedies are constructed.

Sidney's diagrammatic conception of the mental processes is equally evident in his description of the memory. Since the image of heroism "inflameth the mind with desire to be worthy," readers are encouraged, for their moral welfare, to "let Aeneas be worn in the tablet of your memory" (p. 49). Apparently thinking of a kind of tabula rasa, Sidney envisions the memory as a flat screen upon which images may be imprinted. In another passage he points out that nothing is more conducive to memory than "a certain room divided into many places, well and thoroughly known." He adds that poetry is more easily retained in the memory than prose because it situates every word in its "natural seat, which seat must needs make the words remembered" (p. 54). The "art of memory" was extremely fashionable during the sixteenth century, and its vogue can be traced to a source in the broad current of visual epistemology which flowed through so much of Renaissance culture. Sidney was probably familiar with the art in two distinct, yet intimately related, forms. Ramus's topical logic was an emphatically pictorial system of recall in which visualized diagrams provided the "places" or "rooms" where ideas could be stored. Ramus excluded memory from its traditional place in rhetoric and identified it with judg-

31. Ibid., IV, 114.

ment on the assumption that the visualized processes of thought were themselves a simplified recall mechanism.[32]

A second art of memory was advanced by a number of Renaissance Neoplatonists who understood memorization as a process of stamping archetypal images on a mental grid. The mental images were the psychic facsimile of the hieroglyphs and were purported to reflect the order of the cosmos. The Neoplatonist, like the Ramist, thought of memory as an essentially visual activity in which the objects seen (and remembered) were not words but things.[33] Sidney probably encountered this system in the work of John Dee, who included it, among other Hermetic mysteries, in his *Monas Hieroglyphica* (1564).

Although he was probably aware of both arts of memory, Sidney seems to have borrowed his ideas almost exclusively from the Ramist camp. A poem is like a "room divided into many places" because each word has a "natural seat," an easily memorized relationship with other words in a statement. Now the natural seat, like the divided room, cannot be an external thing, an object seen in the phenomenal world. Rather, the seat of the word is natural because it is that word's place (in the logical sense) on the graphic fore-conceit underlying the poem. In short, memorization is a visual rather than an aural process. The words of a poem are remembered only because they can be seen plotted out on a mental chart. Each word is bracketed in a logical (and visible) relationship with other words. Taken together in a poem,

32. Walter J. Ong, *Ramus, Method, and the Decay of Dialogue* (Cambridge, Mass., Harvard University Press, 1958), p. 280.

33. I have an obvious debt here to Frances Yates, *The Art of Memory*. Miss Yates (p. 234), in discussing the memory system implicit in Ramism, argues that with Ramus, "the 'natural' stimulus for memory . . . is not the emotionally exciting memory image; it is the abstract order of dialectical analysis." What Miss Yates fails to recognize, however, is that "the abstract order" of Ramus's "dialectical analysis" is itself a distinctly visible diagram, admittedly not "emotionally exciting," but nevertheless the instrument of cool, visual calculation.

they give verbal expression to the Idea upon which they are visibly arranged and to which they are ultimately referable.

Although Dee's memory system has no clearly discernible influence in the *Apology*, the recurrent appearance of this controversial scientist in Sidney's intellectual background is an indication that his ideas bore more weight with the young poet than is generally recognized. Dee's interest in mathematics brought him into the mainstream of visual epistemology, and it is therefore not surprising that he and Ramus found each other intellectually compatible. They appear to have met first in Paris in 1547, when Dee earned the Frenchman's praise for his lectures on Euclid. It was Dee's turn to listen three years later when, during a successful year of study in Paris, he heard Ramus lecture on logic.[34] These early meetings led to the exchange of letters in which Ramus encouraged Dee in his fruitless attempt to introduce mathematics and geometry into the curriculum of the English universities. Because of this close personal and intellectual affinity, it is not inconceivable that Dee had a hand in arranging the meeting between Sidney and Ramus in 1572.

Conjecture aside, however, we can be certain that Sidney and Dee were well known to each other. The mathematician recorded two occasions when he entertained the young nobleman in his country residence,[35] and Edward Dyer, Sidney's close companion during the late 1570's, became godfather to Dee's eldest son, Arthur, on July 13, 1579. Sidney broadened his own scientific education by pursuing chemistry "with Dee as teacher, and with

34. E. G. R. Taylor, *The Mathematical Practitioners of Tudor and Stuart England* (Cambridge, England, Cambridge University Press for the Institute of Navigation, 1954), p. 18; and *The Compendious rehearsal of John Dee* (1592), appended to *Johannis Glastoniensis Chronica sive Historia de Rebus Glastoniensibus* (1726), II, 504.

35. *The Private Diary of Dr. John Dee*, ed. J. O. Halliwell-Phillipps (London, Printed for the Camden Society, 1842), pp. 2 and 20. The visits took place on January 16, 1577, and June 15 ("abowt 5 of the clok"), 1583.

Dyer as companion." [36] He was deeply interested in the mathematical sciences from an early age, particularly since he considered them essential to the art of war. Sidney expressed his enthusiasm for both geometry and astronomy in letters to his mentor Languet and encouraged his younger brother to follow a similar course of study.

Although Sidney mentions geometry only twice in the *Apology*, his generally visual approach to mental activity must have found confirmation in the principles of that discipline. The relationship between geometrical images in the mind and their representation in external nature (as described by Dee) is identical to the one that exists between the poet's fore-conceit and his finished poem. Both the poet and the geometrician think of the objects of their arts as visible shapes, abstract patterns, and not the phenomena of external nature or words. Indeed, Sidney's description of poetic composition is in many ways similar to what must have been Dee's conception of drawing a geometrical figure. The poet's hand, like the geometrician's, traces out the form of an Idea viewed within the mind. The result is a pictorial fusion of the particular with the general, for the individual speaking picture and the individual triangle or circle are thought to reflect the universal image before the mind's eye. Thus the main similarity between the poet and the geometrician is in the nature and function of their concepts; the main difference is that the geometrician illustrates his inward conceits with lines, while Sidney's artist must do it with words.

THE GROUND-PLOT

The poetic process, as I have condensed it from the *Apology*, commences with the arrangement of "reasons" on a conceptual

36. Thomas Moffett, *Nobilis or A View of the Life and Death of a Sidney*, trans. Virgil B. Heltzel and Hoyt H. Hudson (San Marino, Calif., The Huntington Library, 1940), p. 75.

skeleton in the writer's mind; the poet then imitates this mental frame with vivid language, and the result is a poem. But beneath the carefully erected veneer of verbal particulars resides the universal form upon which the artifact was modeled. The poem is merely a verbal medium through which the poet's mental pictures are made delightfully accessible to the eyes of his audience. An adept reader will invert the creative procedure: he will "use the narration but as an imaginative ground-plot of a profitable invention" (p. 58). The ground-plot is the poet's fore-conceit as it appears in the speaking picture of a poem. Sidney assumes that the reader will use the verbal image of the artifact as a basis for the reconstruction ("invention" in the rhetorical sense — "to find" or "to come upon") of the full-scale Idea as seen in the poet's mind. In short, the ground-plot is the poet's way of letting us see what he means.

The word "ground-plot," like "idea" and "conceit," had visual implications for Sidney which are probably not immediately obvious to the modern reader. The term is a conjunction of the two words "ground" and "plot," both of which were in fairly common use, particularly in mathematics books, by the time of the *Apology*. But the compound form was relatively unknown in English, and Sidney's near innovation provides us with a useful insight into what he expected his readers to see in a poem.

During the Renaissance the word "plot" was generally employed to describe a plan or structure that could be expressed in visual form. It has an obvious connection with the notion of a plot of ground — and a perhaps less obvious relationship to the literary (or criminal) plot, where the visual connotation is lost, or at least submerged, in the familiarity of the metaphor. The word appears several times in Thomas Digges's *Pantometria* (1571), a fully illustrated handbook describing the spatial relationships that exist between natural bodies and offering instruction in the use of various scientific instruments for reducing those relationships to quantitative proportions. Digges also explains that the numerical results of observation can be represented on a pictorial "platte" (at other times called a "mappe" or "carte"). A further refinement is "to reduce many plattes into one, and to make a fayre carde or mappe of an whole province or region." [37]

The plot of the mathematicians, then, is a collocation of ideas or intellectually determinate relationships presented in visible form. Sidney generally uses the term in this way, although he always assumes that the plot is a conceptual diagram, a map seen in the mind. Pyrocles, for example, pleased with the success of his plans, boasts that the situation is just as his "owne plot could have laide it." [38] The mental plot is a psychic grid where the details of an argument or a poem can be arranged. Pyrocles, disguised as an Amazon, hopes that his/her speech will be persuasive to Philoclea, "having alredy plotted out in her [his] conceite, how she [he] would deale with her." [39] In effect, then, plot, as the structural model upon which all thoughts are patterned, is nearly synonymous, in Sidney's usage, with conceit and Idea.[40]

The first half of the contraction, "ground," was also rich with visual and conceptual implications. In one of its simplest connotations it signifies a base or foundation and was often used to describe the background of a painting. Sir Thomas Elyot, for example, praises "the way of a cunnynge paynter" who "maketh the grounde of his worke of the depest blacke colour that he may

37. Thomas Digges, *Pantometria*, Sig. Li*ᵛ*. "Plot," "plotte," "plat," and "platte" are orthographic variations on the same word. Cf. Robert Recorde's *Pathway to knowledg*, "To The Reader": "This candle did I light: this lighte have I kindeled: that learned men maie se, to practice their pennes, their eloquence to advaunce, to register their names in the booke of memorie I drew the platte rudelie, whereon thei maie build."

38. *Prose Works*, I, 86.

39. Ibid., I, 480.

40. "Plot" is also synonymous with "model." In the early version of the *Arcadia*, Sidney writes "a Moddell of the heavenly dwellinges" (*Prose Works*, IV, 13). In the revised version, in the same context, the phrase is altered to "a plotte of the celestiall dwellings" (*Prose Works*, I, 57).

come by." [41] Sidney often employs the term in this sense, describing Amphialus's jacket as "more rich than glaring, the ground being black velvet." Similarly, Pamela's needlework is a "marvaile to see" in part because "the colours for the grounde were so well chosen." [42]

"Ground" could also signify a base or foundation in the context of logic and science, meaning an initial assumption or point of intellectual departure. Robert Recorde defines geometry as the foundation of all the mathematical sciences, "the grounde of all theyr certeintie." [43] Thomas Digges, comparing the cosmologies of Aristotle and Copernicus, opts for the latter because of his sound mathematical hypotheses. "There is no doubte," argues Digges, "but of a true grounde truer effects may be produced then of principles that are false." [44] Sidney was familiar with this sense of "ground" and put it to constant use in his prose. Musidorus reminds Pyrocles that "a mind wel trayned and long exercised in vertue . . . doth not easily chaunge any course it once undertakes, but upon well grounded & well wayed causes." [45] Having escaped from Arcadia with Musidorus, Pamela pauses to reconsider her actions, anxious to "weighe with what wynges shee flewe oute of her Native Contry and upon what grounde shee buylt her Determinacyon." [46] "Ground," then, like "plot," bears with it both the suggestion of something seen, and of a foundation for rational arguments or judgments.

"Ground-plot," as it appears in the *Apology*, is verbally redundant. The individual components of the term have almost exactly the same connotation, and either "ground" or "plot" alone would have conveyed Sidney's intention without significant

41. Sir Thomas Elyot, *Of the Knowledge which Maketh a Wise Man*, ed. Edwin Johnston Howard (Oxford, Ohio, The Anchor Press, 1946), p. 53.
42. *Prose Works*, I, 367 and 402.
43. Recorde, *Pathway to knowledg*, "The Preface."
44. Thomas Digges, *A Prognostication euerlastinge* (1576), Sig. Mi^v.
45. *Prose Works*, I, 55.
46. Ibid., IV, 185.

loss in precision. Although Sidney frequently employs both "ground" and "plot" in his writing, the compounded form is very seldom found. The term is thus conspicuous for its rarity. The *New English Dictionary* lists Sidney's as the second recorded usage of "ground-plot" in the history of the English language. Its first appearance occurs in John Dee's preface to Billingsley's translation of Euclid's *Elements* (1570). Dee's "Groundplatt" is not only a word but a large diagram of the "Sciences, and Artes Mathematicall" (Figure 1). The various branches of the general subject are divided and redivided in orderly brackets across the page. Dee explains that the impressive chart is designed for the reader's benefit: "That you may the easier perceive, and better remember, the principall pointes, whereof my Preface treateth, I will give you the Groundplatt of my whole discourse, in a Table annexed: from the first to the last, somewhat Methodically contrived." [47] Dee's assurance that his graph will be an aid to perceptual and mnemonic clarity and his allusion to method are the unmistakable signs of the influence of Ramus, whose "methodical" diagrams serve identical objectives. Furthermore — and again we should think of Ramus — Dee's emphasis on the pedagogical utility of his speaking picture should not obscure the prior assumption that the shape of his graph exactly duplicates the structure of the arts and sciences of mathematics. In short, the simple act of looking at his graph amounts (from Dee's point of view) to an insight into a transcendent order of being.

Since Sidney knew Dee, both personally and as a student and since he pursued mathematics with some enthusiasm, it would have been a remarkable oversight to have ignored his teacher's preface to the first English translation of Euclid's *Elements*. In other words, there can be little doubt that he was well acquainted with Dee's picture. Because of his highly diagrammatic approach

47. John Dee, Preface to Euclid's *Elements*, trans. John Billingsley (1570), Sig. Aiiii^r.

to the conceptualizing processes and his interest in Ramus, Sidney must have been deeply impressed with Dee's "somewhat" methodical "groundplatt." In fact, it is quite probable that the mathematician's memorable chart was in the back of Sidney's mind when he used the word "ground-plot" in the *Apology*. The similarities between the speaking picture of poetry and the abstract diagram were too close to be missed. In a poem, as in Dee's graph, visual structure is more eloquent than language, for it penetrates and possesses the "sight of the soul" in the way that a "wordish description" never can (p. 27).

The process is clearly illustrated in a description of the amorous misadventures of Pyrocles. The young prince is disguised as an Amazon, in love with Philoclea and desperately attempting to conceive a plan for diverting the affections of Basilius and Gynecia, Philoclea's parents.

With hasty handes shee gott her self up turning her sighte, to every thinge, as yf Chaunge of object mighte help her Invention. So went shee ageane to the Cave, where forthewith yt came into her heade, that shoulde bee the fittest place to performe her exployte, of whiche shee had now a kynde of Confused Conceypte, allthoughe shee had not sett downe in her fancy the meeting with eche particularity that mighte falle oute: Butt, as a Paynter dothe at the first shewe a Rude proportion of the thinge hee imitates, whiche after wth more Curyous hande hee drawes to the representing eche Lineament; So had her thoughtes (beaten aboute yt Continually) receyved into them, ground plott of her devyse, allthoughe shee had not in eche parte shapte yt according to a full determeynacyon.[48]

Since conceits enter by the eyes, Pyrocles begins his thinking with looking, as an aid to invention. The reader begins in a similar fashion by looking at the poem. The cave, like the poem after a first reading, produces a 'Confused Conceypte," a general pattern of an idea without the full array of details. The "ground plott of her devyse" ("devyse," or "device," a variation on an emblem) is a "Rude proportion," comparable to the painter's

48. *Prose Works*, IV, 203.

initial outline of the things he imitates. The reader's ground-plot is similarly visible and serves exactly the same purpose, for it is his first conceptual response to the poem, a proemial pattern upon which the subsequent particularities of his "invention" can be "shapte." If the poem is sufficient in its "reasons," the reader's efforts should result in a perfect re-vision of the poet's fore-conceit. He will see exactly what his author means.

ENERGIA

At about the same time that he was composing the *Apology*, Sidney wrote a long letter to his brother, Robert, in which he mentions that the "ethick part" of moral philosophy has "vertues or vices and the natures of Passions" [49] as its main subject matter. This trinity of topics, as assigned to poetry in the *Apology* (p. 29), may not sit very well with us today, inclined as we are to make rather rigid distinctions between abstractions like *superbia* and *prudentia*, on the one hand, and floods of powerful feeling, or passion, on the other. With good reason, perhaps, we are given to the view that generalizations about human behavior are false and incomplete in their application, for they overlook the irrational rags and unexpected bones of mental activity and practical experience that appear so prominently in modern interpretations of life, not to mention literature. Or, to put it another way, we are accustomed to a psychology that gives a wide berth to the unconscious, and in some ways unseen, forces that shape individual lives.

For men of Sidney's time, however, this distinction between the rational and the irrational, the seen and the unseen, was in no way as absolute as it is today. The currency of "humors" comedy and the advent of Character books are a small fraction of the evidence that could be presented to show that men of the Renaissance regarded passions as no less conventional than ab-

49. *Prose Works*, III, 131.

stract virtues and vices and accordingly no less susceptible to
analysis and generalization. The difference between virtuous and
passionate behavior could be understood psychologically as the
difference between virtuous and passionate ideas or conceits.
Fulke Greville takes exactly this position in "A Treatie of Humane Learning," arguing that when the imagination is misled by
the senses, "our affections cast/False shapes, and formes on their
intelligence," with the result that passion or affection holds sway.

> Hence our desires, feares, hopes, love, hate, and sorrow,
> In fancy make us heare, feele, see impressions,
> Such as out of our sense they doe not borrow;
> And are the efficient cause, the true progression
>   Of sleeping visions, idle phantasmes waking,
>   Life, dreames; and knowledge, apparitions making.[50]

According to such an explanation, passion is a variety of mental
experience distinguishable in degree, but not in kind, from other
forms of psychic activity. And the degree of difference arises
largely from the kinds of images present before the mind's eye.
Once false impressions, generated by the affections, have over-
taken the mind, passionate thought and presumably passionate
action will follow.

The literary results of this more or less unified conception of
human experience were, of course, profound. Where today we
might think of the poet as the narrator of individual human
passions and the philosopher as the voice of a more general view
of human life, the Renaissance position was much less dichotomous. For Sidney at least, the poet and the moral philosopher
have exactly the same domain: they both concern themselves
with virtues, vices, and passions. The two differ only in their
mode of presentation: the philosopher deals in words, the poet
in pictures.

50. "A Treatie of Humane Learning," stanzas 12–13, from *Poems and
Dramas of Fulke Greville*, ed. Geoffrey Bullough, 2 vols. (New York, Oxford University Press, 1945), I, 157.

That Sidney considered passions psychologically similar to virtues and vices is crucial to his handling of emotion in general and to his conception of *energia* in particular. Toward the end of the *Apology* Sidney turns his attention to "that lyrical kind of songs and sonnets," remarking characteristically that the poets of the day are far from felicitous in the composition of amorous verses. "So coldly they apply fiery speeches," he argues, that the reader is left with the impression that such poets are imitating other writers rather "than that in truth they feel those passions, which easily (as I think) may be betrayed by that same forcibleness or *energia* (as the Greeks call it) of the writer" (p. 81). The crux of the objection is credibility; English love poets lack credibility because they have imitated poetic conventions rather than their own passions and thus lack *energia.*

Others have charted the errant course of *energia,* and it is unnecessary to recount all of their discoveries here. The concept has proved a knotty one, to say the least. To begin with, the major classical and Renaissance sources for the term are very often inconsistent in their interpretations of its meaning. Furthermore, the modern commentators, while agreed that the sources offer contradictions, have further complicated matters by adding a number of explanations for the term which differ on important points. The mounting confusion, particularly among contemporary scholars, has resulted from the fact that interpretations of *energia* vary according to the text selected and according to the context in which the term is considered. The lesson seems to be that any definition of *energia* will be subject to manifold exceptions, with the corollary that we may do best to treat the term as it appears in specific instances and leave the general concept in its inevitable obscurity.[51]

51. Classical discussions of *energia* include Aristotle, *Rhetoric,* 1411^a ff.; and Quintilian, *Institutio Oratoria,* VIII, iii, 89. Among Renaissance commentators, see particularly Julius Scaliger, *Poetices Libri Septem,* III, 26 (*efficacia*); Joachim Du Bellay, *La Deffence et Illustration de la Langue Fran-*

By far the most extensive treatment of *energia* to date and certainly the most crucial for students of Sidney, appears in Neil L. Rudenstine's *Sidney's Poetic Development*. Convinced that *energia* provides the key to the theory of the *Apology* and also that it goes far in explaining Sidney's poetic technique, Mr. Rudenstine develops a definition of the concept. Throughout his discussion he emphasizes that *energia* derives from two things: first, "from the poet's intense and imaginative involvement in his theme"; and second, from the successful "effort to discover forms at every level of language — rhythm, sound, syntax, rhetoric, stanza, genre — forms which draw their energies from a writer's strong feelings and release them with such force as to move, convince, and teach (in the broadest sense) an audience." [52]

This analysis tends to cast a romantic coloring over Sidney's more or less neoclassical aesthetic. For example, while it is undeniable that *energia* or, for that matter, any laudable quality in poetry, results from the writer's personal involvement and while Sidney did compose sonnets in which his own strong feelings may have surfaced, it is my contention that the author of *Astrophil and Stella* was not the poet, or the aesthetician, of intense personal and "imaginative" art. Almost the entire emphasis of the *Apology* falls on the poet's perfect pattern, his clearly conceived fore-conceit of an abstract virtue, vice, or pas-

---

coyse, ed. Henri Chamard (Paris, M. Didier, 1948), p. 35 and Chamard's note; Torquato Tasso, *Dell' Arte Poetica* in *Le Prose Diverse di Torquato Tasso*, ed. Cesare Guasti, 2 vols. (Florence, 1875), I, 56–57; and George Puttenham, *The Arte of English Poesie*, ed. G. D. Willcock and A. Walker (Cambridge, England, Cambridge University Press, 1936), p. 143. For modern views of the concept, see Madeleine Doran, *Endeavors of Art* (Madison, Wis., Wisconsin University Press, 1954), pp. 233 and 242–243; Jean H. Hagstrum, *The Sister Arts* (Chicago, Chicago University Press, 1958), p. 12; Paul J. Alpers, *The Poetry of the Faerie Queene* (Princeton, N.J., Princeton University Press, 1967), pp. 104–105; and Neil L. Rudenstine, *Sidney's Poetic Development* (Cambridge, Mass., Harvard University Press, 1967), chap. 10.

52. Rudenstine, *Sidney's Poetic Development*, pp. 151 and 159–160.

sion, rather than on the verbal expression of personal feelings. The poet derives his materials, not from his experiences in the phenomenal world, but from an internally viewed universe of more ideal, more general truths. Accordingly, his manner of expression "is not wholly imaginative," for he is determined to convey a general Idea — "to bestow a Cyrus upon the world to make many Cyruses" — and not "a particular excellency, as nature might have done" (p. 16). Therefore, I believe it is a mistake to confuse Sidney's notion of passions as abstractions like Hope, Fear, Hate, and Love, which are conceptually similar to virtues and vices, with the more modern sense of passions as strong feelings, personal emotions, which defy generalization.

Moreover, I would argue that *energia* should not be so closely associated with the verbal and technical aspects of poetry. While it is true that Sidney discusses language in the section on *energia*, he also makes it clear that his principal topic is "the right use of the material side of poesy" (p. 81). By "material" he means the "inside" of a poem, its conceptual structure, "matter to be expressed by words" (p. 73). Only in the passage following the one on *energia* does he turn to "the outside of it, which is words" (p. 81). When he does discuss language in the context of *energia* — coldly applied "fiery speeches" and "swelling phrases" — he is pointing to the fact that the overblown rhetoric of contemporary verse is false and implausible because it lacks precision and directness. These qualities, so essential to Sidney's notion of *energia*, are absent because the verbal surface of the poetry rests on no clearly conceived Idea of passion but is simply an accumulation of conventional phrases without a controlling concept. Although he does not use the term, George Gascoigne prescribes the same kind of *energia* when he argues that "pleasant woordes" and "apt vocables" are secondary and insists that "the first and most necessarie poynt that ever I founde meete to be considered in making of a delectable poeme is this, to grounde it upon some fine invention." [53]

Such differences in the interpretation of detail account partially for Mr. Rudenstine's description of what it is that the reader is expected to see in a good poem. "Energia," he says, "is above all a means of giving feeling a visible form." Poetry "makes us see revenge, anger — indeed all passions — expressed in such a way that we understand them for what they are." [54] But he comes no closer than this to explaining *exactly* what he means by "visible form" and *precisely* how we "understand" passions "for what they are." The important point, in my opinion, is the epistemological thrust of Sidney's use of the verb "to see" and the fact that for Sidney the understanding of a concept was simply a special way of seeing it. When, for example, we read that the poet enables us "not to hear of" virtues, vices, and passions, "but clearly to see through them" (p. 29), Sidney means that inside the verbal outside of the best poetry there resides a concrete universal, an image of Cyrus or Lucretia or Gnatho wherein the mind's eye can discern the outlines of a general concept. Such a process will occur, of course, only when the poet has clearly conceived the Idea (of a particular virtue, vice, or passion) to which the words of his poem conform.

In this light the conclusion that Sidney's definition of poetry is "largely in terms of dialogues, tales, the motions and whisperings of the people, the 'setting' of a banquet or a walk, and the vivid scenes, actions, or images from dramatic and narrative verse," and that such a definition includes "the main constituents of energia" [55] explains only a part of Sidney's approach. While

53. George Gascoigne, *Certayne Notes of Instruction,* in *Elizabethan Critical Essays,* ed. Smith, I, 47.
54. Rudenstine, *Sidney's Poetic Development,* p. 157.
55. Ibid., p. 158. In developing his definition of *energia,* Mr. Rudenstine reviews the ideas of two of Sidney's probable sources. He begins by referring

it is beyond dispute that vivid descriptions of specific scenes and actions constitute the "delight" of good poetry, they are only the superficial first impressions which draw "children from play and old men from the chimney corner" (p. 38). Once given such a colorful narrative, the reader is expected to use it as the ground-plot of his own invention, his own visualization of the poet's fore-conceit. And it is this kind of seeing, the seeing that amounts

---

to Aristotle's remarks on *energia* in the *Rhetoric* (1411ᵃ ff.), pointing out that Sidney translated "at least two books, if not all, of the *Rhetoric,* and he must have known this passage well." He summarizes the section in Aristotle by noting that "it emphasizes 'activity' and the sense of things being present before one's eyes, as well as more general visual effects" (p. 154). John Hoskyns, in a familiar passage from *Direccōns for Speech and Style* (in Osborn, *The Life, Letters, and Writings of John Hoskyns,* p. 155), states that he has seen Sidney's translation of Books I–II of Aristotle's *Rhetoric;* but surely this is not evidence that Sidney knew a specific passage "well," particularly when that passage appears in Book III. Furthermore, even if Sidney did translate part of the *Rhetoric,* we have no real reason to suppose that he had done so before he began to write the *Apology.* If we were to judge from the Aristotelian allusions in the *Apology,* we would conclude that Sidney made little or no use of the *Rhetoric* but shows great familiarity with the *Poetics* and the *Ethics.* In the latter of these there appears a discussion of *energia* which comes much closer to the sense of the term as it appears in the *Apology* than the passage in the *Rhetoric.* Discussing the active expression of character, Aristotle points out that "it makes quite a difference . . . whether we conceive the supreme good as the mere possession (*hexis*) of virtue or as its employment (*energeia*) — i.e. as a state of character or as its expression in conduct" (*Nicomachean Ethics,* I, viii, trans. Philip Wheelwright, in *Aristotle* [Garden City, N.Y., Doubleday, Doran & Co., Inc., 1935], p. 123). This use of the term couples the idea of an abstraction in operation with an emphasis on the relationship between *gnosis* and *praxis* which is equally typical of Sidney.

Mr. Rudenstine then turns to Scaliger's *Poetices Libri Septem* (III, 26) and concludes that exclamation, direct address, and other rhetorical forms conveying "the sense of vivid dramatic action" (p. 155) are the qualities that Scaliger selects as the most conducive to *energia.* What should also be noted, however, is Scaliger's argument that *energia* (or *efficacia,* as he translates the Greek term) is a quality, "not of words, but of Ideas, which are the species of things" (*non verborum virtutem, sed Idearum, quae rerum species sunt*). In short, while words are capable of conveying *energia,* the term, as Shepherd (*An Apology for Poetry,* p. 226) points out, "refers not to the words used in presenting the subject but to the vivid mental apprehension of things themselves."

to knowing, that Sidney emphasizes and that *energia* is designed to produce.

Energia, then, bears the implication that the poet's most important work is completed before he puts pen to paper — or, to repeat a quotation from the *Apology*, that "the skill of the artificer standeth in that *Idea* or fore-conceit of the work, and not in the work itself" (p. 16). The term, in brief, means conceptual clarity for Sidney and arises in a poem only when the writer has his moral abstraction — whether of a virtue, vice, or passion — clearly in view before he begins to write. Without such conceptual clarity the poem "becomes a confused mass of words with a tingling sound of rhyme, barely accompanied with reason" (p. 74) — which is another way of saying that the poem gives our minds nothing to see.

SUMMARY

The *Apology*, though an internally consistent critical argument, represents the confluence of a wide variety of literary and philosophical ideas. Sidney's unequivocally visual epistemology, in many ways the key to his poetic theory, might have derived from any one of numerous possible sources. It is much more likely, however, that the persistent equation of thinking with seeing in the *Apology* and throughout Sidney's works resulted from the unconscious assimilation of many related ideas to a single, almost magnetic, intellectual disposition. Sidney reconciled a love of literature with an esteem for learning by trying to prove that poetry is a science — indeed, the mother of all the arts and sciences. Plato's assertion that the sight of virtue would automatically produce the love of virtue conformed perfectly to Sidney's ethical and epistemological predispositions. Ramist logic, the doctrines and methods of contemporary methematics, and the familiar critical traditions of European art and literature provided him with the scientific substructure that he considered essential to the "defence of poor Poetry," and at the same time reinforced his fundamentally visual approach to the human mental processes.

Sidney was not a "homely and familiar poet" addressing his plea to the purely literary sensibilities of his fellow poets. The *Apology* reflects its author's deep submergence in all levels of contemporary European culture. Its intellectual latitude is an expression of Sidney's firm conviction that poetry is a science and that it should be accepted as such by the entire community of artists and scholars to which the treatise was directed. Accordingly, we should recognize that the *Apology* is not so much a handbook on poetry as it is a scientific theory of communication. The transit from fore-conceit to ground-plot involves a poet, an audience, and a medium through which conceptual pictures can be transmitted. Sidney's real innovation was not that he altered the ancient premises of visual epistemology but that he gave them a new application. Thinking is seeing, and ideas are pictures, but Sidney proposes to communicate those mental images, not through external pictures, but through the speaking picture of a poem. The theory, as we have shown, is consistent; but it remains to be seen how Sidney applied the theory in his own poetry and prose.

4

The Speaking Picture
of Sidney's Prose
and Poetry

THE PROSE

The theory of the *Apology* left its impression on both the manner and matter of everything that Sidney wrote. In spite of the variousness of its impact, we can generalize that the main effect of the *Apology* was to give definition to Sidney's central creative conviction — that it is the poet's most urgent task to render philosophical truth visible through poetry and prose that minimize the gap between written word and pictorial idea. This, according to Fulke Greville, was Sidney's objective in the *Arcadia*, where the author's "intent, and scope was, to turn the barren Philosophy precepts into pregnant Images of life." [1] The poetic pictures that Greville refers to are almost certainly in the *New Arcadia*, Sidney's incomplete revision of the original, or *Old Arcadia*, which was completed in 1580. [2] The later version was

1. Fulke Greville, *Life of Sir Philip Sidney*, ed. Nowell Smith (Oxford, The Clarendon Press, 1907), p. 15.
2. I follow Ringler's dating throughout. Greville (*Life of Sidney*, p. 14) registers his regret that Sidney had not "liv'd to finish, and bring to perfection this extraordinary frame of his own Common-wealth." Since the *Old Arcadia* was in fact finished and since Sidney's death brought an end to his revisions, it is unquestionably to the *New Arcadia* that Greville makes reference.

not begun until 1584 and thus follows in the wake of the *Apology* and *Astrophil and Stella*, both of which were finished by 1582. Since it is a massive revision and was begun after the crystallization of critical theory in the *Apology*, the *New Arcadia* is the obvious place to look for the speaking picture of Sidney's prose. Although the discussion of the prose before the poetry somewhat violates the chronology of the Sidney canon, a preliminary excursion into *Arcadia* will help to illuminate the more subtle and sophisticated texture of *Astrophil and Stella*.

The extant fragment of the *New Arcadia* is considerably longer than the complete *Old Arcadia*. Had Sidney finished the revision, it would have been more than twice as long as the original. "The final purpose of this amplification," writes one of Sidney's recent commentators, "is to show the universal applications, or the philosophical underpinnings, of the plot of pastoral romance established by Montemayor — in a word, to moralize plot." [3] This objective was, of course, in perfect agreement with the doctrines set forth in the *Apology*. At the same time that he filled his romance with philosophical pictures, however, Sidney endowed the members of the Arcadian community with new powers of vision — powers acquired since the composition of the *Apology*. In effect, the *New Arcadia* not only provides the reader with a full gallery of moral images but also offers him exemplary instruction in how those images are to be viewed. This instruction, not surprisingly, duplicates that already given in the *Apology*.

Although he concurs with Plato and Cicero that "who could see virtue would be wonderfully ravished with the love of her beauty" (p. 49), Sidney is alone in the assurance that virtue — not to mention vice and passion — can be presented in visible form. In the *New Arcadia* the results of his optimism are fully evident. We read, for example, that the Arcadians see more than a man in Pyrocles: "All that beheld him (and al that might be-

3. Walter R. Davis, *A Map of Arcadia: Sidney's Romance in Its Tradition* (New Haven, Conn., Yale University Press, 1965), p. 56.

hold him, did behold him) made their eyes quicke messengers to their minds, that there they had seene the uttermost that in mankind might be seene." [4] The mere sight of the young noble-man is sufficient to stir the Arcadians into an awareness that Pyrocles represents the pinnacle of human virtue. In another pas-sage that is unique to the *New Arcadia*, Pyrocles explains that by simply seeing Musidorus he acquired both the *gnosis* and *praxis* of virtue. "He taught me by word, and best by example, giving me in him so lively an Image of virtue, as ignorance could not cast such mist over mine eyes, as not to see, and to love it." [5] Pyrocles takes instruction in virtue by seeing it in his friend's example. Knowledge — the penetration through the "mist" of ignorance — which is the product of his seeing, has its result in love. The lesson has accordingly met with both of Sidney's peda-gogical requirements: *gnosis* follows upon sight, and *praxis* de-velops out of the knower's positive disposition toward the object known. We can be sure that the lesson would have failed had Musidorus given Pyrocles a moral treatise to read. His student would have complained, as he does further on in *Arcadia*, "if we love vertue, in whom shal we love it but in a vertuous creature? without your meaning be, I should love this word *vertue*, where I see it written in a book." [6]

The regal inhabitants of Arcadia, then, are not the products of brazen nature but the denizens of a poetic golden world where ideal concepts take on flesh and march forth in full daylight. These passages show that the Arcadians look upon each other much as Sidney would have us look upon his poetry and prose. Like Pyrocles, we must disregard words. Instead, the reader is expected to penetrate beneath the verbal particulars that describe Musidorus to the general concept of virtue that the words reflect; or, to cite one more example, we must be prepared to see that

---

4. *Prose Works*, I, 48.
5. Ibid., I, 264.
6. Ibid., I, 80. Cf. IV, 19.

"if ever Vertue tooke a bodie to shewe his (els unconceaveable) beautie, it was in *Pamela*." [7]

Sidney's policy in revising the *Old Arcadia* was to flesh out his narrative with a variety of characters and events through which he assumed his readers would be able to see moral universals. He introduced this new material in dozens of short verbal portraits that unite the general type with a particular personage or event. These brief pictures are so numerous and so consistent in their contours that they can be isolated with relative ease. The King of Pontus, for example, has a malcontent as an adviser. He is described as "a man of the most envious disposition, that (I think) ever infected the aire with his breath: whose eies could not looke right upon any happie man, nor eares beare the burthen of any bodies praise: contrary to the natures of al other plagues, plagued with others well being; making happines the ground of his unhappinesse, & good newes the argument of his sorrow: in sum, a man whose favour no man could winne, but by being miserable." [8] This character has almost no narrative function but appears as a kind of digression, a moment when the story pauses and the artist inserts an illustration. The description is designed to catch the lineaments of a philosophical type rather than a complex, individual personality. Sidney is portraying an extreme example of a certain vice, as the superlative "the most envious disposition" makes clear. Superlatives, which are a common feature in these portraits, function as the verbal agents of conceptual precision, for they push the significance of the word to its connotative limit. We can mentally picture or imagine qualities best when they are described in their extremes — when, by becoming the poles or boundaries of a quality, they also take on certain quantitative characteristics. The paradoxical constructions have a similar effect, for they reduce the complexity of real character

7. Ibid., I, 472.
8. Ibid., I, 203.

to a formula of dichotomous extremes. The paradox, "plagued with others well being," is the pattern for the succeeding phrases. For this man, "well being" in others corresponds to his own "plague." Similarly, "happines" in others corresponds to his own "unhappinesse," and "good newes" in others corresponds to his own "sorrow," and so his "favour" arises because others are "miserable." Antithesis and repetition are employed, not for their decorative effect, but in order to give definition to an idea. Beneath the verbal wit is a strict conceptual ground-plot, a nonverbal conceit that regulates the disposition of the language. The picture achieves precision by divesting words of their suggestiveness, by subordinating verbal subtlety to that kind of clarity we tend to associate with vision. We do not see a man here; we see through the details of the particular example to the universal idea upon which it is patterned.

Sidney often summarizes his moral pictures in a terse, at times pointed or paradoxical, phrase or sentence. As might be expected, these summary pictures generally fall at the end of a description and are sometimes prefaced by "in sum" or "to conclude." As in the case of the malcontent ("in sum, a man whose favour no man could winne, but by being miserable"), these epitomes compress *multum in parvo* and often contain the conceit upon which the details of the description are arranged. Pamphilus, the embodiment of "disguised falshood," is characterized as "one, whose head one would not think so stayed, as to thinke mischievously." But, "to conclude, such a one, as who can keepe him at armes ende, neede never wish a better companion." [9] Lycurgus is a bold braggart, constantly parading his amorous and military exploits to the world — "In summe, in all his speeches, more like the bestower, then the desirer of felicitie." [10]

Fulke Greville explains that Sidney's objective in his poetic

9. Ibid., I, 266.
10. Ibid., I, 507.

portraits "was to limn out . . . exact pictures, of every posture in the minde," [11] as a kind of moral gallery for his readers. John Hoskyns says as much, but he also sheds some important light on Sidney's technique. In a section entitled "To Illustrate," Hoskyns remarks that "Men are discribed most excellentlie in *Arcadia*," adding, "hee that will truely set downe a man in a figured storie, must first learne truely to set downe an humo[r]. a passion, a virtue, a vice, & therein keeping decent pporcōn add but names, & knitt togeather the accidents & incount[ers]." Hoskyns then goes on to give a long list of "notable & lively portracts" that appear in the *Arcadia* and concludes that in sketching them it was "*Sidney's* course . . . to imagine the thinge pnte [painted] in his owne brayne, that is [his] pen might the better pnte [paint] it to yo[w]." [12]

Hoskyns's comments claim our attention for at least two reasons. First, and most obviously, his description of Sidney's method of composition is identical to the one prescribed in the *Apology*. The artist — an emphatically visual artist — proceeds by painting his fore-conceit clearly in his own mind, thereby ensuring that the reader's ground-plot will develop into a precise, and thus profitable, invention. Like Sidney, Hoskyns thinks of words, not as verbal phenomena primarily to be heard, but as conceptual counters that point to, and are ultimately dissolved in, the pictorial ideas they make us see. Furthermore, the notion that character description involves the preliminary selection of humors, passions, virtues, or vices — in short, abstractions — which are then fleshed out with names, "accidents & incount[ers]," accords perfectly with Sidney's assertion that "whatsoever the philosopher saith should be done, he [the poet] giveth a perfect

11. Greville, *Life of Sidney*, p. 16.

12. John Hoskyns, *Direccōns for Speech and Style* in Louise Brown Osborn, *The Life, Letters, and Writings of John Hoskyns*, Yale Studies in English, LXXXVII (New Haven, Conn., Yale University Press, 1937), pp. 155–156.

picture of it in some one by whom he presupposeth it was done, so as he coupleth the general notion with the particular example" (p. 27). Exactly this method informs the speaking picture of the malcontent that I have analyzed already.

Consistent with his argument that the poet should concern himself with politics as well as ethics, Sidney also packed the *New Arcadia* with portraits of various political characters and events. These include, as Greville points out, "the growth, state, and declination of Princes, change of Government, and lawes: vicissitudes of sedition, faction, succession, confederacies, plantations, with all other errors, or alterations in publique affaires." [13] Perhaps the most impressive of these political pictures appears in Book II of the *New Arcadia*, when Musidorus portrays Evarchus to the princess Pamela. He describes his uncle as "A Prince, that indeed especially measured his greatnesse by his goodnesse: and if for any thing he loved greatnesse, it was, because therein he might exercise his goodnes. A Prince of goodly aspect, and the more goodly by a grave majestie, wherewith his mind did decke his outward graces; strong of body, and so much the stronger, as he by a well disciplined exercise taught it both to do, and suffer." At the beginning of his reign Evarchus found his country "disjoynted" by "the worst kind of *Oligarchie*" and was "forced to establish" order by "some fewe (but in deede notable) examples" of "extreme severitie." But with peace restored to the monarchy, Evarchus "vertuouslie and wisely" acknowledged that

he with his people made all but one politike bodie, whereof himselfe was the head; even so cared for them, as he woulde for his owne limmes: never restrayning their liberty, without it stretched to licenciousnes, nor pulling from them their goods, which they found were not imployed to the purchase of a greater good: but in all his actions shewing a delight to their welfare, broght that to passe, that while by force he tooke nothing, by their love he had all. In summe

13. Greville, *Life of Sidney*, p. 15.

(peerelesse Princesse) I might as easily sette downe the whole Arte of governement, as to lay before your eyes the picture of his proceeding.[14]

Submerged in the portrait is Menenius Agrippa's comparison of the state to the body. The union of greatness and goodness in Evarchus, the head of the state, has its fruition in the union of power and love in the body of a just society. Aristotle's brief sketch of the monarch in the *Ethics* — a work that Hoskyns designates as one of Sidney's main sources — may also have added something to the poet's fore-conceit.[15] According to Aristotle, the ideal king is so perfect in himself that he is without needs or desires and so takes the good of his subjects as his sole objective. Regardless of its source, however, it is clear that from Musidorus's narration the reader is expected to proceed to a profitable invention of his own; we are meant to look beneath the fiction to the political Idea that forms its base. Musidorus even suggests that his description, were it complete, would amount to the ground-plot of the whole art of government. If such were the case, we could perform a complete Ramist analysis of the noble king's natural example. The result would be a full-scale diagram of the monarch's art, parsed out into its logical divisions and subdivisions. From Musidorus's point of view — and, as Sidney intends, from ours — Evarchus is a speaking picture whose actions, taken together, represent the sum of the political virtues. The assumption here, as in all the portraits, is that by confronting the general concept wrapped in a particular fable, we shall see it clearly and naturally with the eyes of our "judging power" and that we shall therefore know it and love it.

One from among Sidney's many descriptions of Pamela may be taken as a typical example of virtue. In this passage, which

14. *Prose Works*, I, 185–187.
15. See Aristotle, *Nicomachean Ethics*, VIII, 10; and Hoskyns, *Direccōns* in Osborn, *The Life, Letters, and Writings of John Hoskyns*, p. 155.

was added to the *New Arcadia,* we are meant to see the Idea of
Devotion in the young princess.

> This prayer, sent to heaven, from so heavenly a creature, with such
> a fervent grace, as if Devotion had borowed her bodie, to make of it
> self a most beautifull representation; with her eyes so lifted to the
> skie-ward, that one would have thought they had begunne to flie
> thetherward, to take their place among their felow stars; her naked
> hands raising up their whole length, & as it were kissing one another,
> as if the right had bene the picture of *Zeale,* and the left, of *Humble-*
> *nesse,* which both united themselves to make their suites more ac-
> ceptable.[16]

This description, like all of the Arcadian portraits, is virtually
overflowing with what Sidney thought of as *energia.* The passage
is a digression, bringing the narrative to a complete halt. It is
devoid of action and dialogue. While it does give a specific passion visible form, that form is hardly concrete. What we can
actually visualize from the details of the picture is a girl praying
with words written on her arms — which is about as concrete
as a political cartoon. The description has *energia* because, on
Sidney's terms, it makes an abstraction visible. Within this extraordinary aggregation of words we are expected to see, and
therefore to understand, the nonverbal, emphatically noncon-
crete, fore-conceit of Devotion. If we leave the description with
the feeling that no princess ever looked quite like this one, we
shall be moving in the right direction. The next and final step
will be to discover that Pamela, like Donne's Elizabeth Drury,
is not a person at all. Her personality is a thin tissue of particularities that scarcely obscure the cold, bare bones of the Idea
that is her raison d'être.

The highly conceptual quality of Sidney's poetic pictures leaves
the reader with the sense that there is an enormous pressure of
intellect pushing up from beneath the verbal surface of the prose.
This occurs in the portrait of Pamela primarily because Sidney

16. *Prose Works,* I, 383.

is not content merely to describe; rather, he injects the details with a heavy dose of abstract meaning as he proceeds. An arm is not an arm — it is Zeal. The same kind of thing very often happens in descriptions of events or situations, and again we are left with the impression that the projector operator has stopped his camera in order to expand on the meaning of the objects before our eyes.

This simultaneously abstract and photographic technique is at work in a startling description of a shipwreck near the beginning of the *New Arcadia*. Having been separated from Pyrocles by a disaster at sea — a disaster "which had driven both him & his friend rather to committe themselves to the cold mercie of the sea, then to avide the hote crueltie of the fire" — Musidorus and some friendly shepherds return to the scene of the accident.

When they came so neere as their eies were ful masters of the object, they saw a sight full of piteous strangenes: a ship, or rather the carkas of the shippe, or rather some few bones of the carkas, hulling there, part broken, part burned, part drowned: death having used more then one dart to that destruction. About it floted great store of very rich thinges, and many chestes which might promise no lesse. And amidst the precious things were a number of dead bodies, which likewise did not onely testifie both elements violence, but that the chiefe violence was growen of humane inhumanitie: for their bodies were ful of grisly wounds, & their bloud had (as it were) filled the wrinckles of the seas visage: which it seemed the sea woulde not wash away, that it might witnes it is not alwaies his fault, when we condemne his crueltie: in summe, a defeate, where the conquered kept both field and spoile: a shipwrack without storme or ill footing: and a wast of fire in the midst of water.[17]

The "in summe" conclusion should be an immediate warning that we are in the presence of Sidney the painter-moralist, with the obvious difference that we are viewing a landscape instead of a portrait. Clearly, too, the language of the passage bears a close resemblance to the speaking pictures that I have already

17. Ibid., I, 9–10.

discussed. But what is most striking here is the degree to which Sidney has interpreted his own description. The prevailing rhetorical figures are paradox and antithesis. "The cold mercie of the sea," for example, is the perfect antithesis of "the hote crueltie of the fire," while the phrases are themselves paradoxes; "humane inhumanitie" pretty well catches the paradoxical moral sentiment of the entire scene, as does "a wast of fire in the midst of water." The general tone is of "piteous strangenes" — "piteous" for reasons all too obvious, and strange because of juxtapositions like "precious things" and "dead bodies." A similar effect is produced by the succession of qualifications, "a ship, or rather the carkas of the shippe, or rather some few bones of the carkas," where each modification renders the scene more disastrously heavy with human implication and thus narrows and clarifies our moral focus. At the same time, of course, the series of modifications, like the paradoxes and antitheses, is a verbal reminder that we are in the presence of a very discriminating narrator.

Near the conclusion of this extraordinary passage we come upon one of the most arresting pictures in the *Arcadia*, the personification of the sea as an old man with human blood settled into the wrinkles of his face. While we are initially startled with the rather macabre scene, Sidney, with characteristic promptness, tells us what his image means. It means that the sea is free from responsibility for the dreadful slaughter and that the full weight of blame rests on human shoulders. In the most literal way, this bizarre personification contains and makes visible the significance of the entire passage, for it graphically confirms the impression of "humane inhumanitie" that the narrator has hinted at from the very outset. Although this much is clear, we may wonder why Sidney chose to make his point in quite this fashion. The image of the bloodstained visage is of the most metaphysical variety; the scene as it appears — a wrinkled face full of blood — and the scene as it means — "humane inhumanitie" — have no more in common than a flea and a marriage bed. Like the picture of Devotion in Pamela, this personification of the sea seems grotesque and almost incomprehensible when visualized as a concrete thing, but it achieves pristine clarity and perfect decorum when seen as the picture of an Idea.

The explanation of this disparity between concrete and abstract significance in the same image brings us back to Sidney's visual epistemology, more specifically to his background in the techniques of the emblem writers. That he was familiar with such techniques and prepared to employ them is manifest in the profusion of emblems and impresas that appear throughout the *Arcadia*.[18] The impresa is usually a heraldic shield that exhibits a visual symbol, or device, and a brief *mot*, or motto. Together the illustration and motto make the meaning of the device clear, while either alone would be obscure. Although Sidney makes abundant use of the impresa in this conventional form, he also adapts it to his own artistic purposes. Musidorus, for example, while addressing his words to the clownish Mopsa, wishes to address his meaning to Pamela. His solution, as he explains it to Pyrocles, was to take "a Jewell, made in the figure of a Crab-fish, which, because it lookes one way and goes another, I thought it did fitly patterne out my looking to *Mopsa*, but bending to *Pamela*: The word about it was, *By force, not choice*." [19] For Pamela at least the crab has considerable *energia*. The trick works because, with the help of the motto, she is able to penetrate the details of the jewel to their unspoken, but emphatically visible, meaning.

Emblems are more complex than impresas, involving a picture,

18. See my discussion of the emblems and Sidney's awareness of them in Chapter 2, pp. 79–88. It is noteworthy that the emblems and impresas in the *New Arcadia* vastly outnumber those in the original. See, for example, *Prose Works*, I, 75, 90, 101, 105, 107, 189, 238, 356.

19. *Prose Works*, I, 164–165.

a motto, and a poem, and they generally have a moral rather than a military subject. Ideally the picture is obscure in itself but fully clear when seen in conjunction with the poem. One of the most obvious examples of an emblem in Sidney's work is the poem "Poore Painters oft with silly Poets joyne," which appears in both versions of *Arcadia*.[20] In the *Old Arcadia* the poem is sung by Dicus, a shepherd who enters with a whip in one hand and a naked Cupid in the other, symbolizing his hatred of love. On his chest Dicus bears "a paynted Table," which is intended to make his contempt even more graphically clear. The picture shows Cupid as a hangman enticing lovers to the gallows. With horns on his head, long ears, cloven feet, and a "body full of eyes," this Cupid is something of a departure from what we are accustomed to in the god of love. In his right hand he holds a crown of laurel, in his left a money purse, and from his mouth pictures of a handsome man and woman are suspended. This painting, though expressed verbally rather than visually, forces us to seek a figurative rather than a literal interpretation of its significance. In short, we must bring an Idea to our viewing before it will become the vision of understanding.

As in all emblems, the poem that follows provides the key to the meaning of the picture. Cupid emerges as a god of deceit who tempts lovers to their doom with false hopes of gain or honor or satisfied desire. The central conceit of the image — that Cupid's brand of love is false because it "Rules the eyes" — underpins the sense of the various visual details. The eyes, ears, horns, and cloven feet, for example, are the legacies of Cupid's parents, Argus and Io, and signify the deceitful, rumor-ridden, overweening, and unstable condition that Dicus chooses to conceive of as love. Once these meanings have been grasped, our way of looking at the picture undergoes a radical change. Instead of gazing in puzzlement at what appears to be an incommensu-

20. *Prose Works*, I, 238–240; IV, 60–62; *Poems*, pp. 20–22.

rate collection of visual particulars, we see with the eyes of the mind, viewing the details as segments of meaning that collectively mirror the general Idea of false love that Dicus is trying to set forth.

By closing our eyes to the literal, concrete image, then, and by accepting an abstract, figurative alternative, we are able to see what the poet-painter means. An identical process takes place in our final understanding of Pamela and of the shipwreck, though in these passages the separation between picture and explanation is not strictly maintained. The sum of Pamela's arms and eyes is not the "bodie" of a princess in prayer but a bloodless abstraction, the conjunction of Humility and Zeal in the concept Devotion. Similarly, in the description of the sea the concrete details have been selected and disposed, not to create a realistic picture, but in order to mirror an Idea. The "in summe" conclusion — which functions as the motto of the description — and the actual scene and the poet's explanation of its meaning are all related emblematically and create the illusion that the acts of seeing and understanding are simultaneous. Such an illusion obviously fulfills the main aesthetic impulse of the *Apology*, for it closely approximates what Sidney considered the actual process of thought. We seem, not to hear of "humane inhumanitie," but rather to see through it.

The *New Arcadia* is crowded with more than eighty poetic pictures similar to the ones I have just discussed. Since most of them do not appear in the *Old Arcadia* and, moreover, since they illustrate so clearly the critical manifesto set forth in the *Apology*, it is difficult to resist the conclusion that Sidney revised and expanded his romance in order to bring it into alignment with the main principles of his critical treatise. This impression becomes even stronger if we turn from the conceptual pictures of the *New Arcadia* to the prose that gives them outline and definition. In the most general terms this unusual prose can be described best as anti-Ciceronian in texture.

One of the main objectives of the anti-Ciceronians was to disengage rhetoric from its traditional mooring in oratory and to ground it in a philosophical theory of composition. Oratory was essentially an art of public speaking, and as such it was designed to be persuasive by sound and gesture as much as by sense. The anti-Ciceronians had little interest in speechmaking but were concerned to develop a mode of composition which could express reality more clearly and more accurately than oratory. This concern, when coupled with a philosophical idealism that prescribed that truth and reality are accessible only to the mind, issued in the notion that literary style can succeed only by its precise fidelity to the actual forms of thought. Fulke Greville, for example, argues that "those words in euery tongue are best,/Which doe most properly expresse the thought," and adds that true eloquence "is not this craft of words, but formes of speech" designed "to declare/What things in Nature good, or evill are." [21] Truth, according to such standards, is most eloquent in its bare simplicity and need only be seen to be persuasive. The accompanying theory of language, with its heavy emphasis on the communication of clearly defined concepts, has little or nothing to say about what we recognize today as the sensuous and emotive qualities of words. Rather, it proceeds almost entirely from assumptions about terms and their (usually mental) referents and thus overlaps with the philosophy of knowledge.

The theory of literary composition outlined in the *Apology*, as I have explained it, is constructed on a conscious and consistent epistemological foundation. It is therefore not surprising that

21. Fulke Greville, "A Treatie of Humane Learning," Sts. 109–110, in *Poems and Dramas of Fulke Greville*, ed. Geoffrey Bullough, 2 vols. (New York, Oxford University Press, 1945), I, 181.

its author was a confessed anti-Ciceronian. Languet warned him against the excesses of the Ciceronians, and it is well known that Sidney considered "Ciceronianisme the cheife abuse of Oxford, *Qui dum verba sectantur, res ipsas negligunt.*" [22] Accordingly, critics have looked for intellectual rather than oratorical patterns in Sidney's rhetoric, and in the main they have come up with the expected discoveries. Like the more generally recognized anti-Ciceronians, Sidney tends to employ linear and logical rhetorical figures, tropes, which enhance the sense, and to avoid the *schemata verborum*, which embellish the sound.[23]

Sidney's gravitation to anti-Ciceronian rhetorical practices, while a prominent and discernible feature of his style, should not be construed as evidence that he considered himself a member of the anti-Ciceronian school of writers. His writing is character-ized by intellectual rather than verbal figures, not because he labored self-consciously to include the former and exclude the latter, but because his fundamental approach to composition pre-cluded alternatives to the stylistic patterns that we recognize as typically his own. As the *Apology* makes clear, a poem is the verbal extension of a pictorial concept; and it is therefore the thought behind the words that must be finally accountable for style. Language is the apparel of thought; it dresses up ideas, but it does so without obscuring the visible form of naked truth.

An identical approach to the relationship between language and thought was current among the Ramists, to whom, as I have

22. *Prose Works*, III, 132. Languet's admonition is in *The Correspond-ence of Sir Philip Sidney and Hubert Languet*, ed. S. A. Pears (London, 1845), pp. 22–23.

23. On Sidney's rhetorical practices, see P. A. Duhamel, "Sidney's *Arcadia* and Elizabethan Rhetoric," *Studies in Philology*, 45 (1948), 147; and Simon Scribner, *Figures of Word-Repetition in the First Book of Sir Philip Sidney's Arcadia* (Washington, D.C., Catholic University of America Press, 1948), p. 96. My thoughts on anti-Ciceronianism are derived in good part from Morris Croll's essays, which have recently been collected under the title *Style, Rhetoric, and Rhythm* (Princeton, N.J., Princeton University Press, 1966).

remarked, Sidney owed a considerable intellectual debt. The spirit of what I have termed anti-Ciceronianism is clear, for example, in Gabriel Harvey's criticism of those who concentrate on the verbal figures in their analysis of literature, "without indicating the stores of arguments, the quantities of proofs, and the structural framework." [24] Ramus divided the traditional five parts of rhetoric between logic and rhetoric; invention and disposition and memory were the functions of dialectic, while elocution and delivery were reserved for rhetoric. In addition, he drastically reduced the number of rhetorical figures, largely ignoring the verbal schemes and relating the figures of thought to the logical topics from which they derived. The remaining thought figures ("shapes") and tropes ("turnings," as Fraunce calls them) were conceived of in spatiovisual terms as rhetorical manipulations of visible intellectual objects.[25] The Ramist rhetoric, then, is almost completely indistinguishable from the highly visualized epistemological base upon which it rests. Words are not thoughts, but they are considered useful only insofar as they can be relied upon to trace out the true contours of conceptually visible ideas.

24. *Gabriel Harvey's Ciceronianus*, Introduction and notes by Harold S. Wilson, English trans. Clarence A. Forbes (Lincoln, Neb., The University, 1945), p. 87. Croll (*Style, Rhetoric, and Rhythm*, pp. 188–189) points out the "professed Anti-Ciceronian" position of Nashe and Harvey but adds that "neither of these writers had philosophy or authority enough to lead his age." Aside from the fact that Nashe and Harvey are unlikely literary bedfellows, Croll failed to recognize the impact of Ramism in England during the 1570's and 1580's and thus missed an important stage in the development of English rhetorical theory. Indeed, the notion that English anti-Ciceronianism begins with Bacon is a modern confusion that probably stems from a similar error among the Ramists themselves. In the *Ciceronianus*, for example, Harvey is quite confident that he is defending the true Cicero, but at the same time he expounds doctrines that are fundamentally opposed to traditional Ciceronian rhetoric.

25. Walter Ong, *Ramus, Method, and the Decay of Dialogue* (Cambridge, Mass., Harvard University Press, 1958), p. 281. For Fraunce's views on tropes, cf. *The Arcadian Rhetorike*, Sig. A2ᵛ. A much fuller account of Ramist rhetoric than there is room for here can be found in Sister Miriam Joseph's *Shakespeare's Use of the Arts of Language* (New York, Columbia University Press, 1947), pp. 13 ff.

The Arcadian rhetoric, like that of the anti-Ciceronians in general and the Ramists in particular, is more deeply rooted in ideas than it is in words. For Sidney the art of composition begins and nearly ends in the first stage, invention. Once the concept is clear, the elocution will more or less take care of itself. This attitude toward writing rests heavily on the assumption that meaning is something separate from language — something as I have indicated in the moral portraits, to be seen independently of the words on the page — and demands of the reader that he see through the verbal surface to the concept that stands behind it. The common notion that Sidney's is a florid, decorative style arises from the failure to recognize that the outside of the Arcadian rhetoric is what it is only because of the inside.

This decidedly conceptual quality in Sidney's prose is perhaps most obvious in his numerous descriptions of the victory of passion over reason. The subversion of man's rational powers, according to Sidney, almost always results in a form of moral disorder best described by the Latin *cupiditas,* the helpless submission to sin doubling and redoubling upon itself. This is the condition, for example, of the paranoiac tyrant of Phrygia, in whom "suspition bred the mind of crueltie, and the effectes of crueltie stirred a new cause of suspition." [26] The important nouns in this sentence are repeated in a kind of chiasmus: suspicion/cruelty//cruelty/suspicion. The repetition is clearly a figure of wit rather than words, for there is a logical relationship between suspicion and cruelty that is prior to, and in fact explains, the disposition of the language. The word "suspicion" precedes the word "cruelty" because they are related causally; suspicion breeds cruelty. Thus in the next unit the word "cruelty" precedes the word "suspicion" because once cruelty has become dominant, it creates suspicion. The prose takes the form it does, not in order that we may be impressed with the author's rhetori-

26. *Prose Works,* I, 197. Cf. also I, 152, 205, 262, 278, and 324.

cal sweep, but because the words, in their relationship to each other, represent the relationship of cruelty to suspicion in Sidney's conception of this variety of *cupiditas*. By their conformity to the pattern of the poet's Idea, the words are quite literally a speaking picture.

Sidney often objectifies the concept *cupiditas* by projecting it into the texture of his prose. Its effects in a battle, for example, are set forth in a display of verbal disorder.

The clashing of armour, and crushing of staves; the justling of bodies, the resounding of blowes, was the first part of that ill-agreeing musicke, which was beautified with the griselinesse of wounds, the rising of dust, the hideous falles, and grones of the dying. The verie horses angrie in their maisters anger, with love and obedience brought foorth the effects of hate and resistance, and with minds of servitude, did as if they affected glorie. Some lay deade under their dead maisters, whome unknightly wounds had unjustly punished for a faithfull dutie. Some lay uppon their Lordes by like accidents, and in death had the honour to be borne by them, whom in life they had borne. Some having lost their commaunding burthens, ranne scattered about the field, abashed with the madnesse of mankinde. The earth it selfe (woont to be a buriall of men) was nowe (as it were) buried with men: so was the face thereof hidden with deade bodies, to whome Death had come masked in diverse manners. In one place lay disinherited heades, dispossessed of their naturall seignories: in an other, whole bodies to see to, but that their harts wont to be bound all over so close, were nowe with deadly violence opened: in others, fowler deaths had ouglily displayed their trayling guttes. There lay armes, whose fingers yet mooved, as if they woulde feele for him that made them feele.[27]

The picture of war and slaughter is augmented by the "ill-agreeing musicke" of the language itself. Nouns are juxtaposed in absolute contradiction ("beautified with griselinesse," "love and obedience" with "hate and resistance"), and phrases display a variety of paradoxes ("unjustly punished" against "faithfull dutie"). The harmony of reason is inverted as mental chaos spreads into external nature ("the verie horses angrie in their maisters

27. Ibid., I, 388.

anger"); and there is a grim sort of wit in the punning conceits (horses "borne" by their masters, the "face" of nature "masked" in death, and fingers that "feele" without feeling). The words are thick with *b* and *d* and *s* sounds that roll in a deep bass under the breathless movements of the participles, the polysyllabics, and the ironic alliterations ("the madnesse of mankinde"). The rhythms might be from a nursery rhyme:

> The clāsh/ing of arm̄/our, and crūsh/ing of stāves;
> The jūst/ling of bōd/ies, the resōund/ing of blōwes.

The dactyls and the repetitions of the *ing*'s lend the lines a completely inappropriate singsong cadence. Indeed, everything in the passage is out of step; the rhythm contradicts the sounds, the nouns contradict their adjectives, the images other images. The sense of *cupiditas*, the frantic rise of disharmony, is represented not only in the objects described but in the way they are described. Beneath the speaking picture of chaos is the poet's foreconceit, the paradox of ignoble nobility, which regulates both the matter and the manner of the painter's brush. The words transcend their individual connotative values by adhering to a more general pattern, to the overriding Idea of war as a grotesque contradiction. Accordingly, they are the details for the reader's graphic ground-plot, verbal units that point to and define a concept. The language of the passage is pictorial not only in the sense that it describes a visualizable battle but also because the words limn out the conceptually visible structure of thought itself.

Sidney's picture of war is intended to leave us with a distinct impression of disorder, of actual chaos represented in verbal chaos. From the maker's point of view, however, and from the reader's as well, there is a definite logic to the language of disorder, just as there is a logic to the fact of moral chaos. The Idea of ignoble nobility is a contradiction, but it is also a pattern, a rhetorical figure of wit upon which the details of disorder can be laid out in an orderly fashion. To understand the passage, we must look through the superficial confusion to the conceit that regulates the relationships of the words and ultimately explains them. In short, the meaning of the narrative is more than the sum of its verbal parts—meaning is indivisible from the graphic conceptual framework that determines the structure of those parts. It is only through seeing this conceit that we know what Sidney is saying about war.

The verbal logic of the battle portrait carries with it the implication of intellectual distraction ("disinherited heades") and consequent moral anarchy ("the madnesse of mankinde"). The alternative to disorder is, of course, harmony. And for Sidney the Idea of harmony is almost indivisible from the exercise of right reason in a life of moral rectitude. The prose of concord, as might be expected, is a verbal emblem of unity which, by its orderly rhetorical texture, traces out the nonverbal fore-conceit of harmony in the ground-plot of the narrative. This is well illustrated in Sidney's description of the young princes in their first day at sea.

The winde was like a servaunt, wayting behind them so just, that they might fill the sailes as they listed; and the best saylers shewing themselves lesse covetous of his liberalitie, so tempered it, that they all kept together like a beautifull flocke, which so well could obey their maisters pipe: without sometimes, to delight the Princes eies, some two or three of them would strive, who could (either by the cunning of well spending the windes breath, or by the advantageous building of their mooving houses) leave their fellowes behind them in the honour of speed: while the two Princes had leasure to see the practise of that, which before they had learned by bookes: to consider the arte of catching the winde prisoner, to no other ende, but to runne away with it; to see how beautie, and use can so well agree together, that of all the trinckets, where with they are attired, there is not one but serves to some necessary purpose. And (o Lord) to see the admirable power & noble effects of Love, whereby the seeming insensible Loadstone, with a secret beauty (holding the spirit of iron in it) can draw that hard-harted thing unto it, and (like a vertuous mistress) not onely make it bow it selfe, but with it make it aspire to so high a Love, as of heavenly Poles; and thereby to bring foorth the noblest deeds, that the children of the Earth can boast of.[28]

The passage opens with two similes, proceeds through some fairly straightforward narrative, and concludes with an abrupt transition to a metaphorical comparison of love with a loadstone. Our initial impression is probably one of general harmony, of an orderly disposition of objects in the pursuit of a useful end. But a closer inspection of Sidney's figurative language should raise certain questions. Although the wind may be "like a servaunt," and the fleet "like a beautifull flocke," what is the connection between the similes? Indeed, what is their function in the first place? And, aside from the fact that love is perhaps comparable to a loadstone, what is there to explain the sudden shift in subject at the end of the passage? In short, what is it about this apparently disorganized description that justifies our sense of general harmony?

We can find the beginning of an answer to these questions in the *Apology*. "The force of a similitude," writes Sidney, is not "to prove anything to a contrary disputer, but only to explain to a willing hearer." Metaphors and similes prove nothing in themselves, but they are a way of "informing the judgment" (p. 83). According to this scheme similitudes are one of the poet's most useful aids in his delightful teaching, for they clarify ideas by rendering them visible to the "sight of the soul" in a way that the philosopher's wordish discourses cannot. George Puttenham points out that such figures make their effect "by certaine intendments or sence . . . working a stirre to the mynde." He adds that they give language "efficacie by sence," that they "serve the conceit onely and not th'eare," and classifies them under the

28. Ibid., I, 191–192.

quality that they all exhibit, *energia*.[29] It is this same quality of *energia* — what I have defined as conceptual clarity — which explains the "force of a similitude" for Sidney. While words are not ideas, they are capable of making ideas visible and thus of "informing the judgment," by reflecting the structure of concepts. When this phenomenon occurs, as it does in the passage under discussion, we can expect that the connotative force of individual words will be sacrificed to the conceptual picture that they collectively mirror.

The apparent disorder of the figurative language in the description of sailing is directly related to Sidney's conception of the function of similitudes. Though the passage is superficially descriptive of several things in several ways, it is regulated by a single Idea. In other words, although the similes and the subject of love have no obvious connection with sailing, the topics are similar in that they all reflect the same fore-conceit. The wind is "like a servaunt" because the sailors use it to their advantage in filling the sails and are thus able to exercise "the honour of speed." Similarly, the fleet is "like a beautifull flocke" because the mariners are able to "temper" the wind's "liberalitie" in the same way that a shepherd restrains and orders his sheep. The concept common to the similes is one of relationship: more specifically, the subordination of means to natural authority in the achievement of a constructive and harmonious end. Useful harmony is attained through the just subservience of the servant to his master, the sheep to their shepherd, and the wind to the mariners. In the same way, and as the princes observe, the "beautie" of the ship results from the harmonious economy of its parts ("all the trinckets" serving "some necessary purpose"), just

29. George Puttenham, *The Arte of English Poesie*, ed. G. D. Willcock and A. Walker (Cambridge, England, Cambridge University Press, 1936), pp. 142–143. Puttenham's discussion also includes the *schemata verborum*, or figures of words, which "serve th'eare onely," and which he classifies under the term *enargia*.

as the proper end of things "learned by books" is their realization in "practise."

The transition to the subject of love hinges on the fact that the "noble effects of love" are produced by essentially the same relationship between master and servant as those of sailing, sheepherding, and so on. The comparison with the loadstone functions as a thematic link and also provides the similitude by which the operations of love are presented to our powers of judgment. The lover, by submitting to his "vertuous mistresse," aspires to a heavenly love that results in "the noblest deeds, that the children of the Earth can boast of." Similarly, the compass ("that hard-harted thing"), by responding to the attraction of the loadstone, is directed to "the heavenly Poles" and thus aids the mariner in determining his course. The harmony of utility, then, for the sailor, the shepherd, the compass, and the lover is the fruition of a just relationship between the powers of authority and the things subject to those powers. The metaphorical latitude of the description bears the implication that the principle of hierarchy is a natural law stretching through all levels of human experience.

The superficial and apparently unrelated topics of this passage, sailing and love, while dominating the actual narrative, are mere auxiliaries to Sidney's central theme. The meaning of the description is ultimately indistinguishable from the Idea of harmony that informs and hence unifies the seeming irregularity of the parts. In the same way, the superficial inconsistencies of the figurative language arise from their adherence to the presiding conceit. The similitudes have no argumentative force but merely illustrate the fore-conceit that coordinates the entire passage. In effect, then, the narrative is a succession of illustrations or speaking pictures of the same Idea. Narrative or thematic consistency is sacrificed to conceptual consistency, to the common pattern regulating the structure of the individual parts; or, to put it another way, the theme of the narrative is its conceptual structure. We see the harmony of sailing, the harmony of the flock, and the harmony of love; but from the accumulated particulars we should progress to the general Idea of harmony itself. This is what Sidney is trying to make us see.

To this point I have argued that Sidney's narrative prose is pictorial in two senses: in the sense that it is used to describe abstractions visible to thought and in the sense that the patterns of his language conform to the structure of concepts seen in the mind. The speaking pictures make a third and much more dramatic appearance in the prose dialogue of the *Arcadia*. In much the same way that third-person descriptions figure forth ideas, dialogue functions as the verbal emblem of a character's state of mind. This phenomenon occurs primarily because most of the Arcadian actors are personified moral abstractions, with the result that their speech is usually a kind of word picture of the Idea that they represent. Not surprisingly, the speech of the heroes and heroines in Arcadia is generally characterized by fluent elegance and logical precision. These qualities are evident, for example, in the flow of Pamela's reasoning: "But *Dorus* (sayd she) you must be so farre maister of your love, as to consider, that since the judgement of the world stands upon matter of fortune, and that the sexe of womankind of all other is most bound to have regardfull eie to mens judgements, it is not for us to play the philosophers, in seeking out your hidden vertues: since that, which in a wise prince would be counted wisdome, in us wil be taken for a light-grounded affection." [30] Her graceful feminine humility, the submerged complimentary force of "maister of your love" and "your hidden vertues," all contribute to the delicate power of her persuasion. She moves logically from premises to conclusion, securing her auditor's assent by the appealing correctness of what she says. Musidorus

30. *Prose Works*, I, 158.

can hardly disagree, for to do so would be illogical and to his own discredit. Sidney clinches our feelings about the speech by describing the reaction of Musidorus, who finds his "soule refreshed with her sweetly pronounced words." [31]

The equation of logical speech with mental clarity may be another reflection of Sidney's background in Ramist dialectic. Since logic is natural to the soul, argued the Ramists and since the patterns of thought ideally regulate all forms of expression, it follows that speech should be a verbal emblem of concepts in the mind. As one Ramist puts the matter, "the more logicall a man is, the more he is like a man, and the lesse logicall, the lesse like a man who is a reasonable Creature." [32] In the same vein, John Hoskyns argues that a man's mind cannot "bee thought in tune, whose wordes doe iarr, nor his reason in frame whose sentences are preposterous nor his fancie cleare and pfect, whose utterance breakes it selfe into fragments, and uncertaintyes." [33] By such standards the unobtrusive "natural" logic of Pamela's speech is the verbal image of the orderly disposition of her mind.

By the same standards, of course, broken and dismembered speech without a basis in logic is the verbal image of a disorderly mental state. We can observe the development of such disorder in a speech delivered by Pyrocles in Book III of the *New Arcadia*. Disguised as a woman (Zelmane) and the captive of Cecropia, the prince racks his brain for a plan to save Philoclea, who is also a prisoner. He decides to persuade Philoclea that she must feign submission to Cecropia's evil devices, with the condition that he (Pyrocles/Zelmane) be released. Only then will he be able to arm himself and rescue the helpless princess. With his plan "already plotted out in her [his] conceite, how she [he]

31. Ibid., I, 158.
32. Thomas Spencer, *The Art of Logick* (1628), Sig. A3ᵛ–A4ʳ.
33. Hoskyns, *Direccõns for Speech and Style*, in Osborn, *The Life, Letters, and Writings of John Hoskyns*, p. 116.

would deale with her," Pyrocles is taken to Philoclea's chamber. When finally alone with his beloved, however, Pyrocles is overcome with such a flood of emotion that his speech is reduced to the "eloquence of amazement: for all her [his] long methodized oration was inherited onely by such kinde of speeches. Deare Ladie, in extreame necessities we must not. But alas unfortunate wretch that I am, that I live to see this day. And I take heaven and earth to witnesse, that nothing: and with that her [his] brest swelled so with spite and griefe, that her [his] breath had not leasure to turne her selfe into words." [34] From Sidney's point of view, Pyrocles' procedure in preparing his speech is absolutely flawless. A good Ramist, he has "plotted out" his arguments on the graph of his mind and thus "methodized" what he has to say. In theory, of course, since its outside is guaranteed to reflect the clarity of its inside, the oration should abound in *energia*. What no Ramist can predict, however, is emotion. Pyrocles' fore-conceit is inundated by a fog of confusion so thick that only the most minute beams of reason can penetrate it. The result is a speaking picture of "amazement," a speech whose disconnected stops and starts perfectly reflect the obscurity of the speaker's mind.

Anger, a more specific variety of passion, makes several appearances in the *New Arcadia*. Angry characters usually speak in the manner recommended by Abraham Fraunce, the Ramist rhetorician, who prescribes "shrill, sharpe, quicke, short" speech.[35] Much the same prescription appears in the *Apology*, where Sidney points out that Cicero, when "inflamed with a well-grounded rage" against Catiline, often employed repetition in his oration, forcing the words to "double out of his mouth" (p. 83). Sidney was probably using Cicero as a model when he com-

34. *Prose Works*, I, 480–481.
35. For a full survey of the "affections," see Fraunce's *The Arcadian Rhetorike*, Sig. I2ʳ–I7ʳ.

posed Pamela's retort to Cecropia, a speech whose doubling language takes its source in justifiable rage.

Pamela (whose cheeks were died in the beautifullest graine of vertuous anger, with eies which glistered forth beames of disdaine) thus interrupted her. Peace (wicked woman) peace, unworthy to breathe, that doest not acknowledge the breath-giver; most unworthy to have a tongue, which speakest against him, through whom thou speakest: keepe your affection to your self, which like a bemired dog, would defile with fauning. You say yesterday was as to day. O foolish woman, and most miserably foolish, since wit makes you foolish. What dooth that argue, but that there is a constancie in the everlasting governour? Would you have an inconstant God, since we count a man foolish that is inconstant? [36]

Pamela's passion, an eminently rational anger, is "well-grounded" in the assurance of an eternal God. Her wrath is the expression of righteous indignation in the face of what she considers the patent irrationality of Cecropia's godlessness. Her sharp, quick sentences have a passionate kind of *energia*, for they are brisk figures of thought, logically based repetitions designed to expose the paradox of atheism in all its contradictions. Cecropia's irreverent breath and tongue are employed in the defiance of the power that makes her speech possible in the first place. Her inconstancy and miserable foolishness are doubly contemptible because they are seated in wit, in the God-given powers of *recta ratio*, man's stronghold of wisdom and constancy. Pamela's anger, then, is expressive of all the virtues she finds lacking in her adversary. Her speech, in its bristling rectitude of wit, sets forth a picture of balanced and reasonable faith.

The taut clarity of Pamela's argument is to be compared with Cecropia's rhetoric of dissimulation. In trying to deceive the innocent Philoclea, the wicked woman speaks with all the artfully controlled guile of Milton's Satan.

Cecropia . . . came in, and haling kindnesse into her countenance, What ayles this sweete Ladie, (said she) will you marre so good

36. *Prose Works*, I, 407.

eyes with weeping? shall teares take away the beautie of that complexion, which the women of *Arcadia* wish for, and the men long after? Fie of this peevish sadnesse; in sooth it is untimely for your age. Looke upon your owne bodie, and see whether it deserve to pine away with sorrow: see whether you will have these hands (with that she tooke one of her hands and kissing it, looked uppon it as if she were enamoured with it) fade from their whitenesse, which makes one desire to touch them.[37]

The rhythms are somnolent, each clause moving with smooth fluidity to a feminine ending ("countenance," sweete Ladie," "weeping," "complexion," "wish for," and "sadness"). The mellifluous harmonies are broken only by the incessant sting of sibilants—"what ayles this sweete Ladie, (said she)," or "this peevish sadnesse; in sooth" — which function as a malicious counterpoint weaving through the seeming simplicity of the speech. The specious arguments (urging vanity and pride) are artfully submerged in compliments. The cumulative effect of Cecropia's language is perversely suggestive, for her interests are manifestly carnal ("good eyes," "that complexion," "men long after," "your owne bodie"). Hers is the most threatening of mental aberrations, for it expresses itself with fine and tempting subtleties. The slippery rhetoric limns out a mentality so familiar with sin as not to recognize the extremity of its own deception. Even when presented with an "image of Vertue" (as Sidney relates in another passage), "what the figure thereof was her hart knew not." [38] Because of the shape of her mind, then, it is little wonder that Cecropia's speech is the speaking picture of evil.

In the four or five years preceding 1584 Sidney seems to have recognized the value of dialogue as a medium for the expression of emotional states of mind, for the *New Arcadia* contains a relatively greater proportion of dialogue than the *Old Arcadia*. This recognition may have emerged with the composition of

37. Ibid., I, 376–377.
38. Ibid., I, 384.

Astrophil and Stella, an amorous monologue almost entirely in the first person. He appears to have realized that while an omniscient narrator is best suited to the description of abstract vices and virtues, passions seem stiff when viewed objectively. Dialogue serves to iron out such stiffness by uniting thought and expression in the same voice, thus lending greater plausibility to the extreme reaches of passion and also throwing the reader's view of the character's feelings into a more dramatic perspective. We can observe this crucial difference between first- and third-person narration by comparing parallel passages from the two versions of the *Arcadia.* In the original, Philoclea is described by an omniscient narrator.

But, when the Ornament of the earthe, younge *Philoclea* appeared in her nymphelike apparell, so nere nakednes, as one might well discerne parte of her perfections: And yet so apparelled as did shewe, shee kept the best store of her beautyes to her self, her excellent faire hayer drawen up into a nett, made onely of yt self, A nett in deede to have caughte the wyldest Disposicion, her body covered with a lighte taffita garment, so cutt, as the wrought smock came throughe yt in many places, ynoughe, to have made a very restrayned imaginacyon have thoughte what was under yt.

In the *New Arcadia* the same passage, with significant additions, is part of a dialogue between the two princes in which Pyrocles describes Philoclea to his friend, Musidorus. (The additional material has been underscored in order to facilitate comparison.)

But when the ornament of the Earth, *the model of heaven, the Triumphe of Nature, the light of beauty, Queene of Love,* young *Philoclea* appeared in the Nimphe-like apparell, so neare nakednes, as one might well discerne part of her perfections: & yet so apparelled, as did shew she kept best store of her beuty to her self: her haire (*alas too poore a word, why should I not rather call them her beames*) drawen up into a net, *able to take Jupiter when he was in the forme of an Eagle;* her body (*O sweet body*) covered with a light taffeta garment, so cut, as the wrought smocke came through it in many places, inough to have made your restraind imagination have thought what was under it.[39]

39. Ibid., IV, 33; I, 90.

In the first passage the object described is appealing enough, but the mind behind the description is completely impersonal, and we have no way of evaluating the nature of the observations made. If anything, we may be a trifle uncomfortable with this account of Philoclea; the objective view of frankly sexual beauty is not a particularly happy one, and our narrator may seem a bit of a voyeur. In the revision, on the other hand, we are in the company of an identifiable personality, an enthusiastic young lover. The new descriptive details, particularly the lover's view of Philoclea as "the modell of heaven, the Triumphe of Nature, the light of beauty, Queene of Love," are reminiscent of *Astrophil and Stella*, where the "star lover" often describes his beloved as a brilliant heavenly body, a celestial spirit influencing nature from above. We are also reminded of the sonnets by the fact that the picture of Philoclea is purely subjective, the point of view of one only too ready to expand on the details of her charm. The added exclamations are completely cogent in the dialogue, for they merely intensify our sense of the lover's zealous agitation. But they would have been awkward in the earlier version, where increased gusto would only confirm our misgivings about the narrator's enthusiasm. Above all, the description has gained dramatic interest by being cast in the first person. In hearing Pyrocles' voice, we seem to see his passion from the inside; the breathless additions catch the tempo of his passion and function as its emblem.

"Love," writes Sidney, "is better then a paire of spectacles to make every thing seeme greater, which is seene through it." [40] His metaphor is instructive, for it emphasizes the fact that love, like all other passions, is for Sidney primarily a state of mind, a way of looking at the world, and only secondarily a manner of speaking. As Pyrocles explains it to Musidorus, after a period of "uncertaine wishes" and "unquiet longings," love had its inevita-

40. Ibid., I, 144.

ble effect: "I could fix my thoughts upon nothing, but that within little varying, they should end with *Philoclea:* when each thing I saw, seemed to figure out some parts of my passions." [41] At the same time that his world is transformed into a kind of picture gallery of his most compelling thought, the passionate person is himself transformed into an image of that thought. Gynecia, for example, is so beset with passion "that al her countenances, words and gestures, are miserable portraitures of a desperate affection." [42] It follows quite naturally that when such characters speak, their words will tell us more about themselves than about the objects of their discourse. This is generally true of the dialogue in the *Arcadia:* more often than not it is Sidney's way of letting us see a speaker's mind. In Pamela's speeches, for example, we have seen sweet reasonableness and well-grounded rage, and in Cecropia's, slippery guile. The same phenomenon occurs in Pyrocles' case, for his words describe Philoclea, not as she is, but as she appears through the spectacles of his passion.

Reality undergoes a similar enlargement when Pyrocles, having recently fallen in love, describes the Arcadian country side to Musidorus.

And Lord (dere cosin, said he) doth not the pleasauntnes of this place carry in it selfe sufficient reward for any time lost in it? Do you not see how all things conspire together to make this country a heavenly dwelling? Do you not see the grasse how in colour they excell the Emeralds, everie one striving to passe his fellow, and yet they are all kept of an equall height? And see you not the rest of these beautifull flowers, each of which would require a mans wit to know, and his life to expresse? Do not these stately trees seeme to maintaine their florishing olde age with the onely happines of their seat, being clothed with a continuall spring, because no beautie here should ever fade? . . . Is not every *eccho* therof a perfect Musicke? and these fresh and delightfull brookes how slowly they slide away, as loth to leave the company of so many things united in perfection?

41. Ibid., I, 85.
42. Ibid., I, 94.

and with how sweete a murmure they lament their forced departure? Certainelie, certainely, cosin, it must needes be that some Goddesse enhabiteth this Region, who is the soule of this soile.[43]

Mr. Rudenstine quite correctly finds abundant *energia* here, arguing that the style of the passage is animated, vivid, an energetic expression of Pyrocles' passion. He notes that all the key devices of *energia* are present: apostrophe, a strong dramatic voice, exclamation, repetition, direct address, personification, and speech directed to inanimate objects. "Everything," he concludes, "breathes life; everything is animated and vivacious, in a state of activity, present 'before the eyes.' " [44]

While it is undeniable that this passage is an eloquent example of *energia*, my explanation for the actual function of the concept differs in important detail from Mr. Rudenstine's. Obviously, the qualities that he describes as characteristic of *energia* are evident in Pyrocles' speech. On the other hand, those same qualities are notably absent from most of the third-person passages that I have analyzed in terms of the same concept. But what does this dialogue have in common with, say, the speaking picture of Pamela/Devotion that can be described as *energia*? The answer, I would argue, is conceptual clarity. As I pointed out in the last chapter, and as I have illustrated in succeeding discussions, the term *energia*, in Sidney's usage, is descriptive of the clarity of the concepts that underlie good writing, and not the words per se. Accordingly, while the various rhetorical devices that we find in this speech do express Pyrocles' passion vividly, they are merely the effects of *energia*, and not its cause. The cause of the *energia* is the clear and compelling conceit that presses itself in upon the speaker's mental vision.

My point, and the full meaning of Pyrocles' speech, will be clearer if we consider the dialogue in its dramatic context. Un-

43. Ibid., I, 57; cf. IV, 12–13.
44. Neil Rudenstine, *Sidney's Poetic Development* (Cambridge, Mass., Harvard University Press, 1967), pp. 160–161.

known to the reader, the prince has fallen in love. The first major effect of his state is the desire to be alone in the woods. Musidorus finds his friend and reminds him, in a long, eloquent speech, that "a mind wel trayned and long exercised in vertue . . . doth not easily chaunge any course it once undertakes." The man of true virtue, he continues, "doth shew forth Images of the same constancy, by maintaining a right harmonie betwixt it and the inward good, in yeelding it selfe sutable to the vertuous resolution of the minde." Pyrocles, whose thoughts are "fixed upon another devotion," only half grasps the sense of what has been said and replies in a confused manner, insisting that he has just cause for his retreat and defending his solitariness by the passionate appeal to the beauty of his surroundings. The reader, by this point in the narrative, has begun to sense Pyrocles' distraction and concurs in the judgment of Musidorus, who notices a "store of thoughts" in his friend, "rather stirred then digested," and who remarks to himself that Pyrocles' speech is not directed "to one constant end, but rather dissolved in it selfe, as the vehemencie of the inwarde passion prevayled." With these observations in mind, Musidorus carries on, hoping to bring the pattern of his friend's passion into clearer focus. He suggests, perceptively, that Pyrocles has filled his solitude "with the conceites of the Poets," who "set up every thing to the highest note; especially, when they put such words in the mouths of one of these fantasticall mind-infected people, that children & Musitians cal Lovers." Whatever doubts may have remained as to the nature of the situation disappear; Pyrocles, "with the verie countenance of the poore prisoner at the barr, whose aunswere is nothing but guiltie," admits that he is in love.[45]

When viewed against this background, Pyrocles' passionate speech has a decidedly analytic function. By this I mean that his debate with Musidorus should be regarded as a narrative

45. *Prose Works*, I, 54–59.

ground-plot upon which the reader can perform his own analysis and thereby reach a profitable invention. In the most general sense the section develops a contrast between the "vertuous resolution of the minde" to the life of heroic action and the solitary meanderings of "mind-infected" love. This contrast is most obvious as the explicit theme of the debate, but it also is expressed in the quality of thought that each of the speakers betrays. The clear, well-organized succession of Musidorus's arguments is the verbal image of keen rational vision, while Pyrocles' errant logic and impassioned language is the emblem of his inner disorder.

But the passage is analytic in a more specific, dramatic sense. In following the narrative, the reader, like Musidorus, becomes engaged in the search for Pyrocles' secret. We are initially impressed with Musidorus's discourse on constancy and with its obvious application to his friend. We may also pause over the fact that Pyrocles' mind is intent on "another devotion," and we should begin to suspect that the desire for solitude is not his only reason for retiring to the woods. The result of his state of distraction is eminently clear in his long dialogue of self-defense, which, as Musidorus remarks, is logically chaotic, the product of a powerful "inwarde passion." The heaven that he sees in his surroundings is clearly the picture of nature, not as it is, but as it appears through the medium of his love. His view of the world has more basis in "another devotion" — in the heavenly mental image of Philoclea — than it does in geographical fact. It is this amorous conceit that the dialogue — indeed, the entire section — is designed to make the reader see.

Viewed in this way, the speaking picture of Pyrocles' passion is quite literally the ground-plot for our profitable invention. We have regarded his words, not as a literal description of the natural scene, but as verbal emblems that, by which their passionate uniformity of tone, collectively represent the Idea of love in the prince's thoughts. Such analysis, or invention, is perfectly in keeping with Sidney's aesthetic objectives. We have learned about this apparently crippling passion, not by hearing it set out in a lifeless verbal definition, but by seeing the concept of love limned out in a particular example. That we do see the amorous conceit beneath the concrete details of Pyrocles' speech is, as I have already suggested, the result of *energia*. Without such conceptual clarity the dialogue, however vivid and animated, would be a confused mass of words barely accompanied by reason.

While the maker's most important task in writing dialogue is to reach a clear preconception of the Idea that he wishes to figure forth, the finished speech inevitably creates the illusion that what the reader is seeing is a picture of the speaker's fore-conceit, and not the poet's. The same is true of Sidney's poetry, most of which is in the first person. That Sidney should have been so successful at creating this illusion is not difficult to explain. A comparison of the *Apology* with the *New Arcadia* reveals that Sidney's conceptions of passion in general, and love in particular, are almost identical to his conception of the psychology of artistic creation. Most crucially, love, like poetry, has an important basis in visual epistemology. The good poet composes from a clearly visualized concept of vice, virtue, or passion; in the same way the passionate words of the lover are derived from the image that he sees within his mind. Like the poet, the lover sees things, not as they are, but in their ideal proportions, as they might be. Accordingly, good poems and the utterances of passionate characters are alike speaking pictures, both offering the reader a ground-plot for his own invention. It is because of this nucleus of similarities between poetry and passion that we, as readers, are content in the illusion that Pyrocles' amorous conceits are his own, and not Sidney's.

The passionate lover, then, like the good poet, is distinguished by the clarity of his inner conceptions, his *energia*. It is hardly surprising, therefore, that Sidney's lovers turn out to be good poets. Nor is it surprising that his poet-lovers take it as their most urgent obligation to make their conceits clear. Indeed, it is not too much to say that Sidney's amorous poetry, to which I shall now turn, is a simultaneous meditation on the general themes of love and aesthetics.

THE POETRY

The notion that lovers are mindless, muddleheaded people, borne along by blind, if benign instincts, is distinctively modern. While we may be right in giving love its source in a kind of visceral fog and in reserving the uppermost region of the human anatomy for the clairvoyant operations of reason, we are wrong if we assume that such a dichotomous model accurately describes the view of the Renaissance in general, or of Sidney in particular. "Love," as it is defined in both versions of *Arcadia*, is "the refiner of invention." [46] Whether or not their inventions are moral or profitable, Sidney's lovers spend much of their time gazing upon well-defined conceits, which have nothing to do with their abdomens. When the compelling clarity — the *energia* — of the lover's amorous Idea is accurately set forth in words, the result is good love poetry.

Exactly this set of amorous and aesthetic assumptions informs the first sonnet in *Astrophil and Stella*. Deeply in love and hopeful that an eloquent expression of his affection will win Stella's favor, Astrophil has some momentary difficulties in converting his powerful feelings into equally powerful words.

> I sought fit words to paint the blackest face of woe,
> Studying inventions fine, her wits to entertaine:
> Oft turning others' leaves, to see if thence would flow

46. Ibid., I, 86; IV, 9.

Some fresh and fruitfull showers upon my sunne-burn'd braine.
  But words came halting forth, wanting Invention's stay,
Invention, Nature's child, fled step-dame Studie's blowes,
And others' feete still seem'd but strangers in my way.
Thus great with child to speake, and helplesse in my throwes,
  Biting my trewand pen, beating my selfe for spite,
   'Foole,' said my Muse to me, 'looke in thy heart and write.' [47]

This Muse might well have written the *Apology*, for the heart that Astrophil is referred to is not the locus for vague, undifferentiated feelings but the seat of all the faculties, a kind of screen where the image of Stella will be visible to the mind's eye.[48] Astrophil's mistake, like the mistake of the love poets criticized in the *Apology*, is to conceive of poetry as the imitation of other writers. Such a method of composition, he discovers, lacks what is essential to all good poetry, "Invention's stay." Only when the poet has his invention — in this case the image of Stella — clearly before his mind can true imitation occur; for only then will the verbal outside of his poem mirror a precisely defined Idea. As the sonnets that follow in the sequence make clear, the Muse's exhortation becomes Astrophil's manifesto.

This initial sonnet is a fine example of the way aesthetic and amorous intentions overlap in Sidney's love poetry, for the poem is at once a description and an illustration of the way love refines invention. The aesthetic intention is the most obvious: Astrophil takes the problem of poetic invention as his explicit theme. At the same time, however, the poem is an indirect and extraordinarily graceful compliment to Stella and may be viewed as the product of the speaker's amorous invention. With the possible exception of Coleridge, no English poet was ever more eloquent about his own lack of eloquence than Astrophil. His painstaking search for appropriate words, his candor, his breath-

47. AS, 1 (Ringler, p. 165).
48. See Ringler's note, p. 459.

less frustration, and his almost surprised discovery that Stella is not only the object but the source of his art, all add up to the speaking picture of formidable passion.

Before turning to a detailed discussion of *Astrophil and Stella*, it will be useful to dwell for a while on the poetry of Sidney's apprenticeship. Here we can observe the individual strands that were later woven together in the more subtle fabric of the sonnet sequence. In these early compositions there is an important relationship between the theme and the technique, the description and the illustration, of amorous invention. Much of the love poetry written before the sonnets is concerned with the process and products of knowledge; it takes invention as its theme. Both of the young princes, for example, expound upon the nature of love in what might be called the poetry of amorous discourse. Pyrocles weeps with frustration at his own rebellious passion.

> In vaine, mine Eyes, you labour to amende
>   With flowing teares your fault of hasty sight:
> Since to my hart her shape you so did sende;
>   That her I see, though you did lose your light.
>
> In vaine, my Hart, now you with sight are burnd,
>   With sighes you seeke to coole your hotte desire:
> Since sighes (into mine inward fornace turnd)
>   For bellowes serve to kindle more the fire.
>
> Reason, in vaine (now you have lost my hart)
>   My head you seeke, as to your strongest forte:
> Since there mine eyes have played so false a parte,
>   That to your strength your foes have sure resorte.
>   And since in vaine I find were all my strife,
>   To this strange death I vainely yeeld my life.

And Musidorus persuades his mistress with a lover's logic.

> Since so mine eyes are subject to your sight,
> That in your sight they fixed have my braine;
> Since so my harte is filled with that light,
> That onely light doth all my life maintaine;

Since in sweete you all goods so richly raigne,
That where you are no wished good can want;
Since so your living image lives in me,
That in my selfe your selfe true love doth plant;
 How can you him unworthy then decree,
 In whose chiefe parte your worthes implanted be? [49]

Both poems develop the theme of vision in its relationship to knowledge and to two very different kinds of love. The "hasty sight" of Philoclea has become an inward vision for Pyrocles, and the shape seen in his mind is fuel for the furnace of passionate love. Desire is accompanied by a flood of tears, which blur his external eyes, and by a mental fixation on the image of Philoclea, which blinds his rational power of moral vision. The presence of Pamela's "living image" in Musidorus's thoughts, on the other hand, is the basis for his claim to her respect. Since she is the embodiment of all that is worthy and since her virtues are seen in his "chiefe parte," Musidorus's love is the function of rational vision, which issues in the ennoblement of the lover. Although the products of love in these two poems are radically different, the process is essentially the same. The princes see and therefore know and therefore love; that they look at similar things in very different ways is merely an illustration of the potential extremes of amorous vision.

Sidney's consistent association of spiritual love with reason and carnal love with passion is evidence that he had read one or more of the Italian *trattati d'amore* and that he understood their full epistemological implications. One of the most frustrating problems for the Arcadian lovers is to refine their vision of the *bella donna* beyond mere lust of the eye to an intellectual apprehension of ideal beauty. Sidney's male protagonists are painfully aware that only the latter kind of vision — the cool gaze of *recta ratio* upon a Platonic abstraction — can result in virtuous action; and yet, as their adventures illustrate, they are

49. OA, 14 and 16 (Ringler, pp. 38–39).

almost completely powerless to abandon the image of a body for the image of an Idea.[50]

In spite of the fact that he never allows the themes of rational and irrational love to reach their traditional Christian conclusion, Sidney invests his love poetry with a definite religious aura through the use of a conventionally Christian vocabulary. When viewed in her ideal dimension, the beloved is like an angel, a heavenly creature, a spirit influencing the course of mortal affairs, or a bright light illuminating the lover's mind. From a carnal point of view, she is darkness, night, the denizen of caves where the absence of light symbolizes moral myopia. These and similar metaphors were traditionally employed to set forth the dependence of the human mind on the divine intellect operating through second causes. Sidney retains most of the subtleties of this visual theory of knowledge, but he submerges them in the nominally pagan structure of Arcadian religion.

The Christian spirit underlying the theme of amorous invention is most obvious in a series of poems spoken by Basilius, the king of Arcadia. In each of five poems Basilius addresses himself to the sun, the timeworn symbol for God in his capacity as *intellectus agens*, the eternal light of human reason. The first poem is a hymn in which Sidney's acquaintance with the conventions of visual epistemology is fully evident.

> Apollo great, whose beames the greater world do light,
> And in our little world dost cleare our inward sight,
> Which ever shines, though hid from earth by earthly shade,
> Whose lights do ever live, but in our darknesse fade.[51]

Here, as I argued in the Introduction, a veil of classical myth does little to obscure the poem's Christian theme. Apollo, like

---

50. Cf. *Prose Works*, I, 78; IV, 17. For a discussion of the tensions between ideal and real love in *Arcadia*, see Mark Rose, *Heroic Love* (Cambridge, Mass., Harvard University Press, 1968), pp. 48, 54–56.

51. OA, 26 (Ringler, p. 44). Basilius recites the hymn with Gynecia, Pamela, and Philoclea.

the God of the Christian tradition, illuminates both the external world of nature and the internal vision of the human intellect. Equally traditional is the qualification that the divine light appears only dimly to the eye of man's fallen mind. With this qualification, it is perfectly appropriate that the poem should conclude with a plea for moral strength and the admission that "nothing winnes the heaven, but what doth earth forsake."

The four poems that follow this hymn retain the initial religious associations, but the spirit of devotion quickly gives way to love of a different kind. As the plot of the romance progresses, Basilius becomes passionately aroused by Cleophila (the prince Pyrocles disguised as an Amazon), whose heavenly charms inspire the old king to take a radically altered view of his god.

> *Phaebus* farewell, a sweeter Saint I serve,
> The high conceits thy heav'nly wisedomes breed
> My thoughts forget: my thoughts, which never swerve
> From her, in whome is sowne their freedome's seede,
> And in whose eyes my dayly doome I reede.
>
> *Phaebus* farewell, a sweeter Saint I serve.
> Thou art farre off, thy kingdome is above:
> She heav'n on earth with beauties doth preserve.
> Thy beames I like, but her cleare rayes I love:
> Thy force I feare, her force I still do prove.[52]

This poem has much more to do with the speaker's thoughts, or conceits, about things, than it does about the things themselves. In the mind of Basilius, Apollo (Phaebus) has been replaced by a mortal, and the promise of God's heavenly "kingdome" has been abandoned for an earthly paradise. The lofty conceits of divine wisdom are overlooked as Basilius turns his thoughts to the "cleare rayes" of a decidedly sublunar variety of beauty. His ludicrous apostasy is of special interest here because it illustrates the crucial importance of Sidney's visual epistemology to the theme of amorous invention; the transition from

52. Ibid., 38 (Ringler, p. 72).

divine to carnal love is effected through a shift in the conceits visible to the eyes of Basilius's mind.

The movement from religious to amorous vision is carried even further in the third poem, where Apollo (now called "Titan"), "the giver of the daie" and "author of our sight," sinks beneath the conceptually visible horizon. At sunset, however, there arises a new sun (Cleophila/Pyrocles), "a heavenly sparke" in "earthly clothes" whose beams replace those of the sun-god.[53] The same dichotomies of light and dark, day and night, represent the lover's irreverent conceits in the fourth poem. "Looking still uppon *Cleophila*, (whome nowe the Moone did beutify with her shyning all moste at the full) as yf her eyes had beene his Songebooke," Basilius sees the disguised prince as a second sun, unhappily cloaked in "darke envious night." The moon, however, saves the day, sending gentle beams to illuminate "the face, which nothing can amende." [54]

The transition to night in the third and fourth poems is the factual basis for Basilius's "sun" conceits, but it also signifies the gradual movement from the light of reason and virtue to the shadows of irrational lust. The final poem in the series completes the transition by absolutely contradicting the first. Basilius, having arranged what he supposes to be a midnight rendezvous with Cleophila, is tricked into an act of passion with his wife, Gynecia. Still deceived by the bed trick, the absurd old lecher gloats over the assumed consummation of his lust in a hymn to darkness.

> O Night, the ease of care, the pledge of pleasure,
> Desire's best meane, harvest of hartes affected,
> The seate of peace, the throne which is erected
> Of humane life to be the quiet measure,
>
> Be victor still of *Phoebus'* golden treasure:
> Who hath our sight with too much sight infected,

53. Ibid., 52 (Ringler, p. 80).
54. *Prose Works*, IV, 201; OA, 55 (Ringler, p. 82).

> Whose light is cause we have our lives neglected
> Turning all nature's course to selfe displeasure.
>
> These stately starrs in their now shining faces,
> With sinlesse sleepe, in silence, wisdome's mother,
> Witnesse his wrong which by thy helpe is eased:
>
> Thou arte therefore of these our desart places
> The sure refuge, by thee and by no other
> My soule is bliste, sence joyde, and fortune raysed.[55]

In the dead of moral and intellectual night, Basilius is now completely without the "inward sight" of the opening hymn. As a result of his lust the light of reason is cut off from his inner conceits, just as Phoebus is hidden from the earth by "earthly shade." Images of light dominate the opening poem, the emblems of reason's just dominion in the microcosm of the mind; but images of darkness prevail at the conclusion, signifying the complete submission to immoral thoughts. The poem's specious logic — that divine illumination should infect the sight and divert "nature's course to selfe displeasure" — indicates the speaker's total blindness to the guiding light of *recta ratio*. In short, the poem is a speaking picture of Basilius's mind, a verbal canvas mirroring the lusterless mental obscurity of sin itself.

Viewed as independent poems, Basilius's hymns convey little more than conventional sentiments; viewed as a sequence, however, they give dramatic expression to the speaker's gradual moral degeneration. The initial prayer, by drawing upon the traditional Christian associations of God, the sun, light, moral probity, and religious devotion, establishes the thematic and metaphorical terms by which the succeeding poems are evaluated and understood. The unity of the sequence results from the fact that the terms of the poetry are more or less constant: God, the sun, and light figure in every poem. What changes, however, is the point of view that Basilius brings to these essentially fixed phenomena.

55. *OA*, 69 (Ringler, p. 108).

The drama of the sequence, in other words, like the drama of the first sonnet in *Astrophil and Stella,* is psychological; for the poems both describe and illustrate love's effects on the speaker's invention. In the second hymn, for example, Basilius describes the actual mechanics of his thought processes, explaining that he has forgotten the "high conceits" of heavenly wisdom, that Phoebus's "Image is defaste," and that he dwells exclusively on the picture of Cleophila, which fills his thoughts. In the third poem, while there is no mention of specific mental contents, Basilius's arguments are an emphatic illustration of the disastrous moral effects that his new conceits have had. The notion that Titan, "the author of our sight," should hasten away for fear of being compared with Cleophila, is a decided step down from the pious rectitude of the first hymn, where devotion for Apollo has its corollary in contempt for the world. By reading the two poems together, we discover — what is not at all surprising — that there is a definite relationship between the speaker's conceit and what he has to say. In this light the sequence is of interest not only because it dramatizes the curve of the old king's passion but also because it points up the connection — a connection crucial in Sidney's poetry — between passionate words and equally passionate thoughts.

Basilius illustrates what is generally true of Sidney's lovers, that "infected mindes infect each thing they see." [56] The lover, infected with passion, tends to project his amorous conceits into the things he sees; or, as Sidney puts it, he "seekes to make ech thing badge of his sweet passion." [57] When his projections find their way into poems — and they almost always do — the result is an amorous invention, the verbal "badge" of the lover's state of mind. We find Musidorus uttering such a speaking picture not long after he has abandoned the life of princely heroism in

56. *CS,* 18 (Ringler, p. 147).
57. *OA,* 28 (Ringler, p. 47).

order to pursue the affections of the princess Pamela. In an attempt to convey his passion to the princess, he sets up an equation between his mental contents and the material objects of the pastoral world.

> My sheepe are thoughts, which I both guide and serve:
> Their pasture is faire hilles of fruitlesse Love:
> On barren sweetes they feede, and feeding sterve:
> I waile their lotte, but will not other prove.
> My sheepehooke is wanne hope, which all upholdes:
> My weedes, Desire, cut out in endlesse foldes.
>> What wooll my sheepe shall beare whyle thus they live,
>> In you it is, you must the judgement give.[58]

Musidorus's sheep are thoughts because, as he understands it, his relationship to the flock and to his amorous conceits is essentially the same. Since Musidorus is in love with Pamela, he guides his thoughts to her and serves his thought through the constancy of his affection. The pasture of his mind is fair because Pamela is fair, and so on. We are presented here with the rural landscape, not as it is in itself, but as seen through Musidorus's mind; he sees things, but we see his thoughts about those things presented in words. The poem's invention — the expressed equivalence between external things and internal thoughts — has no narrative value but simply serves as a formula for the rest of the poem. Once the connection between things and thoughts has been established, the actual sheep, pasture, hills, sheephook, and weeds become irrelevant to the conceptual potency of the words "sheepe," "pasture," "hilles," "sheepehooke," and "weedes." By their association with the prince's state of mind, the words become the verbal emblems for concepts that have no obvious relationship to the objects of the shepherd's profession. Following Musidorus's example, we must

58. Ibid., 17 (Ringler, p. 39). Pyrocles draws a similar correlation between thoughts and things in OA, 2 (Ringler, p. 11), "Transformd in shew, but more transformd in minde," as does Musidorus in OA, 4 (Ringler, p. 13), "Come shepheard's weedes, become your master's minde."

be prepared to sever the connection between words and things (between the word "sheepehooke" and an actual implement, for example), to ignore the things, and to accept the concepts associated with the words ("sheepehooke" with "wanne hope") as their new meanings. Once we have taken this step, the invention of the poem becomes a ground-plot for our own invention, and by substituting thought for thing, we can proceed to a full understanding of the passionate Idea in Musidorus's mind.

Somewhat later in the narrative of the *Arcadia* Musidorus receives signs of Pamela's favor and expresses his joy in another poem about sheep.

> Feede on my sheepe, my chardge my comforte feede,
> With sonne's approche your pasture fertill growes,
> O only sonne that suche a fruite can breede.
>
> Feede on my sheepe, your fayer sweete feeding flowes,
> Eache flower eache herbe dothe to your service yeeld,
> O blessed sonne whence all this blessing goes.[59]

Again we are presented with a speaking picture of Musidorus's passion, but this time the invention of the poem is implicit. Sidney has assumed that in reading the word "sheepe" we shall forget about furry, four-footed animals and perceive the previously established connection between sheep and thoughts. If this relationship is borne in mind, we shall see through the details of the description to the passionate fore-conceit which regulates Musidorus's point of view. Accordingly, we shall ignore the words as descriptive of things and treat them as units of thought, an aggregation of emblematic objects that collectively limn out the speaker's passionate joy.

While Musidorus's invention may be clear, it is hardly felicitous. The poems illustrate one of the deepest pitfalls of the emblem technique, for they go beyond what we ordinarily think of as metaphor — the discovery of likeness between things — to

59. Ibid., 23 (Ringler, p. 43).

the arbitrary assignment of equivalence where none, by any stretch of the imagination, exists. In other words, a sheephook is no more or less appropriate as a symbol for wan hope than a dump truck. Such lapses in decorum, however, are not common in the *Arcadia*. Characters do find their thoughts taking shape throughout the countryside, but more often than not there is some intrinsic connection between thought and thing that makes the discovery of likeness plausible and even illuminating.

Such is the case in a pair of poems spoken by one of Sidney's happiest characters, Philoclea, a person for "whom the not knowing of evill serveth for a ground of vertue." [60] In spite of her natural innocence, Philoclea is not immune to the infection of passion. In the second book of the *New Arcadia* we find her falling in love with Pyrocles, who, so far as she knows, is Zelmane, an Amazon. Overpowered by this mysterious and unwonted affection, she takes a midnight stroll in the forest. In a short time she comes upon a white marble stone that she had inscribed with a personal testimonial a few days before the arrival of Pyrocles/Zelmane in Arcadia. Her inscription, a hymn to chastity, is the first of the companion poems.

> Yee living powres enclosed in stately shrine
> Of growing trees, yee rurall Gods that wield
> Your scepters here, if to your eares divine
> A voice may come, which troubled soule doth yeld:
> This vowe receave, this vowe ô Gods maintaine;
> My virgin life no spotted thought shall staine.
>
> Thou purest stone, whose purenesse doth present
> My purest minde; whose temper hard doth showe
> My tempred hart; by thee my promise sent
> Unto my selfe let after-livers know.
> No fancy mine, nor others' wronge suspect
> Make me, ô vertuous Shame, thy lawes neglect.
>
> O Chastitie, the chiefe of heavenly lightes,
> Which makes us most immortall shape to weare,

60. *Prose Works*, I, 169; cf. IV, 103.

Holde thou my hart, establish thou my sprights:
To onely thee my constant course I beare.
Till spotlesse soule unto thy bosome flye,
Such life to leade, such death I vow to dye.[61]

As the narrative has already made clear, this was not a particularly prudent vow. In the present context the poem is interesting because of its obviously emblematic qualities. Not inappropriately, Philoclea has perceived a relationship between the unblemished purity of her thoughts and the white marble. The stone, as she sees it, "doth present" the state of her mind. As in any emblem, the precise significance of the concrete detail — in this case the stone — is explained in the poem accompanying the picture. However, this emblem is unusual for the fact that the poem is actually inscribed on its most important emblematic detail. Philoclea's words, by virtue of their union with the concrete object she beholds, have taken on an emblematic quality of their own. They not only explain the relationship between thought and pictorial detail — between the concept of chastity and the stone — but are themselves a part of the symbol they explain. In short, the words have become things that, like sheephooks and marble stones, can be assigned an emblematic significance. This is precisely what happens in the second of Philoclea's poems.

Musing on her lapse from chastity, Philoclea moves to within view of the marble stone. "The inke," she discovers, "was alreadie foreworne, and in many places blotted: which as she perceaved, Alas (said she) faire Marble, which never receivedst spot but by my writing, well do these blots become a blotted writer." [62] Then, her thoughts turning to the relationship between her new state of mind and the altered condition of the stone, she conceives a retraction to her original vows.

61. OA, 18 (Ringler, p. 40).
62. *Prose Works*, I, 173; cf. IV, 105.

My words, in hope to blaze my stedfast minde,
This marble chose, as of like temper knowne:
But loe, my words defaste, my fancies blinde,
Blots to the stone, shame to my selfe I finde:
    And witnesse am, how ill agree in one,
    A woman's hand with constant marble stone.

My words full weake, the marble full of might;
My words in store, the marble all alone;
My words blacke inke, the marble kindly white;
My words unseene, the marble still in sight,
    May witnesse beare, how ill agree in one,
    A woman's hand, with constant marble stone.[63]

Very much in the manner of her maker, Philoclea explains that the words of her first poem were intended to "blaze" her mind. "Blaze," a shortened version of "emblazon," is a term clearly related to the emblem tradition. A blazon is a heraldic shield designed to give pictorial expression to the qualities possessed by its owner. The marble stone in the first poem is obviously a blazon for the simple reason that it is a pictorial symbol assigned with a very definite meaning. Less obviously, but as Philoclea insists, the words in the first poem can also be understood as a blazon; in fact, they "blaze" Philoclea's mind in two different ways. First, of course, they are a speaking picture of her thought; they make what is emphatically a state of mind and a concept — chastity — apparent to the reader. Second, as I have already suggested, by their position on the stone Philoclea's words actually symbolize the abstraction that they explain. Thus her words present simultaneously an abstract and a concrete picture of her mind.

In the second poem, discovering that the words of her hymn have been smeared and blotted, Philoclea declares that she was wrong in associating her words with the marble "as of like temper known." Ironically, the dramatic alteration that her

63. OA, 19 (Ringler, pp. 40–41).

words have undergone perfectly coincides with the alteration that has taken place in her condition. Most apparently, since her vow has proved false and since the marble remains the symbol of chastity, it is absolutely appropriate that her words should have disappeared from the face of the stone. More important, however, is the way the inscription on the stone functions emblematically as the blazon of Philoclea's state of mind. The relationship between language and thought is hinted at in the first stanza, when Philoclea equates the "words defaste" with her "fancies blinde." Her affection for Pyrocles/Zelmane, which has issued in the loss of chastity, has its psychological basis in her submission to the immoral illusions of fancy, which are blind, not because they offer nothing for her mind's eye to see, but because her vision is unenlightened by the chaste rays of right reason. In short, she views this handsome Amazon with eyes of love. In the same way that reason, the source of chastity, has been extinguished, so Philoclea's words, the verbal expression of her condition, are also obscured. Accordingly, the words formerly legible on the marble still "blaze" her mind, her moral blindness, precisely because they have become blurred and illegible. But in retaining their emblematic function the words have ceased to be verbal symbols, written words that point to a definite concept, and have become concrete visual symbols, things seen and understood as analogous to certain mental contents. In effect, this second poem is asking us to forget about words altogether and to picture mentally a white stone with ink spots covering it. The image so visualized is a nonverbal emblem bearing starkly visual witness to the paradox that our speaker is setting forth — that her mind does not agree with the purity and constancy of a marble stone. The first poem, now viewed as a concrete rather than a verbal thing, is very precisely the picture of Philoclea's blind fancy.

The assumption that words are effective only to the degree

that they make ideas visible takes on a new dimension in Philoclea's companion poems. The language of the second poem figures forth Philoclea's passionate conceit — her blind fancy — not by a direct discussion of the speaker's mental contents, but by referring us to the words of the first poem, illegible blots on a slab of marble. When our inner gaze rests squarely on these (in the conventional sense) meaningless words, we are quite literally looking at Philoclea's passionate fore-conceit. The gap between language and thought is minimized in such a configuration because words no longer point to concepts but instead begin to look like them.

More often than not, however, the lovers of *Arcadia* are less ingenious than Philoclea and display inventions quite similar to those achieved in the prose. Musidorus's poems on sheep are similar to the description of Pamela as Devotion, for example, in that the details of the lover's monologue are emblematic, or figurative, rather than literal; no sooner does Musidorus describe an object than he assigns it an abstract meaning. In this respect Sidney's poetry and prose are similar to the verse in Giordano Bruno's *De Gli Eroici Furori*. Bruno's poems follow a regular pattern. First an emblem is described in words; a poem then follows in which the details of the emblem appear; and finally there is a prose commentary in which the meaning of the poem and its relationship to the emblem are explained. Frances Yates makes the point that the conceits of Bruno's poems are contained in the emblems that precede them and speculates that in *Astrophil and Stella* Sidney was also "using the conceits emblematically." [64]

While there is a germ of truth in this conjecture, it fails to recognize the much deeper intellectual sympathies that Sidney shared with Bruno and that ultimately account for the similar-

64. Frances A. Yates, "The Emblematic Conceit in Giordano Bruno's 'De Gli Eroici Furori' and in the Elizabethan Sonnet Sequences," *Journal of the Warburg and Courtauld Institutes*, 6 (1943), 102 and 112–113.

ities in their verse. Both writers proceed from the assumption that thinking is seeing, and both make it their task to express mentally visible concepts through the medium of words. Bruno makes it clear at the beginning of his treatise that his "ultimate design" is to "signify divine contemplation and present the eye and ear with other frenzies." [65] The poems are a manifestation of Bruno's design in that the emblems are assumed to contain and give visible expression to ideas that are clarified and enlarged upon in the subsequent prose commentaries. Sidney's procedure is fundamentally the same in much of the Arcadian verse, although he unites Bruno's tripartite structure within the boundaries of single poems. In the first monologue on his sheep, for example, the Idea visible to Musidorus's mind is the emblem regulating the disposition of the conceits in the song. Although Sidney does not offer a full explanation of the poetry, the invention in the first line (that "sheepe are thoughts") serves as a commentary by providing the key to the poem's meaning. Where Bruno explains his visible fore-conceit in a long, verbal exegesis, Sidney simply embeds his in the narrative as a ground-plot for the reader's profitable invention. In a sense, then, Bruno's poems are speaking pictures of philosophical concepts in which the author refuses to let the pictures speak for themselves.

Although Sidney and Bruno had somewhat similar conceptions of poetry, there is good reason to doubt that the latter had any significant influence on *Astrophil and Stella*. Sidney's sonnets are the final fruition of techniques and themes developed in the Arcadian poetry, and not the result of a sudden inspiration. Furthermore, the almost naïvely emblematic structure of Bruno's verse has more in common with Sidney's early writing, where ideas are woven into the tapestry of the natural landscape, than with *Astrophil and Stella*. In the sonnet cycle the emblems and

65. Giordano Bruno, *The Heroic Frenzies*, trans. Paul Eugene Memmo, Jr. (Chapel Hill, N.C., University of North Carolina Press, 1966), p. 66.

the concepts they represent are united in the consciousness of Astrophil himself. The poems are emblematic only in the sense that they are speaking pictures of Astrophil's passionate thought.

In the *Arcadia*, particularly in the revised version, Sidney was more interested in *stasis* than *kinesis*, more concerned with making moral distinctions than with creating situations in which moral distinctions have to be made. The Arcadians leave us with the impression that in the very act of experiencing lust or magnanimity they are also offering us a precise analysis of their state of mind. The motion of thought is thus sacrificed to fixed meanings: Pamela is not devout — she is Devotion. By comparison, the best poems in *Astrophil and Stella* succeed because they capture mental movement without forcing it to a halt. The sonnets are moving pictures of a living consciousness. True, Astrophil can manipulate moral abstractions, but more often than not virtuous logic resolves itself in explosive passion. And while self-analysis is one of Astrophil's most enduring preoccupations, the results of his scrutiny are rarely reliable. In fact, we learn a great deal about him by observing the shortcomings, the oversights, the gross rationalizations that make up his point of view. To complete the analogy, then, the only fixed meanings in *Astrophil and Stella* are those that the reader can abstract from the flux of the speaker's consciousness.

From the moment that Astrophil looks into his heart and begins to write, we are expected to regard him as a *persona*. The failure to observe this important fiction has been the cause of a good deal of needless debate about the inconsistencies in Sidney's style. His professed anti-Petrarchism, for example, is said to be inconsistent with the numerous Petrarchan conceits in the poetry. But to blame Sidney for lapses in poetic technique is to miss completely the nature of that poetic technique. The style of the sonnets, like the style of most of Sidney's poetry, is designed to set forth a speaking picture of thought. But *Astrophil and Stella* is unique in that all of the poems, with their admitted inconsistencies, limn out the conceits of a single, fictional, inconsistent personality. Accordingly, the lapses in Sidney's technique must be recognized as an index to Astrophil's state of mind before the drama of the sonnets can be appreciated for what it is: the perfectly consistent portrait of a lover's passionate inconsistency.

Like the hypothetical poet in the *Apology*, Astrophil sees the fore-conceits for his poems within his mind. "In *Stella's* face" he reads "what Love and Beautie be," and his task "but Copying is, what in her Nature writes." [66] Her image is the "right badge" of his love, the refiner of invention that is "worne in the hart" [67] ("hart" meaning the mind in general). Since the Idea before his mind's eye is almost always the same, Astrophil assures us that his poems are straightforward variations on a single theme.

> When I say '*Stella*', I do meane the same
> Princesse of Beautie, for whose only sake
> The raines of *Love* I love, though never slake,
> And joy therein, though Nations count it shame.
> I beg no subject to use eloquence,
> Nor in hid wayes to guide Philosophie:
> Looke at my hands for no such quintessence;
> But know that I in pure simplicitie,
> Breathe out the flames which burne within my heart,
> *Love* onely reading unto me this art.[68]

As the result of fluctuations in Stella's actual behavior, however, Astrophil's invention, his view of the Idea in his mind, is subject to considerable variation. Very often Stella is described as a celestial spirit in whose beams the lover sees virtuous beauty. But she is also Astrophil's "disgrace"; his love for her is a "poison," and her "*Vertue*" is no more than a disguise for "ungratefulnesse." [69]

66. AS, 3 (Ringler, p. 166).
67. Ibid., 54 (Ringler, p. 192). Cf. AS 15 and 90.
68. Ibid., 28 (Ringler, p. 179).
69. Ibid., 19 (Ringler, p. 174); 16 (Ringler, p. 173); and 31 (Ringler, p. 180).

Certainly these are striking inconsistencies, even more striking, perhaps, than those in the style of the sonnets. Like the variations in technique, however, such shifts in point of view are Sidney's way of letting us see Astrophil's passion.

We never see the real Stella; rather, we see her as she is refracted through the lenses of Astrophil's mind. Within the apparent chaos of these contradictory reflections, distortions, and magnifications, there is a definite formula that regulates the way the lover views his beloved, and the estate of love in general. Astrophil outlines this formula in the Fifth Song.

> While favour fed my hope, delight with hope was brought,
> Thought waited on delight, and speech did follow thought:
> Then grew my tongue and pen records unto thy glory:
> I thought all words were lost, that were not spent of thee:
> I thought each place was darke but where thy lights would be,
> And all eares worse then deafe, that heard not out thy storie.
>
> I said, thou wert most faire, and so indeed thou art:
> I said, thou wert most sweet, sweet poison to my heart:
> I said, my soule was thine (ô that I then had lyed)
> I said, thine eyes were starres, thy breasts the milk'n way,
> Thy fingers *Cupid's* shafts, thy voyce the Angels' lay:
> And all I said so well, as no man it denied.
>
> But now that hope is lost, unkindnesse kils delight,
> Yet thought and speech do live, though metamorphosd quite:
> For rage now rules the reynes, which guided were by Pleasure.
> I thinke now of thy faults, who late thought of thy praise.
> That speech falles now to blame, which did thy honour raise,
> The same key op'n can, which can locke up a treasure.[70]

The Stella that we encounter here is seen, not as she is in herself, but as she appears to the mind of Astrophil. When she provides grounds for hope and when hope results in delight, thought and speech follow to record her glory. In another mood, however, when delight has been shattered by unkindness, Astrophil sees Stella, and thus describes her, through the prism of his

70. Ibid., Fifth Song (Ringler, pp. 212–213).

rage. At all times, of course, Stella remains the same person; but her actions produce radical alterations in the state of Astrophil's mind. And since speech is designed to make thoughts visible, the poetic records that grow out of Astrophil's thoughts are not pictures of Stella as she is but pictures distorted by a prevailing passion. It follows, then, that the reader should regard the variations in Astrophil's point of view as ground-plots from which to invent a broad range of passionate mental states.

While Astrophil's intellectual habits illustrate the poet's assurance that thoughts — most notably passionate thoughts — are things to be seen in the mind, his behavior also indicates that the sight of beauty is not always guaranteed to issue in virtuous action. He knows about the Platonic ladder and even tries to climb it, but more often than not he stumbles at the second rung and falls. The *Apology* is clearly one of his favorite books, though he discovers again and again that beauty in Stella, unlike beauty in poems, is not easily translated into a cool, internally viewed abstraction. Astrophil makes just such a discovery in Sonnet 25.

> The wisest scholler of the wight most wise
> By *Phoebus'* doome, with sugred sentence sayes,
> That Vertue, if it once met with our eyes,
> Strange flames of *Love* it in our soules would raise;
> But for that man with paine this truth descries,
> While he each thing in sense's ballance wayes,
> And so nor will, nor can, behold those skies
> Which inward sunne to *Heroicke* minde displaies,
> Vertue of late, with vertuous care to ster
> Love of her selfe, takes *Stella's* shape, that she
> To mortall eyes might sweetly shine in her.
> It is most true, for since I her did see,
> Vertue's great beautie in that face I prove,
> And find th'effect, for I do burne in love.[71]

The first quatrain is Astrophil's version of "the saying of Plato and Tully" that we have already encountered in the *Apology*:

71. Ibid., 25 (Ringler, p. 177).

"That who could see virtue would be wonderfully ravished with the love of her beauty" (pp. 48–49). The "wight most wise" is Socrates, and his "wisest scholler" is obviously Plato. Having consulted the Delphic Oracle, Plato discovers that the sight of virtue, were it visible, would cause its beholder to love it immediately. It will be recalled that Sidney's defense of poetry as the supreme moral teacher rests squarely on the assumption that poetry can make virtue visible to the mind's eye. This poem, like so many I have discussed, illustrates the profound degree to which Sidney's aesthetics are rooted in Renaissance love theory.

The second quatrain introduces arguments suggesting that Plato's saying may be unduly optimistic. Most men, dwelling only on the illusory images of sensation, have no access to that world of ideal beauty that would render them lovers of virtue. But, Astrophil continues, virtue, recognizing this deficiency in men and anxious that she should be loved, has taken Stella's shape. In other words, Stella has been transformed into a concrete universal, a mortal mirror of a transcendent Idea. To this point in the argument the analogies between poetry and love are absolute. If Astrophil can see in Stella what Sidney's readers are expected to see in his speaking pictures of virtue, the results will be exactly the same.

The climax of the poem occurs in the last line. If, as the product of seeing Stella, Astrophil burns with the "Strange flames" of line 4, then we may conclude that his love is virtuous. On the other hand, if the final line is intended ironically — which is surely the more likely interpretation — then the argument of the preceding lines collapses. Whatever scholars may say, passion seems to be the outcome of Astrophil's vision. In spite of the fact that he understands the amorous theory in all of its detail, it is strongly suggested that his burning love is something less than divine and that the beauty he sees in Stella is far from abstract.

Astrophil is a learned and courtly young man, at home with the traditions of European poetry, and apparently aware of his responsibilities to virtue and heroic endeavor. As his final equivocation makes clear, however, the paradoxical difficulties of love have begun to separate the plates of his moral and intellectual armor. The reader's perception of this tension between what Astrophil knows (that he should love virtue in Stella) and what he seems, almost reluctantly, to feel (that he is afire with a very sublunar passion) constitutes the poem's meaning. In arriving at this perception, we have viewed the verbal outside of the poem, not as an end in itself, but as a medium through which to see a decidedly nonverbal inside.

Astrophil's fruitless attempt to win Stella's favor is the dominant theme in the sonnets, but it is also the occasion for interludes of debate in which the poet meditates on the problem of love in its relation to the rest of his life. As I have already suggested, Astrophil is a well-bred and well-educated nobleman, a soldier, a courtier, and a poet with strong convictions about the nature of his craft. He is thoroughly acquainted with the ancient equation of knowledge with virtue, measures his manhood by his valor and learning, and scorns all that is not noble, pious, prudent, or useful. In short, love comes as something of a shock to him.

> It is most true, that eyes are form'd to serve
> The inward light: and that the heavenly part
> Ought to be king, from whose rules who do swerve,
> Rebels to Nature, strive for their owne smart.
>   It is most true, what we call *Cupid's* dart,
> An image is, which for our selves we carve;
> And, fooles, adore in temple of our hart,
> Till that good God make Church and Churchman starve.
>   True, that true Beautie Vertue is indeed,
> Whereof this Beautie can be but a shade,
> Which elements with mortall mixture breed:
> True, that on earth we are but pilgrims made,

And should in soule up to our countrey move:
True, and yet true that I must *Stella* love.[72]

We have encountered these truisms before, most notably in the theory of knowledge that underlies the *Apology*. It is to Sidney's credit that he was willing to put *gnosis* to the rude test of *praxis*, for Astrophil has made the discovery that there are more things in Stella's eyes than in all his philosophy. Much later in the cycle, in Sonnet 71, after a rehearsal of almost identical truths, Astrophil is able to pinpoint the rift between his knowledge and his feeling with much greater intensity: " 'But ah,' Desire still cries, 'give me some food.' " [73] For the moment, however, we are in the presence of one learned in almost everything but the facts of love, whose desire is as undefined as his doubt. The conclusion of the poem is much less abrupt than Sonnet 71, and Astrophil's admission of love is the function of candor rather than cynicism, awe rather than bitter self-reproach. A second reading reveals that his awareness of renegade emotion is implicit from the very beginning. Each new assertion of truth increases our sense of an impending and inevitable qualification. His assurance that reason "ought to be king" and that the soul should be directed to heaven implies that he is all too aware of the alternatives to wise piety. Indeed, the dutiful regimentation of the arguments against irrational and irreligious love suggests that the foe is afield and prepared for conflict. Accordingly, we are not surprised when Astrophil, in spite of his learning, joins the fools who adore Cupid in the temple of their hearts.

Astrophil addresses himself in the language of wordish philosophy, definitions and distinctions slipping from his tongue like the memorized rules of anyone's wisdom but his own. He is as impressed with the paradox of contradictory truths as he is with the personal implications of his new emotional involvement. The

72. Ibid., 5 (Ringler, p. 167).
73. Ibid., 71 (Ringler, p. 201).

poem achieves its effects through implication and suggestion rather than explicit statement. At its face value it is a learned and coolly objective analysis of a paradox. The conclusion reveals Astrophil's awareness of the contradiction, but it also reveals that his awareness is as yet an academic one. The strident regularity of his thoughts and the occasional hint of perfunctory self-rebuke suggest that he knows something is wrong with love but that he is not sure — definitions notwithstanding — what that something is. Astrophil's poem, like his love, is an assemblage of bookish convictions whose true mettle will be apparent only after they have stood the test of experience.

In Sonnet 5 Astrophil is experiencing almost the same paradox that he later discovers in Sonnet 25. In the latter poem, however, the passion is more bristling, even though only implied. In the earlier poem the pressure of real feeling has not yet begun to push up against the tight verbal paradox that rounds out the last lines. Astrophil is awed and confused, the realization of his situation has knocked his intellectual hat off, but the gales of passion have not yet arisen to blow it away. He is more amazed and befuddled than impassioned. Looking ahead from Sonnet 5, through Sonnet 25, we can see in Sonnet 52 a more complete and self-conscious expression of Astrophil's passionate state of mind.

> A strife is growne betweene *Vertue* and *Love*,
>   While each pretends that *Stella* must be his:
>   Her eyes, her lips, her all, saith *Love* do this,
> Since they do weare his badge, most firmely prove.
> But *Vertue* thus that title doth disprove,
>   That *Stella* (ô deare name) that *Stella* is
>   That vertuous soule, sure heire of heav'nly blisse:
> Not this faire outside, which our hearts doth move.
>   And therefore, though her beautie and her grace
> Be *Love's* indeed, in *Stella's* selfe he may
> By no pretence claime any maner place.
> Well *Love*, since this demurre our sute doth stay,

> Let *Vertue* have that *Stella's* selfe; yet thus,
> That *Vertue* but that body graunt to us.[74]

The poem, as William Ringler points out, is constructed on a legal conceit. Love argues that Stella is his possession because she displays his badge. "Virtue enters a demurrer — admits the facts but denies that they establish legal title, by raising the question whether the essential Stella is her inside or outside; this stops the action (stays the suit) until the court can decide the legal point." [75] Given this delay, the impetuous Astrophil prefers to settle the case out of court, siding with apparently physical love and leaving Stella's essence to virtue. Again we are in the presence of a lover all too familiar with amorous theory, with the distinction between heavenly and earthly love and with the ends of each. And, as I have observed of other poems, the debate here — between virtue and passion — is an objectification of Astrophil's inner state, a speaking picture of the forces operative in his own consciousness.

What is strikingly new about this poem, however, is its tone. There is something decidedly cavalier about the speaker here. The elaborate and sophisticated legal conceit suggests a certain detachment on Astrophil's part, an ability to stand back and survey his situation with control and with a witty kind of resignation. We have no doubt that he is in love, but he is neither so awed as he was in Sonnet 5 nor so undecided and at cross-purposes as he was in Sonnet 25. Here the controlled wit, the familiarity with the personifications, and the almost good-humored readiness of the conclusion present us with a personality more or less at home with the logical and moral inconsistencies of the situation. The irony of the poem's outcome is, to some degree, at Astrophil's expense; but it is also an irony that he controls with the suggestion that he does not regard the expense

74. Ibid., 52 (Ringler, pp. 190–191).
75. Ringler, p. 476.

as a particularly grave one. In fact, the conclusion suggests that the entire legal conceit is a witty design with a prescribed outcome. The logic of the poem may force Astrophil to settle out of court, but the settlement that he accepts merely confirms our suspicion that logic and legality had nothing to do with his objectives in the first place. The drama of "strife" that Astrophil would have us observe here is thus largely undercut by the artfully contrived manner of its presentation. Viewed in this way, the narrative of moral conflict is simply a ground-plot in which we are able to see what the poem really means: that Astrophil is hopelessly — what is even worse, wittily — committed to passion.

The sonnets that I have discussed so far illustrate Astrophil's gradual discovery that rational arguments based on sound authority have little or no sway in matters of passion. At first it is a source of frustration to the learned lover that reason should bring such negligible weight to the balance of feeling. By Sonnet 52, however, frustration has become resignation, and wit has deserted to the ranks of passion. Later on in the sequence Astrophil yields completely to wit's treason, and even revels in the illogic of love's invention.

> *Stella* is sicke, and in that sicke bed lies
> Sweetnesse, that breathes and pants as oft as she:
> And grace, sicke too, such fine conclusions tries,
> That sickenesse brags it selfe best graced to be.
>   Beauty is sicke, but sicke in so faire guise,
> That in that palenesse beautie's white we see;
> And joy, which is inseparate from those eyes,
> *Stella* now learnes (strange case) to weepe in thee.
>   Love moves thy paine, and like a faithfull page,
> As thy lookes sturre, runs up and downe to make
> All folkes prest at thy will thy paine to 'swage,
> Nature with care sweates for her darling's sake,
>   Knowing worlds passe, ere she enough can find
>   Of such heaven stuffe, to cloath so heavenly mynde.[76]

76. AS, 101 (Ringler, pp. 231–232).

The Shape of Things Known

We are impressed with the impossibility of the speaker's seeing anything but perfection in his beloved and yet with the near impossibility of his seeing her as she is. At the poem's conclusion our objective knowledge of Stella is the same as it was after the first three words: "*Stella* is sicke." Everything else is the effusive invention of Astrophil's prevailing passion. Stella is "grace" because he sees her that way, just as "joy" is "inseparate" from her eyes because she is viewed through eyes that can see nothing but joy. We do see whiteness in "palenesse," but that it should be "beautie's white" is a function of Astrophil's vision, and not our own.

By the conclusion of the octave it has become apparent that Stella's illness is less a cause for concern than it is an occasion for the lover's admirable praise. This is confirmed in the sestet, for Astrophil remarks that Stella's "paine" provokes "Love," who in turn "runs up and downe" to alert "all folkes" to her suffering. But Love is also the refiner of invention; Astrophil imagines Love as a "faithfull page" because he is himself in love and poetically "runs up and downe" in his amorous enthusiasm. Similarly, "Nature with care sweates for her darling's sake" only because Astrophil does the same thing — as the giddy tempo of the sonnet illustrates — and therefore conceives of Nature in the way he does.

The couplet clarifies what we have suspected from the outset: Astrophil's view of Stella goes far beyond an objective description of an individual woman sick in bed. Like the lovers of the *trattati d'amore*, he sees Stella as an idealized image within his mind, a heavenly being for whom only "heaven stuffe" is appropriate. Stella is "sweetnesse" and not merely sweet, "beauty" and not merely beautiful, because Astrophil conceives of her as a being who embodies the Idea of "beauty" and the Idea of "sweetnesse." The objectification of his own feelings in personifications

(Love and Nature) not only illustrates the movements of Astrophil's thought but also lends his point of view a magnitude suitable to the object that it beholds. His sense of himself as a "faithfull page" caught up in the transience of passing worlds is in keeping with the humility that he feels is due to a "mynde" so "heavenly" that it exceeds the limits of mere mortality.

Whether or not Astrophil believes in his invention, and whether or not we do, is beside the point. What matters is that the invention is a precise verbal emblem of a very specific state of mind. This is not the academic Astrophil of Sonnet 5, for whom truth could be scanned at arm's length on the page of a book. Truth must in this instance take second place to the feeling of overflowing joy — which is, after all, what the poem is all about. The flight from Stella's sickbed to the regions of heavenly minds is a journey on the wings of amorous thought, the flight of love from the "true" world to another of its own making. In the immense distance between the real Stella and love's invention, we have the measure of Astrophil's passionate conceit, the speaking picture of his Idea of Stella.

The landscape of *Astrophil and Stella* is inhabited by a host of personifications, such as Nature and Love, which engage the poet-lover's attention and comment. Robert Montgomery has observed that "an abstraction that can be spoken to has a vastly different role than one evoked simply in narrative or exposition." "No other element of Sidney's style," he adds, "is so surely responsible for the energy of *Astrophel and Stella*." [77] As in the sonnet just discussed, Astrophil's personified abstractions are the emblems of his own thoughts momentarily thrust into an objective perspective. When Astrophil engages an abstraction in conversation, he is actually talking to himself, reflecting, weighing

77. Robert L. Montgomery, *Symmetry and Sense* (Austin, Tex., University of Texas Press, 1961), pp. 93–94.

one idea against another in active mental debate.[78] The poems that result perfectly illustrate what Sidney meant by *energia*, for they dramatize the interplay of Astrophil's passionate thoughts in characters visible to the eye of the reader's mind. This is the case, for example, when Astrophil addresses himself to Hope.

> Hope, art thou true, or doest thou flatter me?
>   Doth *Stella* now begin with piteous eye,
>   The ruines of her conquest to espie:
> Will she take time, before all wracked be?
> Her eye's-speech is translated thus by thee:
>   But failst thou not in phrase so heav'nly hie?
>   Looke on againe, the faire text better trie:
> What blushing notes doest thou in margine see?
>   What sighes stolne out, or kild before full borne?
> Hast thou found such and such like arguments?
> Or art thou else to comfort me forsworne?
>   Well, how so thou interpret the contents,
>   I am resolv'd thy errour to maintaine,
>   Rather then by more truth to get more paine.[79]

The poem commences with a question whose answer, it is implied, will effect Astrophil's course of action. If Stella's is a "piteous eye," then Hope is "true"; if not, then Hope is a flatterer. Astrophil, thinking of himself as "the ruines of her conquest," has little reason to harbor false optimism, and from the outset we sense that he is himself the best case against Hope. His arguments make it even clearer that Hope is "forsworne" to "comfort" him, and the verdict demanded is obviously one of perjury. Having brought the case to the brink of justice, however, Astrophil resolves to "maintaine" a patent "errour" in order to avoid "more paine."

The drama of the dialogue hinges on the fictional division

---

78. For examples of Astrophil's personified abstractions, see 4 (Virtue), 8 (Love), 10 (Reason), 11 (Love), 12 (Love), 32 (Sleep), 39 (Sleep), 52 (Virtue and Love), 56 (Patience), 72 (Desire), 88 (Absence), 94 (Grief), 106 (Hope).

79. AS, 67 (Ringler, p. 199).

between Astrophil, the probing attorney for the prosecution, and Hope, the personification of Astrophil's own tenuous longings — what he would like to find to be "true." The initial fiction is carefully guarded throughout the poem, and even at the conclusion Astrophil addresses himself to Hope as though he were speaking to another person. As the trial proceeds, the characters in the debate become more clearly defined: Hope is obviously not "true" but a flatterer, while Astrophil seems logical, bent on exposing the facts. But the result of the dialectic is not a just verdict, and our impressions of Astrophil prove to have been illusory. The conclusion exposes the sheer formality of the distinctions between truth and error, logic and sophistry, Astrophil and Hope. The dialogue turns out to have been a monologue in which objective distinctions prove irrelevant to the course of the lover's feelings. By adopting Hope's "errour," Astrophil, "forsworne" to "comfort" himself, becomes guilty of perjury and his own best flatterer. In short, he becomes his own abstraction, the speaking picture of unreasoning, self-deluded Hope.

The technical differences between *Arcadia* and *Astrophil and Stella*, great though they are, do little to disguise the fact that Sidney's artistic and moral objectives in the romance are fundamentally the same as those in the sonnets. In both genres his first and most urgent impulse is to make thoughts and ideas visible to the eye of the reader's mind. In the *Arcadia* this is achieved by painting concepts across the face of external nature, by investing characters and events with definite abstract meanings, and by writing in a prose style that expresses, through the complex texture of its language, the contours of ideas. The high formality of the romance was best suited to fixed concepts, virtues and vices, which could be stenciled into the mindless landscape without provoking nominalists to the inevitable query, "I see the thought, but where is the thinker?"

By allowing Astrophil to speak his own mind, Sidney brought

the critical doctrines of the *Apology* to their creative fulfillment. In the first-person, present-tense internal monologue he discovered a technique that made it possible to figure forth the complex and irregular rhythms of consciousness itself. The primary illusion of the sonnets is that Astrophil is thinking to himself, all the time unaware that we are overlooking every movement of his mind. We see him in the actual process of thought, wrestling with abstractions like Love and Virtue and with personified mental states like Hope, Absence, Grief, and Desire. From the reader's point of view, the result of reading these carefully wrought monologues is a lively and plausible conception of a passionate state of mind. Given our extraordinary insight, we can almost invariably use the narrative of the speaker's ruminations as the basis for our own inventions. For the detached observer Astrophil's experience resolves itself into clear concepts — and all of this in spite of the fact that the lover rarely sees what his experience means. From the point of view of its protagonist, at least, *Astrophil and Stella* is an antidote to the clear-eyed optimism of the *Apology*, for the sonnets append short- and farsightedness, along with a portion of downright blindness, to the ancient equation of thinking and seeing.

5

Reflections
in Seventeenth-century
Literature

Sidney's writing represents the earliest and certainly the most sustained expression of the influence of visual epistemology in English literature. But his example is by no means an isolated phenomenon. The philosophical association of thought with sight had a life of its own; even today it remains an important model for men's habits of thinking about thought. This almost timeless assumption had its most noteworthy literary offspring in neoclassical aesthetics, a tradition that achieved maturity in Sidney's *Apology* and virtually dominated English critical theory from Jonson to Johnson. The neoclassical insistence that poetry should imitate general nature — the Idea of beauty or virtue or truth, something to be seen only in the mind, rather than concrete things — made it inevitable that visual epistemology would continue to play a part in the *gnosis* and the *praxis* of English literature.

It is not my intention to trace this development in anything like its full dimensions. To do so would involve more volumes than I care to write and than anyone could possibly care to read. As a humane and, I think, useful alternative, I have added a pair of brief essays to my discussion of Sidney. Without exhausting the topic, these discussions should at least suggest some of the ways that visual epistemology worked its effects in the literary mind of the seventeenth century.

PICTURAE LOQUENTES: THE ENGLISH CHARACTER WRITERS

A little more than a decade after Sidney's death John Hoskyns noted, in his *Direccōns for Speech and Style*, that Theophrastus had been an important influence on Sidney's Romance. "Hee that will truely set downe a man in a figured storie, must first learne truely to set downe an humo^r. a passion, a virtue, a vice, & therein keeping decent pporcōn add but names, & knitt togeather the accidents & incount^{ers}." This procedure is well illustrated in Aristotle, who served as one of Sidney's models; but, adds Hoskyns, "I thinke alsoe that he had much helpe out of *Theophrasti imagines.*" [1] As he goes on to point out, Hoskyns is referring to the speaking pictures of vices and virtues that appear in the *New Arcadia* and inferring that Sidney had used the *Characters* of Theophrastus as a pattern for his own ethical portraits. Fulke Greville makes a similar suggestion in his *Life* of Sidney, pointing out that his old friend had written a "*Characteristicall* kind of Poesie" and that he had defended his literary practice in the *Apology*. Greville describes such poetry as a "representing of vertues, vices, humours, counsells, and actions of men in feigned and unscandalous Images," [2] apparently referring,

1. John Hoskyns, *Direccōns for Speech and Style* in Louise Brown Osborn, *The Life, Letters, and Writings of John Hoskyns*, Yale Studies in English, LXXXVII (New Haven, Conn., Yale University Press, 1937), p. 155.
2. Fulke Greville, *Life of Sir Philip Sidney*, ed. Nowell Smith (Oxford, The Clarendon Press, 1907), p. 2. While Greville seems to be thinking of Theophrastus here, the evidence is not so decisive as it is with Hoskyns. According to the *Oxford English Dictionary*, the word "character" (*caracte, caracter*) was in use in English as early as the fourteenth century and was very common by the end of the sixteenth century.

like Hoskyns, to the ethical types that appear in the *New Arcadia.*

There are good reasons to commend Hoskyns and Greville in their judgment. Sidney's admiration for Aristotle is evident in almost everything he wrote; accordingly, it is not at all improbable that he would have been impressed by Theophrastus, the master's successor and one of his most famous followers. Furthermore, Sidney's speaking pictures do share certain qualities with the Theophrastan Character. Both writers draw brief, exemplary verbal portraits; both strive for compression; the majority of Sidney's types and all of the Theophrastan Characters are vices; both writers construct their portraits around a general concept (avarice, pride, garrulity) and select details that illustrate that concept; and, finally, both have a tendency to round off their sketches with an "in sum" conclusion.[3] Some of these similarities must have been in the minds of Hoskyns and Greville when they drew their inferences about Sidney and Theophrastus.

Similarities notwithstanding, they were almost certainly wrong. The most crucial date in the history of the Theophrastan Character in England is 1592 — six years after Sidney's death — for in that year the Greek text of Theophrastus's *Characters* with Isaac Casaubon's Latin translation was published at Lyons. Although there had been several earlier continental editions of the ancient *Characters*, it is almost beyond dispute that the first English collection of Theophrastan sketches, Joseph Hall's *Characters of Vertues and Vices* (1608), was the foster child of Casaubon's famous publication. Thus the most compelling evidence points to the conclusion that Sidney's portraits, in spite of their similarities with what was to become a fashionable literary mode, were not specifically Theophrastan in their inspiration. Rather, they can be understood as the products of a long

3. The moralistic summations of some of Theophrastus's Characters are now considered apocryphal, though almost all seventeenth-century imitators copied them.

rhetorical tradition, both classical and native in origin, which prescribed the portrayal of moral types as an aid to instruction.[4] While Hoskyns and Greville were wrong in drawing lines of influence between Theophrastus and Sidney, it remains true that there are striking similarities between the two writers. Even more striking are the similarities between the moral portraits that appear in the *New Arcadia* and the avowedly Theophrastan imitations that appeared by the thousands during the seventeenth century. Like Sidney, and unlike Theophrastus, the English Character writers have a tendency to ground their sketches in conceits, witty metaphors that take their source in an abstract Idea. Overbury, for example, introduces a Dissembler as "an essence needing a double definition, for hee is not that hee appeares"; similarly, the Tymist (timeserver) "is a noune Adjective of the present tense." [5] The details that follow from such beginnings are often more characteristic of Sidney than of Theophrastus. In general, Theophrastus avoids abstractions, selects his illustrations from concrete social situations, and avoids moralizing commentary; in short, he views the Character from without, telling us more about what he does than what he thinks. The English writers, by comparison, are inclined to regard virtues and vices as states of mind, humors or affections, and to select details that figure forth what are clearly either perverse or praiseworthy mental states. In other words, they tend to view their Characters from the inside, construing virtues and vices as abstract psychological conditions rather than concrete activities.

It is not my purpose here to suggest that the English Charac-

4. Throughout this paragraph I am indebted to Benjamin Boyce, *The Theophrastan Character in England to 1642* (Cambridge, Mass., Harvard University Press, 1947); see especially chaps. i–iii. For further light on the influence of rhetoric on character portrayal, see Charles Osborne McDonald, *The Rhetoric of Tragedy* (Amherst, Mass., University of Massachusetts Press, 1966), chaps. i–iii.

5. *The Overburian Characters*, ed. W. J. Paylor, The Percy Reprints, XIII (Oxford, Basil Blackwell, 1936), pp. 6, 9.

ter writers were working with Sidney as one of their models; indeed, there is no evidence to support such an inference. However, I shall argue that the non-Theophrastan similarities between the work of Sidney and men like Hall and Overbury can be explained, to some degree at least, by their common aesthetic assumptions. The tendency to abstraction among English Theophrastans, which manifests itself in a penchant for strong lines, in an almost unanimous preference for an elliptical, pointed Senecan style, and in terse, paradoxical conclusions, results — as I have already suggested — from their conceptions of character, not as a mode of behavior, but as an Idea, a visible mental object. Like Sidney, they felt that their moral sketches offered the reader something to see — something in addition to, and far more important than, mere words. Again and again the Character writers emphasize that their variety of instruction is intentionally knotty and obscure; but, they add, given a modicum of effort and the requisite perspicacity, the reader will be able to visualize and therefore know the ethical concept that the words collectively mean.

In 1608 Theophrastus joined Juvenal on Joseph Hall's shelf of literary revivals. *Characters of Vertues and Vices* initiated the vogue of charactery in England, established Hall as its promoter, and offered the first critical *apologia* for the methods and objectives of the genre. Predictably, the author conceived of his little book as a manual for moral edification. For Hall, as for Sidney, moral instruction was inevitably associated with the Platonic axiom, conveyed to the Renaissance by Cicero, that Virtue, could she be seen, would win a numberless throng of devoted admirers. Given this much, the teacher, with his sights set squarely on the promotion of morality in a society fallen on evil times, had only to make Virtue visible in order to secure his ends. It is just this task that Hall assumes in the "Proeme" to Book I of his *Characters*.

Vertue is not loved enough, because shee is not seene; and Vice loseth much detestation, because her ugliness is secret. Certainly, my Lords, there are so many beauties, and so many graces in the face of Goodnesse, that no eye can possibly see it without affection, without ravishment; and the visage of Evil is so monstrous, through loathsome deformities, that if her lovers were not ignorant, they would be mad with disdaine and astonishment . . . Loe heere then Vertue and Vice strip't naked to the open view, and despoiled, one of her rags, the other of her ornaments, and nothing left them but bare presence to plead for affection: see now whether shall find more suiters.[6]

In the "Proeme" to Book II, which introduces the Characters of Vices, Hall continues in the same vein: "I have shewed you many faire Vertues: I speak not for them, if their sight can not command affection, let them lose it. They shall please yet better, after you have troubled your eyes a little with the view of deformities." [7]

Hall's visual vocabulary might be dismissed as so much hollow verbiage were it not for the fact that he elaborates more precisely upon his intentions in the Preface "To the Reader." Here he analyzes ancient philosophers into three groups, of which the third class

bestowed their time in drawing out the true lineaments of every vertue and vice, so lively, that who saw the medals, might know the face: which Art they significantly termed *Charactery*. Their papers were so many tables, their writings so many speaking pictures, or living images, whereby the ruder multitude might even by their sense learne to know vertue, and discerne what to detest. I am deceived if any course could be more likely to prevaile; for heerein the grosse conceit is led on with pleasure, and informed while it feeles nothing but delight: And if pictures have beene accounted the books of idiots, beholde heere the benefit of an image without the offence.[8]

The phrase "speaking pictures" has exactly the same connotation in this context that it does in the *Apology*; indeed, the entire

6. Joseph Hall, *Characters of Vertues and Vices* (1608), pp. 1–3.
7. Ibid., p. 67.
8. Ibid., Sig. A5^{r-v}.

passage has a strong Sidneian ring to it. By "speaking" Hall means "words," the written words that make up this or that Character; and "pictures" refers to the mental images that the artist copies in his prose and that are formed in the reader's mind as he reads. Language, in such a scheme, is clearly subordinate to the pictorial concept that governs its disposition and that it allows the audience to see and know. Thought and sight are so closely associated in Hall's epistemological assumptions that he describes the reading of a Character as the acquisition of knowledge through visual sensation; and then, almost in the same breath, he argues that the same result can occur ("the benefit of an image") without the sensible picture ("the offence"). The confusion arises, of course, because Hall has failed to clarify what he has obviously assumed — that the knowledge of virtue, or vice, is an intensely visual experience. Only when that assumption has been grasped can we understand fully the constant references to pictures, images, sight, and knowledge in his prefatory excursions.

Joseph Hall's scattered comments on Character writing seem to have provided a point of departure for most of the critical commentators during the next few decades. The inevitable description of the Character as a speaking picture arose, just as inevitably, from the equation of words with thoughts, and of thoughts with things seen. A certain "W.P." wrote *In laudem operis* of Nicholas Breton's *Characters Upon Essays, Moral and Divine* (1615):

> Words are the pencils, whereby drawn we find
> The picture of the inward man, the mind:
> Such thoughts, such words; such words, such is the man.[9]

These equations had a partial source in the word "Character" itself. Hall hinted that the Greek philosophers had employed the term "significantly," and the author of "What a Character is"

9. Nicholas Breton, *Characters Upon Essays, Moral and Divine* (1615), in *Archaica*, ed. Sir E. Brydges, 2 vols. (London, 1815), I, p. vii.

in the Overbury collection, perhaps following Hall's lead, elaborates upon a definition of the Greek root:

If I must speake the Schoole-masters language I will confesse that Character comes of this infinitive moode χαφαζω which signifieth to ingrave, or make a deepe Impression. And for that cause, a letter (as A.B.) is called a Character.
Those Elements which we learne first, leaving a strong seale in our memories.
Character is also taken for an Egiptian Hierogliphicke, for an impresse, or shorte Embleme; in little comprehending much.
To square out a Character by our English levell, it is a picture (reall or personall) quaintlie drawne in various collours, all of them heightned by one shadowing.
It is a quicke and softe touch of many strings, all shutting up in one musicall close: It is wits descant on any plaine song.[10]

At first glance, this happily reluctant pedant seems to be uncertain about the status of the Character. Is it visible to the outer eye or to the inner eye? Under closer scrutiny, however, it becomes obvious that the alternatives amount to the same thing. A letter can be engraved on paper or wood, but its primary virtue seems to be that it leaves a deep impression in the memory. In the same way, a Character can be a picture visible to ordinary sight, like a hieroglyphic or an emblem, or it can be an internal picture, visible to the mind; in both cases the act of looking at the picture amounts to a process of conceptualization. Shakespeare catches the ambiguity in Sonnet 59, asserting that "mind at first in character was done"; and Spenser's Artegall, though separated from his beloved, still loves Britomart,

Whose character in th'Adamantine mould
Of his true hart so firmely was engraved,

10. *The Overburian Characters*, ed. Paylor, p. 92. "What a Character is" was not added to the collection until the publication of the ninth impression, which appeared in 1616, long after Overbury's death. Accordingly, attribution of individual Characters, or even of larger groups, is very tentative. See Paylor's Introduction, pp. xvi–xxxiv.

> That no new loves impression ever could
> Bereave it thence.[11]

Letters and words are Characters because, when disposed in significant ararngements, they can represent a pictorial Idea. Emblems and hieroglyphics bridge the gap between thought and sensation, for they are concepts equally significant, in exactly the same form, to both *oculus carnis* and *oculus mentis*. As such they are ideal analogies for this anonymous author, who cannot think of a Character without thinking of a meaning — the "shadowing" that informs all the "various collours" with a uniform significance — and cannot conceive of meaning independently of something visible.

The aesthetic prescriptions of Hall and the anonymous contributor to the Overbury collection were the models upon which almost all subsequent descriptions of the Character were formed. The volume of such commentary was naturally rather small. The Character collections were rarely any larger than an average address book, and few authors felt compelled to preface their offerings with much more than a genial nod to some now-forgotten dignitary. But, on the occasions when descriptions do appear, they conform to one of two inevitable patterns. Some writers, apparently following the Overburian example, describe their sketches as emblems or engravings. Richard Brathwaite, for example, regards his Characters as *"stampes* or *impressures,* noting . . . an especiall place, person, or office."[12] The second, and more common, approach looks back to Joseph Hall. The writer is viewed as a painter, his pencil is a brush, and he draws pictures. Wye Saltonstall's collection *Picturae Loquentes, or Pictures Drawne forth in Characters* (1631) is probably the most

---

11. Shakespeare, Sonnet 59, line 8; Edmund Spenser, *The Faerie Queene,* V, vi, 2, 6–9. Cf. also *Twelfth Night,* I, ii, 50–51; *Two Gentlemen of Verona,* II, vii, 1–4.

12. Richard Brathwaite, *Whimzies: Or, A New Cast of Characters* (1631), Epistle Dedicatory, Sig. A5$^\text{v}$.

eloquent example of the latter variety. Saltonstall conceives of himself as a painter, his paragraphs as pictures, and expresses the hope that they are "shadowed forth with those lively and exact Lineaments, which are required in a Character." [13] Some readers may dislike his title, objecting that he has used no colors in his pictures; but, the author rejoins, "these Pictures are not drawne in colours, but in Characters, representing to the eye of the minde divers several professions." [14] Richard Flecknoe, writing four decades later, makes a related point in an identical vocabulary, insisting that Characters "differ from Pourtracts, in that they are onely *Pictures of Mind*." [15] Saltonstall's playful self-defense makes explicit the epistemological assumption embedded in almost all descriptions of the Character; whether construed as an emblem, engraving, impression, picture, painting, or portrait, its visibility necessarily implies an intellectual eye.

LIVING EMBLEMS

The influence of visual epistemology on seventeenth-century literature reached a high-water mark in the Jonsonian masque. In a genre that is now seldom read and almost never seen, the visual and the conceptual were completely merged in the extra-mental space framed by the proscenium arch. Jonson's place in the history of the masque is, of course, preeminent. Almost alone among court poets, he treated the masque as serious literature; and, inveterate critic that he was, his recorded attitudes toward the form are extensive and invaluable. In the productions of the first decade of the Jacobean period, before his reluctant conces-

13. Wye Saltonstall, *Picturae Loquentes, or Pictures Drawne forth in Characters* (1631), A4^r.
14. Ibid., A5^r.
15. Richard Flecknoe, *A Collection Of the choicest Epigrams and Characters of Richard Flecknoe* (1673), p. 1. Flecknoe takes the same position in the epistle "To the Reader," in his *Aenigmatical Characters* (1665), and in the Preface to *Heroick Portraits* (1660), Sig. A3^v. See also "The Character of a Character," in *Aenigmatical Characters*, pp. 1–2.

sion to court taste in the antimasque, Jonson valued the masque because it organized a diversity of artistic media into a vision of unity and permanence. Unity results when spectacle, music, dance, and poetry are harmonized in the common expression of a pivotal concept, the "invention" of the masque.[16] The quality of permanence in masques has an identical source, as the familiar preface to *Hymenaei* makes clear.

It is a noble and iust advantage, that the things subiected to *understanding* have of those which are obiected to *sense*, that the one sort are but momentarie, and meerely taking; the other impressing, and lasting: Else the glorie of all these *solemnities* had perish'd like a blaze, and gone out, in the *beholders* eyes. So short-liv'd are the *bodies* of all things, in comparison of their *soules*. And, though *bodies* oft-times have the ill luck to be sensually preferr'd, they find afterwards, the good fortune (when *soules* live) to be vtterly forgotten. This it is hath made the most royall *Princes*, and greatest *persons* (who are commonly the *personaters* of these *actions*) not onely studious of riches, and magnificence in the outward celebration, or shew; (which rightly becomes them) but curious after the most high, and heartie *inventions*, to furnish the inward parts: (and those grounded vpon *antiquitie*, and solide *learnings*) which, though their *voyce* be taught to sound to present occasions, their sense, or doth, or should alwayes lay hold on more remov'd *mysteries*.[17]

It should be stressed that by "invention" Jonson did not mean the words of poetry, whether spoken or written.[18] Rather, he uses the term — as Sidney does — to describe the "inside" of the work of art, the fore-conceit upon which the outside is modeled. In Jonson's usage, "invention" is synonymous with "fable," "fic-

16. This point has been well and extensively elaborated in Dolora Cunningham's "The Jonsonian Masque as a Literary Form," *English Literary History*, 22 (1955), 108–124.

17. Ben Jonson, *Works*, ed. C. H. Herford and Percy and Evelyn Simpson, 11 vols. (Oxford, The Clarendon Press, 1925–1952), VII, 209. Hereafter, when convenient, citations from this edition will be given in the text.

18. For a more detailed discussion, see D. J. Gordon, "Poet and Architect: The Intellectual Setting of the Quarrel Between Ben Jonson and Inigo Jones," *Journal of the Warburg and Courtauld Institutes*, 12 (1949), 154–160.

tion," "soule," "forme," "plot," "device," [19] all of which point to conceptualizing processes preliminary and essential to the effective use of words in poems, or to the effective use of words, scenes, music, and dance in masques. Jonson is also like Sidney in regarding invention as the discovery of abstractions. The titles of some of his masques (*The Masque of Beautie* and *Pleasure Reconciled to Virtue*) make this clear enough, as does the formidable research of D. J. Gordon.[20] Thus the importance of invention to Jonson's conception of the masque cannot be overstated; without it the completed artifact would be devoid of meaning — what Jonson calls "sense" — and its various elements would fall into utter disorder.

Jonson and Sidney had much more in common than their views on invention. An exhaustive comparison of the two critics would reveal myriad similarities, ranging from sources through psychology to aesthetics. For example, both stress the primacy of matter in poetry, arguing that such matter is ethical in content and designed to teach and delight by making virtues and vices visible to the audience. The Chorus in *The Magnetick Lady* defines comedy as "the Glasse of custome . . . so held up to me, by the Poet, as I can therein view the daily examples of mens lives, and images of Truth, in their manners, so drawne for my delight, or profit, as I may (either way) use them." [21] For both

19. See *Discoveries* (*Works*, VIII, 635, 645); and *The Kings Entertainment at Fen-Church* (*Works*, VII, 90–91).

20. See D. J. Gordon's "The Imagery of Ben Jonson's *The Masque of Blacknesse* and *The Masque of Beautie*," *Journal of the Warburg and Courtauld Institutes*, 6 (1943), 122–141; and "*Hymenaei*: Ben Jonson's Masque of Union," *Journal of the Warburg and Courtauld Institutes*, 8 (1945), 107–145.

21. *The Magnetick Lady*, Act II, Chorus (*Works*, VI, 545). See also *Cynthias Revels*, Prologue, ll. 19–20 (*Works*, IV, 43); *Poetaster*, IV, vi, 39–46 (*Works*, IV, 281); *Volpone*, Prologue, l. 4 (*Works*, V, 23); *Every Man in His Humour*, I, ii, 109–110 (*Works*, III, 206); *Every Man out of His Humour*, V, viii, 79–80 (*Works*, III, 591); *The Staple of Newes*, Prologue, ll. 21–24, and Epilogue, ll. 1–4 (*Works*, VI, 282, 382); and *Discoveries* (*Works*, VIII, 595).

poets the abstract component in their speaking pictures is very high; Jonson, while much taken with Plutarch's doctrine that "*Poetry* was a speaking Picture, and *Picture* a mute Poesie," goes on to insist that "the Pen is more noble, then the Pencill. For that can speake to the Understanding; the other, but to the Sense" (*Discoveries*, VIII, 609–610). This common habit of describing the matter or invention of poetry as both abstract and pictorial has its ultimate source in visual epistemology. Like Sidney, Jonson tends to regard thinking as a kind of internal seeing. He quotes in full Hoskyns's argument that "The conceits of the mind are Pictures of things, and the tongue is the Interpreter of those Pictures" (*Discoveries*, VIII, 628–629). Such an attitude toward knowledge, coupled with a poetics as deeply rooted in invention as Jonson's, leads quite naturally to the notion that poetry has its most important function in rendering the poet's pictorial abstractions visible to the reader's (or viewer's) mind.

It is not my concern to press this point very far. Jonson's epistemology is much less clear than Sidney's and therefore less useful in a discussion of his aesthetics. But there is, as I have indicated, a marked tendency toward the visual in his discussions of poetry. This tendency is important because it helps to explain Jonson's interest in masques, a genre that made few demands on what are usually regarded as his greatest artistic assets: his sense for dramatic structure, dramatic action, and his robust dialogue. These qualities, so prominent in Jonson's best comedies, were declining remarkably in the period that just preceded his first courtly entertainments. By 1600, as Jonson's editors point out, the allegorical and abstract sides of the poet's mind were dominant (I, 397). We are impressed, as we read the plays written around 1600, with Jonson's growing insistence on clarity in his moral portraits. *Every Man out of His Humour* is prefaced with brief sketches of the main dramatis personae, each drawn in the terse, balanced style of the later Character writers. Midway in the play, two of the characters engage in a conversation that punctuates their author's intention:

MIT. Me thinkes, *Cordatvs*, he dwelt somewhat too long on this *Scene*; it hung i' the hand.
COR. I see not where he could have insisted lesse, and t'have made the humours perspicuous enough.[22]

The pressure of concepts grows even stronger in *Cynthias Revels*, where dramatic action gives way almost entirely to moral allegory. Jonson takes special care to make his message clear in his Preface to the Court: "It is not pould'ring, perfuming, and every day smelling of the taylor, that converteth to a beautiful obiect: but a mind, shining through any sute, which needes no false light either of riches, or honors to helpe it" (IV, 33). In the lifeless drama that follows, the characters, many labeled with stiffly allegorical names, act out the various abstractions they personify. Their minds — that is, the vices or virtues that they embody — could not be more transparent. Near the end of the play Mercury speaks for Jonson when he remarks on the courtly Vices: "Who sees not now their shape, and nakednesse,/Is blinder then the sonne of earth, the mole" (IV, 157).

Not surprisingly, *Cynthias Revels* concludes with a masque. The characteristics of the play — moral perspicuity, abstract clarity, reduction of character to concept — are, in fact, the characteristics of the Jonsonian masque. The evolution of the plays during this period illustrates Jonson's gradual submission to an idea that we have encountered before, that virtue must be seen in order to be loved. The masques cannot be fully appreciated unless we recognize this crucial literary, and ultimately epistemological, point of departure. Jonson could not have concurred in Samuel Daniel's argument that masque writers are "the poore

22. *Every Man out of His Humour*, II, iii. 288–291 (*Works*, III, 479). In V, viii, 79–80 (*Works*, III, 591), Cordatus remarks: "I, you shall see the true picture of spight anon: here comes the pawne, and his redeemer."

Inginers for shadowes, & frame onely images of no result." [23] To the contrary, his whole energy was devoted to creating images of ideas so clearly conceived and expressed that they could not fail to penetrate the eye of the viewer's mind. Cynthia's response to Crites' entertainment is obviously the ideal Jonson had in mind:

> Not without wonder, nor without delight,
> Mine eyes have view'd (in contemplations depth)
> This worke of wit, divine, and excellent. (IV, 167)

How, then, did Jonson's theory work itself out in practice? How did the various parts of the masque function to make an abstract Idea visible "in contemplations depth"?

If the most persistent theme in Jonson's masques is order, then that theme has its most uniform expression in music. Jonson's understanding of music is essentially Neoplatonic; harmony, grounded in fixed numerical ratios, is supremely rational in its structure and the foundation upon which all order and degree rest. Music, as he puts it in his tribute to Alphonso Ferrabosco, is "the soule of heaven" (VIII, 82). It is with such lofty metaphysical assumptions in mind that we must approach the music in the Jonsonian masque. When we read that the armed Cupids in *The Masque of Beautie* "doe not warre, with different darts,/ But strike a musique of like harts" (VII, 192), the full effect of the words will be lost on us if we do not remember that they were written to be sung. The harmony of "like harts" and the harmony of music have a common cosmic source; accordingly, they are equally expressive of the Idea of cosmic order and love, which is the masque's main theme. Discord, the opposite of order, also has an appropriate musical form. Hymen, a principal speaker in *Hymenaei*, relates that marital union "Winnes *natures*,

---

23. The Preface to the Reader, *Tethys Festival*, in *The Complete Works in Verse and Prose of Samuel Daniel*, ed. A. B. Grosart, 5 vols. (London, 1885–1896), III, 306.

sexes, minds,/And ev'rie discord in true musique brings." His speech is followed by the entrance of the antagonists of union, the Humors and Affections, who are accompanied "with a kind of contentious Musique." This discordant rout is introduced, Jonson notes, so "that afterwards, in *Marriage*, . . . they might more fully celebrate the happinesse of such as live in that sweet *union,* to the harmonious lawes of Nature and Reason" (VII, 212–213). From Jonson's point of view, then, music always implies a set of easily visualized numerical proportions whose expression, regulated by "harmonious lawes," serves as an aural emblem of the poet's invention.[24]

Jonson's comments on the dance, while relatively few, are uniform in their insistence that the performers' movements give expression to concepts. One of the dances in *The Masque of Beautie* is described as "full of excellent device" (VII, 191), while in *Pleasvre reconcild to Vertve* Daedalus informs the audience that

> Daúncing is an exercise
> not only shews ye movers wit,
> but maketh ye beholder wise,
> as he hath powre to rise to it. (VII, 489)

Similar praise falls on a dance in *Hymenaei:* "Here, they daunced forth a most neate and curious measure, full of *Subtilty* and *Device;* which was so excellently performed, as it seemed to take away that *Spirit* from the *Invention,* which the *Invention* gave to it: and left it doubtfull, whether the *Formes* flow'd more perfectly from the *Authors* braine, or their feete" (VII, 220–221). In this final example Jonson is impressed with the fact that the dancers have made the "*Formes*" of "the *Authors* braine" their own. The crucial word here is "*Formes*," for it is the visibility

24. For a more thorough discussion, see John C. Meagher, *Method and Meaning in Jonson's Masques* (Notre Dame, Ind., University of Notre Dame Press, 1966), chap. 3.

of an intelligible pattern in the dance that Jonson values. In this instance the masquers "formed into *Letters*, very signifying to the name of the *Bridegrome*" (VII, 221). Later on in the same masque they range themselves into "a faire *orbe*, or *circle*," the emblem of perfection. To complete the speaking picture, Reason stands in the middle of the circle and begins to recite: "Here stay, and let your sports be crown'd:/The perfect'st *figure* is the *round*." [25]

We turn next to the spectacle, the most graphically pictorial element in Jonson's court entertainments. When the curtain unveiled *The Masque of Blacknesse* in 1605, the spectators beheld a scene constructed on the principles of perspective. All of the objects within the proscenium were organized along the lines of geometrically rationalized visual space. The mere "look" of the setting gave visible expression to the concept of order.[26] What better background for the play of abstractions? By analogy, the geometric grid stretched beyond the masque frame into the philosophical regions of mathematical degree which underlie so much of Renaissance thought. This cluster of ideas takes a special form in *The Vision of Delight*, a masque ending with a celebration of Spring. Wonder, one of the main speakers, is awed by the orderly fruition of the season and asks, "Whose power is this? what God?" Phant'sie replies:

> Behold a King
> Whose presence maketh this perpetuall *Spring*,
> The glories of which Spring grow in that Bower,
> And are the marks and beauties of his power. (VII, 469)

25. *Works*, VII, 224. Meagher (*Method and Meaning in Jonson's Masques*, pp. 95–96) points out that Jonson may have employed geometric choreography in his masques. His argument has some support in the fact that the initial dance in *Hymenaei* is directed by Order, the servant of Reason, whose garments are decorated with arithmetic and geometric figures.

26. Jonson's cognizance of the theory of perspective is evident in *Discoveries* (*Works*, VIII, 611).

Hereupon the whole focus of the entertainment turns to the king, and Jonson's invention is suddenly transparent. James, the symbol of order in the state, is for the purposes of the masque the sun. The metaphor is appropriate in several ways. Most obviously, it has great complimentary value, and it testifies to the king's lavish expenditures in making the masque possible. More importantly, the metaphor links the natural fecundity celebrated on the stage with the principle of orderly change symbolized in the sun and embodied in the monarch. In turning our attention to the king, Jonson is thus asking us to see much more than a man; in fact, we are seeing the Idea of orderly growth which is the masque's invention. The role of the perspective in all of this could not be more subtle. Just as change in nature is unintelligible without the concept of order symbolized in the sun and just as the masque itself, the image of an idealized nature, is unintelligible unless we grasp the allusions to the king, so the actual disposition of the spectacle is in perspective only from the king's chair. The lines of order, whether in the macrocosm of nature, the microcosm of the masque, or the spectacle itself, take their source in James. From this point of view, the perspective — geometrical order working within the objects of sense — is simply a picture of the poet's invention.[27]

The perspective setting of the spectacle served as a background for the "personaters" of the masque, the symbolic characters who limn out the details of the invention. There is nothing dramatic about most of the roles in a Jonsonian entertainment. The characters are static personifications of abstractions whose *energia* would dissolve were they to develop dramatically. In *The Masque*

27. My main debts here are to Allardyce Nicoll, *Stuart Masques and the Renaissance Stage* (London, George G. Harrap & Co. Ltd., 1938), p. 34; and Stephen Orgel, *The Jonsonian Masque* (Cambridge, Mass., Harvard University Press, 1965), p. 66. For a discussion of the use of perspecitve in scenery, see the relevant chapters in Lily B. Campbell's *Scenes and Machines on the English Stage During the Renaissance* (Cambridge, England, Cambridge University Press, 1923).

of Blacknesse, for example, the twelve daughters of Niger appear in pairs, "every couple (as they advanced) severally presenting their fans: in one of which were inscribed their mixt *Names*, in the other a mute *Hieroglyphick*, expressing their mixed qualities" (VII, 177). The names and symbolic lore have their sources in Italian mythological manuals and in such emblem books as Ripa's *Iconologia* and Valeriano's *Hieroglyphica*. The total effect of the procession is emblematic: Jonson intends that by looking at the nymphs and their abstract regalia, we shall understand both their individual meanings and their relationship to the masque as a whole.

The same can be said for the inanimate portions of the spectacle. In *The Masque of Beautie*, one of Jonson's most elaborate productions, the viewers at Whitehall surveyed an island that moved slowly forward toward the land. Mounted on the island was the Throne of Beauty, which rotated from right to left imitating the *motum mundi*, while the base of the structure rotated from left to right, "with *Analogy, ad motum Planetarum.*" A bevy of Cupids surrounded the Throne, "all armed, with *Bowes, Quivers, Wings*, and other *Ensignes of Love.*" Above, situated on an intricate scaffolding of arches and pillars, "were placed eight *Figures*, representing the *Elements* of *Beauty.*" Each of these female figures had an abstract name, each was dressed symbolically, and each bore objects signifying her special role. Germinatio, for example, was dressed in green and carried a branch of myrtle, which, Jonson pointed out in a note, was "the ensigne of the *Spring.*" Above this group stood Harmonia, who represented the union of all the elements of Beauty. Her costume was a composition of figures taken from the robes of the others, and she wore a crown set with seven jewels. These were also explained in a note: "She is so describ'd in *Iconolog. di Cesare Ripa*, his reason of 7. iewels, in the crown, alludes to *Pythagoras* his comment, with *Mac. lib. 2. Som. Sci.* of the seven *Planets* and their *Spheares*" (VII, 186–189). Thanks to the extensive research of D. J. Gordon, the significance of this complex collection of emblems is now clear. "The whole machine," he concludes, "is an image of the turning world, presided over by Harmony, with Beauty set in the wheeling heaven which is its cause, and attended by Love moving like the Planets." [28] What the audience at Whitehall was expected to see, then, was a compendium of Neoplatonic ideas presented in visual form.

Naturally Jonson was not overly sanguine that his spectacles would be viewed in the appropriate way. While striving for lucidity, he was convinced — as the emblem writers were convinced — that art should contain mysteries visible only to the learned. This position emerges clearly in *The Kings Entertainment at Fen-Church*:

Neither was it becomming, or could it stand with the dignitie of these shewes . . . to require a Truch-man [interpreter], or (with the ignorant Painter) one to write, *This is a Dog*; or, *This is a Hare*: but so to be presented, as upon the view, they might, without cloud, or obscuritie, declare themselves to the sharpe and learned. (VII, 91)

Jonson's assurances notwithstanding, it is quite likely that most of his spectacles, were they viewed in isolation, would leave even the most erudite observers completely in the dark. Such potential obscurity was usually avoided, however, primarily because of the light cast by the poetry. The songs in the masques serve much the same function as the *mots* that accompany impresas, or the expository poems that appear in books like Whitney's *A Choice of Emblems*; that is, they clarify the invention and illuminate the details of the visual symbolism. Such is the case with the song of Phant'sie in *The Vision of Delight* (quoted earlier) and with the first lyric in *The Masque of Beautie*: "It was for *Beauty*, that the World was made,/And where she raignes, *Loves*

28. Gordon, "The Imagery of Ben Jonson's *The Masque of Blacknesse* and *The Masque of Beautie*," p. 138, and passim.

lights admit no shade" (VII, 190). In a more extensive manner, the dialogue between Truth and Opinion which concludes *Hymenaei* simply expands upon one of the main themes of the masque.

The analogy between the court shows and the emblem literature is a close one; indeed, the emblem books, with their aesthetics deeply rooted in visual epistemology, were one of Jonson's primary models in his construction of masques. In the early entertainments complete impresas appear. Euphrosyne, in *The Kings Entertainment at Fen-Church,* is dressed in green, surrounded by several "ensignes of gladnesse," and given an appropriate Latin motto (VII, 87). The same pattern is clearly discernible in the symbolic nymphs of *The Masque of Beautie* or in the geometric choreography of *Hymenaei.* In the same vein, Jonson's habit of describing the music, dance, and spectacle as the "body" of a masque and the poetry as its "soul" is a direct reflection of his familiarity with the emblem writers. Based on his general theory on court entertainments, the distinction is perfectly apt. The elements of a masque, like the abstract picture and poem in an emblem — or, for that matter, like the Idea and words in a Character — work together to form a speaking picture of the artist's invention.[29] The remarkable feature of the masque is that it made it possible to go one step beyond the other genres in the equation of thought and sight. In a Character the Idea is still very much an object of thought, something to be reconstructed from the patterns of language. In an emblem the concept is made visible in a picture, but it is still pinned to the page of a book. In the masque, however, the abstractions come out of the mind and off the page and present themselves as perfectly audible and literally visible speaking pictures.

29. This point has been made before. Cf. Don Cameron Allen, "Ben Jonson and the Hieroglyphics," *Philological Quarterly,* 18 (1939), p. 295; and Nicoll, *Stuart Masques and the Renaissance Stage,* p. 155.

Index

Index

Castiglione, Baldassare, 72
Cavalcanti, Guido, 65–66, 74
Chaucer, Geoffrey, 62
Chrysippus, 24–25
Cicero, 25–26, 70, 102–103, 138, 152, 153n, 163, 193, 209
Cleanthes, 25
Colet, John, 56
Cooper, Thomas, 108
Copernicus, Nicolaus, 73, 76, 78, 125
Cortese, Giulio, 109
Croll, Morris, 152n, 153n
Cunningham, William, 77, 112n
Cupiditas, 154–156

Daniel, Samuel, 88, 218
Dante, 66–69, 69n, 70
Dee, John, 77–78, 81, 93–94, 101, 120–122, 126–127
Dialogue, 165–168, 171–172, 181, 203
Digges, Thomas, 78–79, 123–125
Diodati, Charles, 3
Diogenes, 23
Dominicans, 40, 43
Donne, John, 145
Dyer, Edward, 115, 121–122

Elizabeth, Queen, 76, 97
Elyot, Thomas, 76, 124
Emblems, 93–94, 108, 157, 213, 223–225; tradition of, 86–88, 104; influence on Sidney, 148, 148n, 149, 181–183, 185–190
Energia, 128–135, 158–159, 172–173; examples of, 145, 148, 163–164, 169, 201–202, 222
Epicurus, 23–24
Erasmus, Desiderius, 86
Euclid, 77, 121, 126

Ferrabosco, Alphonso, 219
Ficino, Marsilio, 53–56, 65, 71, 83, 83n, 84–85, 85n, 86, 94
Flecknoe, Richard, 214
Florentine Academy, 53–54, 85

Fore-conceit, 108, 116, 120, 128, 131, 134, 136, 188–189, 215; analysis of, 110–111, 118, 122–123; examples of, 144–145, 156–157, 159–160, 163, 171–173, 182–183
Fracastoro, Girolamo, 106, 106n
Franciscans, 40, 42–43, 45, 47–49, 53, 75
Fraunce, Abraham, 87, 107n, 115–117, 153n, 163
Fuchs, Leonhard, 80

Galileo, 9, 49
Gascoigne, George, 132–133
Giardi, Christoforo, 87
Gilbert, Neal W., 89
Gnosis and *praxis*, 98, 134n, 196, 205
Gordon, D. J., 216, 224
Granger, Thomas, 91
Greville, Fulke, 129, 137, 137n, 141–143, 151, 206, 206n, 207–208
Grosseteste, Robert, 42–43, 45, 48–49
Ground-plot, 136, 189, 193; analysis of, 122–128; examples of, 141, 156–157, 171, 183, 199
Guthrie, W. K. C., 15

Hall, Joseph, 207, 209–213
Harmony, 155–161
Harvey, Gabriel, 111, 114, 114n, 153, 153n
Havelock, Eric, 21
Hermeticism, 101, 120
Hilliard, Nicholas, 105, 105n
Hoby, Thomas, 72
Horace, 106
Hoskyns, John, 107, 134n, 142, 144, 162, 206, 206n, 207–208, 217
Hugh of St. Victor, 39, 40
Humanism, 60–61, 70, 86, 89, 93

Impresa, 148, 148n

Index

Index